Word

by

Word

The Maui Writers Conference
Presents

Word by Word

An Inspirational Look at the Craft of Writing

by

John Tullius & Elizabeth Engstrom

and the Presenters of the

Maui Writers Conference

**WRITERS
HOUSE
BOOKS**

ISBN: 09666272-6-1

The Maui Writers Conference Presents:
WORD BY WORD
An Inspirational Look at the Craft of Writing

Library of Congress Catalog Card Number: 00-103158

Writers House Books
TripleTree Publishing, PO Box 5684, Eugene, OR 97405
(541) 338-3184 - www.TripleTreePub.com

Cover art by Robert Glick
Book design by Alan M. Clark
Editorial services by Marti Gerdes
Printed in the United States of America
1 2 3 4 5 6 7 8 9

The Maui Writers Foundation
receives all royalties from the sale of this book.

CONTENTS

Part One: Fiction

Part Two: Nonfiction

Part Three: Screenwriting

FOREWORD

I had no idea when I created the Maui Writers Conference that it would become the phenomenal success that it has. I never dreamed that it would attract the very best writers and screenwriters working today, or a who's who of the film and publishing industries–the top agents, editors, publishers, and film executives in the business.

Year after year the Conference also showcases many of the world's greatest speakers. From the Elmer Gantry-like dramatics of Bryce Courtenay, to the tempered truths of Mitch Albom; from the fall-off-your-seat hilarity of Dave Barry, to the stand-on-your-seat inspiration of Jack Canfield; from master teachers like John Saul, Terry Brooks, and Elizabeth George, to the simple elegant pearls of Ernest Gaines, Tony Hillerman, and David Guterson, the Conference has been blessed with their warmth and their wisdom.

To decide to gather their collective knowledge in this volume was simple. Now it's just left to you to pick it up and read. Then share it with a friend. For contained in these pages is a true treasure house of writing insight for all of us who, day by day, word by word, love and toil with the written word.

Aloha nui loa,
John Tullius
Director

Translating a verbal presentation to a written presentation generates a tremendous number of problems, not the least of which is the quality of the tape recording. Amidst the pops, crackles, sizzles, blank spaces, and misunderstood names, are the things the transcriptionist calls "(unintelligible)".

Then there are the presenters' ums, ahs, ahems, grammatical lapses, asides, personal jokes and visual antics that don't come across. And of course, when you edit some of that out, you also edit out some of the soul of the presentation, some of the graciousness.

The editorial team tried very hard to bring the spirit of the talk, the integrity of the speaker and the liveliness of the sessions to these papers. Since 1993, when The Maui Writers Conference began, we have accumulated a tremendous wealth of information. This initial book represents a tiny fraction of the archives, and more will be forthcoming in subsequent volumes.

We hope you find both inspiration and information in these pages. It has been our extreme pleasure to bring it to you, both in person and on paper.

Elizabeth Engstrom

INTRODUCTION

I knew from the time I was seven years old that I was supposed to be a writer. Writing called to me, and while I listened for nearly twenty years, I finally set the passion aside and addressed myself to other things in life. I worked several jobs, although none of them were the stuff of adventure that could fuel future stories. I was a personnel assistant, a research assistant, a secretary, and finally a teacher. I did well at these jobs, as is my nature. But I was always aware that deep inside me, an anxiety resided because I wasn't doing what I was supposed to be doing. I wasn't writing.

I wasn't writing for several reasons. First, I had no belief in myself. I didn't perceive myself as a writer because I believed that writing was mystery, a sort of arcane religious ceremony engaged in by people ordained with the capability of snatching stories out of thin air. I was not such a person. Additionally, I was someone who let life get in the way of what I wanted to do and who I wanted to be. It was easier to become overwhelmed with responsibilities than to sit down and face the great blank page. And finally, I didn't think I had talent. I knew that I could mold sentences, true; I was able to see how language manipulated correctly can add up to seamless prose. But to tell a story? To create a character? To unleash the passion within and leash the passion on the written page in one deft and simultaneous movement? No, no, no, no. I could not do that.

Still, when writing bites, it bites hard. And I continued to feel the sting of its bite even as I busied myself with teaching, engaging in years of fervent union activity, studying for an advanced university degree, traveling, reading, and becoming an ardent theatre-goer. Occasionally, I wrote. I was called upon by my fellow teachers in times of crisis to construct articles for the newspapers, arguing our positions with regard to contract negotiations. I created a newsletter to keep parents and community members abreast of what was happening in our classrooms. In the classroom itself, I taught my students writing and toward the end of improving their abilities to compose, I wrote example essays for them. I was getting my toes wet, I suppose.

The personal computer was what actually brought me back to writing as a serious endeavor. In 1983, my then husband was writing his Ph.D. dissertation and, unwilling to pay someone to type the behemoth, he bought an IBM PC, and he soon taught me how to use it. Faced with a piece of state of the art equipment, I was also faced with what I've long called put-up-or-shut-up time. I thought about myself on my death bed, and I asked myself what I truly wanted to say with my dying breath: "I could have written a novel" or "I wrote a novel." I went for the latter option. I sat down on June 28, 1983, and began the first project I'd written in more than ten years. On September 3, 1983, my first try at a British suspense novel was done.

I'd like to be able to tell you that that first attempt at a British novel soared, that it soared so high, so long, and so well that it floated right into publication. That didn't happen. What did happen was that I learned I could do it. I discovered that if I suited up and showed up at the computer on a daily basis, and if I had a *plan* and not some vague wish to get in touch with the cosmos, I could write a book. So I wrote another in 1984. In 1985, I wrote a third. It was that novel–*A*

Great Deliverance–that was finally accepted for publication. At that point, I had actually written six books: one as a seventh-grader, a second as a high school student, and a third as a young twentysomething freshly fired from her first teaching job at Mater Dei High School in Santa Ana, California.

Here's what I've come to believe about writing since I finally sat down on June 28, 1983, and began that still-unpublished British novel.

First, to be an *assured* success in writing, a person needs to possess three qualities: talent, passion, and discipline.

Second, to be a *probable* success in writing, a person needs to possess either talent and discipline, or passion and discipline.

Third, to possess talent and passion, *or* talent or passion alone without the discipline will not take a writer to the end of the first page.

And fourth, to possess discipline by itself is often enough to assure success, as is attested to by the publication and worldwide success of many truly terrible books that generally go on to be truly terrible major motion pictures.

I've also come to believe that writing is not an arcane ceremony of any kind. I've learned to see it as not only an art but also, more importantly, as a craft. And just like all of the other art forms–from painting to sculpture to dance to musical composition–writing possesses elements that can be taught.

This belief is largely anathema to my European counterparts, as well as to journalists and literary critics from those same countries. Those individuals believe that writing is an esoteric art form with mysterious properties which only a genius can decipher and use. For this reason, unpublished enthusiasts across the Atlantic, push their pens in the darkness, robbed of the kind of literary tradition we're used to in the United States, a tradition that's rich, varied, and lively, in which some of our finest novelists, poets, playwrights, and journalists pass along their craft to those who will follow. That's why in the United States at one time or another, you could have taken a class from John Irving, Toni Morrison, Maya Angelou, Philip Roth, Saul Bellow, Joyce Carol Oates...and on and on. Even today you can join a class with such craftsmen as instructors, not because these folks are desperate for a dime or in need of having fragile egos fed through the admiration of their students, but because these folks adhere to the greatest literary tradition of our country: Knowledge isn't to be hoarded; knowledge is to be shared.

This is also the belief of John and Shannon Tullius, the creators of the Maui Writers Conference, where for years, neophyte writers, experienced craftsmen, the general public, and the blatantly curious have been able to gather and listen to various masters talk about their processes. At the Conference, writers have spoken freely about their style, their technique, the source of their ideas, and the manner in which they do everything from construct plots to design characters from the soles of their feet to the hair on their heads. Under the guidance of John and Shannon, the Maui Conference has grown in stature and reputation, bringing together literary novelists, genre specialists, commercial novelists, journalists, screenwriters, film makers, and others who share the same passion for the written word.

Here in this volume for the first time, you can read what these people have to say about their craft. From Tony Hillerman's Southwest to Susan Isaacs' Long Island to the magical worlds created by Terry Brooks, you can step into the shoes of these writers and get a better idea of how they do what they do. In reading their words, you can walk their paths and glean from them the combined knowledge of several hundred years of sitting down at the legal pad, the typewriter, or the computer and doing the job on a daily basis. You will have the opportunity to amass a wealth of information about how writers go about developing a character, creating a scene, rendering a setting, honing an idea, measuring conflict, forming dialogue, addressing theme, and writing within a particular field like mystery, suspense, science fiction, or fantasy. And at the end, you'll have a better idea of what it means when someone says, "I'm a writer."

There is no magic cookbook for writing. What there is is the opportunity for exposure to the way a lot of professionals work. If you read through these talks carefully and with an open mind, you might well find yourself on your way to developing a process for yourself. And from that process can come your writing.

Read and enjoy.

Elizabeth George
Huntington Beach, California

PART ONE:

FICTION

Fiction is how we define our existence. We tell ourselves 'It's just a story,' and at that, the magic of the craft has us, frees us to confront the complete spectrum of humanity. The greatest magic, however, is that fiction also turns us inward, allows us to examine ourselves. A good author makes our emotions resonate to the motives and actions of the characters. More than any other art, fiction engages our entire mental landscape. It entwines the minds of the reader, the author, and the characters. Fiction is not mere images of events–it's life crystallized, because fiction is experience. We read, and for a while, however short, we become.

--Don McQuinn

"I must have three characters that I know intimately before I start a book because if you look at any of my books, there are always three major characters. I must know them, so I rehearse them all year."

–Bryce Courtenay

Terry Brooks

The Ten Most Important Things a Writer Can Do

I'm going to talk to you about some things that writers sometimes overlook, sometimes let slide a little bit. Some of these will be familiar and they won't do you any good necessarily, but out of this batch, perhaps one or two will strike a chord, give you some new insight, give you some different way of looking at how the craft is perfected. I actually don't have ten things. I could only come up with nine, so this is actually Nine Tips.

So let's start off with number one: Outline, outline, outline. My mantra of life. The first thing we have to do is disabuse ourselves of the idea that outline, outline, outline needs Roman numeral one, capital A, small a, and so forth. Get rid of all that thinking right now and let's look for a more unstructured approach to what we're talking about.

The second thing is that fifty percent of what's important will take place before you ever put pen to paper. It will take place in the head, while you're dreaming. I tell everybody that when you see me lying on the beach, I am not having fun. I'm working. I'm always thinking. And to a certain extent it's true.

If you're a writer, you never stop thinking about the possibilities—you don't just shut your brain down. You're always trying to fit those pieces together, figure out what that story's going to be about. How it's going to develop. Who the characters are going to be.

It's a process that is at least equally important as the writing itself. Do not rush this process. Let it take its own time. Just when you think you're ready to go out there and write down those first few things and get started with your outlining work, don't do it. Sleep on it. Take a couple days. See if you still remember what you started out with. If you don't remember, chances are it wasn't crucial to what you want to do anyway. It's when you can't stop thinking about it, when you see all those things playing out in front of your eyes, *that's* when it's time to sit down and put it on paper.

It's a two-step process. It's the thinking that allows the information to percolate and shape itself, then it's the writing down of what you're going to do. When you're writing down where you're going to go and what you're going to have happen and how it's going to develop, which is that scene-by-scene, segment-by-segment, chapter-by-chapter approach, it's going to do two things for you.

One, it's going to help you remember what it was that you were going to do in the beginning. This is a long process and it's a complex process if you're doing it correctly, and it's extremely difficult to remember all the details, for, say, eight months, a year, a year and a half, two years, or whatever. If you have this to look back on, you'll have a way of touching base with what it is you hope to accomplish.

It will also help you to think your story through. Every time I hear about writer's block I say, outline, outline, outline, outline and you'll save yourself a huge amount of time and trouble. Think it through in advance. Write it out, see how it lays out. Don't be wedded to it, because you're going to get better ideas, and characters are going to take different paths than you anticipated, so don't be locked in. You can send in those change orders on this blueprint and it doesn't cost you a dime. But if you've got your cohesive outline in front of you, you'll be able to see how to make those changes all the way along the line so that you don't disrupt the flow of your story.

It's hard enough to concentrate on the writing process itself—choosing the words, creating the images, making the story come alive. If you're also burdened with trying to figure out how to make the plot come together in the right way, that's an unnecessary and more difficult process.

Number two: Trust your instincts. This is the most difficult thing to talk about in terms of craft. Instincts are something that writers have. Your instincts tell you what's going to work best. You might hone your instinct by reading what other writers have done, by practicing your craft, but essentially you've either got it or you don't. But you've got to trust it. You have to pay attention to what your instincts tell you. And if you've got this really neat idea and you've got this great scene but some little voice says, "I don't know about this," then pay attention to that voice.

Number three: Get to know your characters, but do not marry up with them. You've heard writers talk about how their characters speak to them? About how they come alive from the pages of their books and step into their lives and begin to dictate where they should go and what they should do? I say this is schizophrenia and it's not a good thing. I also say it's important for writers to remember who's running the asylum. So you want to be sure that your characters don't take over your life. You are the one who controls them, because these characters were created by you, are a part of you, but are not the dominant part of you, and if they start to tell you where to go then you've got big trouble. You have to keep tight control over your characters even when you love them, even when you think they're wonderful.

Number four: Less is sometimes more. A pretty simple phrase. It means that if you are good at this business of writing, when you get your craft down to where you want it to be, you can say twice as much in half the space. You learn not to overwrite so you're paring your story down, making it hard and lean and to the point. Not to where you cut out the descriptive phrases and depictions of scenery and settings that are important to the story, but to the point where you're not slowing the pace. You don't want to spell everything out because then you remove the reader from the process. Readers have imagining going on up in their heads when they read a book. They're picturing the characters and the action through whatever emotional dialogue is going on. You want the reader to be engaged by that, and half of that process is letting them intuit for themselves what's going on.

Number five: See the ball. We all know what that means, from basketball, baseball: If you're going to hit the ball, you're supposed to picture yourself hitting the ball and then you picture the ball flying out of the park. Or if you're shooting the ball in a basketball game, you envision yourself making that jump shot. The ball leaving your fingertips, floating up over there, swish. Visualize what's going on. I want you to treat your creativity as if you were a director in a movie. You need to see the scene in your mind before you write it. You need to picture what's going to happen. Very thoroughly. You need to see the characters, the setting, the weather, the point of view, everything. You need to know where the action will start, where it will finish. This will allow you to decide what things you want to put into your book. And this is very important because again, you don't want to put too much in. So you have to select the things that you need in order to make the story develop. And this is very often a function of the kind of story that you're writing.

Number six: Writer's block is your friend. I'll bet you haven't heard that one before. Writer's block is a term that gets bandied about rather recklessly and has in fact a number of different meanings. It can mean that you're blocked from doing anything. "I cannot write. I've been here for a year. I've been looking at this paper. Nothing's happening. My brain is dead." It can also mean that you're momentarily stumped on a smaller point, which way should you go, what should happen here. Small-term writer's block. Now if you have long-term writer's block, serious problems with sitting down and writing, serious difficulties with breaking through, then of course you maybe shouldn't be doing this. Maybe you should be doing something else with your life. I mean that's the worst case scenario. But we're going to assume for the moment that that's not true of anybody here.

So let's talk about the other ramifications of writer's block. It could also mean that you're not paying attention to what I said earlier which is outline, outline, outline. Outlining, to some extent, will help with writer's block. The possibility I think is most often true is that writer's block is your mind's way of telling you that you need to rethink what you're doing. You need to take a close, analytical look at why it is you can't seem to go on. It may be your writer's instincts telling you that you've taken a wrong path, that you've chosen to depict your character in a wrong or inconsistent way from what went before, or that you have chosen to write the scene from perhaps the wrong point of view. Maybe you have positioned this particular scene wrongly, and something else needs to come first in order to logically lead in to where you're going next. So I think when you are at that point, this is another one of those times when you have to step back, take some time to think about it, let everything settle, maybe go back and reread. Take a look at your outline to see where it was you intended to go and try to pinpoint where it was that the writer's block found a foothold in your thinking. So you need to back away. Go for a bike ride. Take a few days and go to Canada. Do something to break the pattern. You'll come back refreshed, with a little better insight. Don't be so hard on yourself.

Number seven: Free advice is worth exactly what you pay for it. Now this has to do with people looking at your work. I would suggest to you that a good editor is still the best answer. I've been lucky. I've had good editors from the beginning. And most of you do not have good editors because, of course, you're not yet published. In lieu of that, you may be relying on family members, loved ones, friends, helpful readers at work, well-meaning members of your writers' groups, strangers, and professionals like me. Don't trust any of us.

Do not listen to any of us with regard to your work, unless you can answer the following question about whether or not these people offer you this: Do they present a balanced and intelligent view about their craft so that they can talk to you directly and sensibly about what's wrong? Don't ever let anybody tell you that your work doesn't work and then walk away from you. Or that they don't like it and walk away from you. Or that it's too long or too short or too fat or too thin or any of that. You make them tell you exactly why it doesn't work, or you write them off. Because advice that just says, "I don't like this," is of no use to you. You have to find somebody who will give you a reason for the problem.

You want their analysis to be objective and you want it to be well-reasoned and you want it to make you think. If what they're telling you doesn't resonate with you at all, then you need to press the issue, because what they're saying to you should make you question what you're doing, and it should trigger something inside of you that says, "Oh, yeah. Well there is this other approach that I might take."

Number eight: Monogamous reading will stunt your growth. If you're a writer of fiction you have to read in different fields. If I'm a writer of fantasy and all I read is fantasy, how in the heck am I gonna know anything? Because it's not all contained right there. I find in my professional career that most of the really good ideas and the really great inspirations I get come from books written by authors who have nothing to do with what I do. And I'm not talking just about fiction, I'm talking about nonfiction and self-help and how-to and all the different areas. You have got to read widely in this business to be any good. And if you don't, believe me, you are in serious trouble. This is important. You must read widely. You have to write regularly, on a regular basis. On some kind of a schedule. You have to read that way, too. And you have to be familiar with what's out there. And there are some absolutely incredible books, wonderful books, terrific language and imagery being used by writers, that you wouldn't even know about if somebody didn't say, "Hey, have you tried this book?" All the really inspiring, terrific books I read during the past year were not marketed as fantasy. They were marketed as something else altogether and many of them were in fields that were not fiction. So leave yourself open to this and make use of it.

Number nine: Never take your readers for granted. Heaven forbid. Don't be boring. Please. Don't be afraid to take chances. Don't be afraid to do something that seems extreme once in awhile. I don't think you should make a practice of this, of course, but you can't be too timid about how you approach this craft. You can't be reticent to do something that seems a little out of the ordinary, a little different from maybe what you anticipated in the beginning, something that just jumps up and says, "I wonder what the result would be if I did this?" And give it a chance to develop. Sometimes you'll get those brilliant ideas that will tell you midway, or three-quarters of the way through a book, where you need to go, what you need to do that will make this story stand out, that will make it wonderful and memorable for the reader.

Oh, I do have a number ten. I wrote it down during David Guterson's speech. It pays to read your notes over before you give a talk. All right. He said, "Being a writer is more important than being published." Of course, of course it is. Being published is something that comes from being a writer. But the thing that will keep you grounded, the thing that will keep you sane, and the thing that will stay with you forever is the fact that you love what you do. It's being a writer; the crafting of what you do, is crucial to who you are. This defines you. You're not a writer if your craft isn't the most important thing to you. We can make magic happen. We put this great huge massive puzzle together, and we don't even know what it's going to look like until it's all done. We fit all those pieces together and then there we have it.

And you know what we get to do when it's all done? And it's beautiful and it's fair? We don't put it on the wall and admire it. We put it away. Time to build another one. What's next? That's what's exciting.

"There's a terrain to the page. The eye is the traveler over that terrain. And the eye likes variety. The eye likes a lot of white space too, because it's lazy, so I try to use short paragraphs. If I can, I have people talking, so that the eye can move around on a quotation mark."

–Steven Goldsberry

Tony Hillerman

The Last Eagle

The first real conflict I had with my editor concerned a cat. I had never actually met Larry except on the telephone, and I'd never been in his office. Had I been, I don't think I'd have tried this but I had written a book in which I tried to establish the character of a villain who was charged with getting into a fellow's house past a guard dog. I had the guy go to an animal shelter and adopt a cat. Put the cat in a shoe box, throw the cat over the fence and then he wanted to find out if the guard dog made a lot of noise when he attacked the cat. The guard dog didn't.

The next night the guy comes back and gets through the fence, kills the Doberman, and does his job. Larry said, "Tony, I think we ought to change that." He said, "Let's not use a cat. Do it some other way." And I said, "Well, I'm trying to establish this fellow's character. He thinks of himself sort of as a cat and I want to show how coldhearted he is." So we argued awhile and finally he said, "Oh well, go ahead. But we're going to get a lot of static from cat lovers. There's a million of them out there. They have their own magazines, everything."

So I did a book signing on that book and waited for the cat lovers to approach me. No one did. Until finally one day in California, an elderly lady came up and said, "Mr. Hillerman, I've always had quite a bit of respect for your books until this last one. But I really don't go for that animal cruelty." And I said, "Well, my editor warned me about that. He said that so many people loved cats they wouldn't ..." And she interrupted and said, "To hell with the cat. I raise Dobermans." When I finally did meet Larry in his office, it was decorated with photographs of cats.

Since this is a writers conference, it occurred to me that I should use the time I have to talk about a couple of things that would have been useful to me, had someone told me about them. I had been a journalist for seventeen years, so I made my living writing, but I had a yen to write fiction. So I tried to find out how people did it and I checked out all the books, and talked to everybody I could find who had anything to offer. They all told me the same thing: If you're going to write plotted fiction, you need an outline. If you're going to write nonfiction you need to outline the book. Whatever you're doing, you need to have a blueprint. That seemed reasonable.

I struggled through the first three books trying to make an outline. And finally in book four I came to the conclusion that there are two kinds of people who write. In category one are people who are able to outline their books and do so. And in category two are those who wish they could but can't. I'm in category two. And in this particular book, which I had tried to outline, I'd outlined the first four chapters before I gave up. I had adopted a policy of outlining as far as I could before starting to write. I'd write a bit and then I'd push the outline. Or I'd try to. The name of the book was *The Crystal Gazer*. And it was going to be a big, important book.

All of these, this series of books, concern Navajo tribal police and the Navajo people. And in this one, I was going to try to draw a parallel to the part of the Navajo version of Genesis, in which humanity was beginning to exist in the fifth world, the world we now occupy. Also, they had a sort of a Moses figure called Changing Woman, who was a teacher of the Navajo value system and Navajo curing ceremonials and so forth. Changing Woman had two sons. She was visited by the sun and by the water, the mist of the San Juan River, which runs through Navajo country. And she bore two sons. Their names were Monster Slayer and Born for Water. They would play in the Navajo theology, sort of what the heroes of Greek mythology play. As they grew older, they went to the Sun, they stole weapons from the Sun, they returned to Earth. And they set on this odyssey around Four Corners country, killing the monsters to make the landscape safe for the people. One of them was a macho fellow, Monster Slayer, and the other was a thoughtful fellow, Born for Water–to represent a dichotomy in human nature.

OK, so I'm going to take these two guys and I'm going to produce two brothers, twins. And they're going to, in quite different ways, set about the task of helping the tribe. I had this all thought out, see? No novel thought out, but these characters thought out. They're going to be the sons of a broken family. Their mother is an alcoholic, their dad gone. And their maternal grandfather is going to be raising them. One of them has converted to Christianity, goes to St. Michael's, becomes a convert to Catholicism, decides to become a priest, becomes a priest, goes to Rome to study at the American school at the Vatican. The other guy becomes politically active. He joins the American Indian Movement, decides it's far too placid for his taste, joins a more militant group, decides they're too slow, forms his own terrorist group. Monster Slayer soon gets on the FBI's Most Wanted list. The other son in Rome, in my outline, is seduced by a daughter of an American diplomat at the American Embassy. Overcome by a sense of guilt and pleasure, he comes back to the reservation. That's what I've got.

Now, I have to have a murder, I'm going to have to have all kinds of crime, but this is all I've got so far. And I keep trying to think it through but it doesn't go anywhere. So I start writing. I decide I'll have them both return to the reservation, since this is my background and I love to write about it. One of them comes back to meditate. The priest. The other one comes back because he needs a place to hide. And he has a great crime thought up–I don't know what it is yet, he hasn't told me, but I will figure it out. He comes back because he knows a place, a wonderful place as a hide-out. Trouble is, someone else knows it, too. His grandfather. So now I've thought of a crime. I'm going to have this guy kill his grandfather, which would give me a chance to drag people into the Navajo value system. The ultimate, absolute crime among Navajos is doing any offense against your own family, especially killing a relative, or any form of incest.

So I write the first chapter. Everybody, I think, who likes to write likes to grind their own axes. One of my axes that I grind every chance I get is a feeling that the FBI is nowhere near as good as it wants us to think it is. I used to be a police reporter so I saw them up close and personal. And believe me, they're highly overpaid and overrated. OK. So I have a scene, a fairly long chapter in which my Monster Slayer character outwits the FBI and escapes, free and clear. It takes place in Washington, down by the Potomac. Good chapter, I think. But it doesn't lead anywhere. So I keep looking at it and I can't think of how to connect it to a second chapter.

I have a file that's getting thicker and thicker that I call "First Chapters." I stick it in that file. Then, I think, I'll start on the good guy, the priest. I get out my *National Geographic* and look at all those pictures of Rome and the Vatican and write a chapter set in Rome and the Vatican, in which this guy is falling from grace. And this one was not so good but it was passable. It established the character. It gave you a look at this guy. But again, it didn't lead anywhere. So I add it to the First Chapter file. I must say, if any of you need good first chapters, I've got lots of 'em.

OK, now I think I'll go back and introduce the murder victim. So I write a chapter that's set in the canyon country of Arizona, a long, long way from anywhere. I want to establish the isolation of the place because all of this needs to take place in real isolation. I'll start right off by establishing that isolation, letting you know how far it is from everywhere. I write a chapter in which the murder victim-to-be, an old man, is being interviewed by a shaman, a crystal gazer. It's a real short chapter. I give you a little bit of the personality of the murder victim but he's going to be a goner. Dead. I need to put in more of the woman because in this chapter I intend to put in a lot of stuff about Navajo culture and theology that will be germane to the plot. But I blank that in because I don't know what the plot's going to be yet. I can always come back to first chapters and insert stuff and take stuff out. I write it. And I thought I did a pretty good job. There are a lot of blank spaces but what was in there was pretty good.

And I go to bed–it was after midnight–and I'm lying there thinking about it and it dawns on me that it has only one flaw and that is, in my opinion, a fatal one for first chapters. It is dull. If you want to write mystery novels you don't want dull first chapters. So, I think about it a long time without coming to a solution. And finally, I think, I could have the Monster Slayer, the bad guy, come out of the canyons. I planned to have the murder happen off-camera, between chapter one and chapter two. In chapter two, you'd hear about the murder only in the fact that it was unsolved and nobody knew who did it or why. I think, no, I'll have the killer show up out of the canyon and kill my victim. And that would make it less boring. Besides, people like to see people killed.

Trouble with that was, if he kills the victim, why wouldn't he kill the shaman, too? He probably would. Then I've got a short story at best.

So here's where I'm going to make another point to writers. There's absolutely nothing too trivial that's not worth remembering. I think about writers as I think about bag ladies– with the grocery cart, going around picking up stuff, you never know, you don't need it today but maybe tomorrow. You remember all kinds of stuff. So I'm thinking, how can I solve this? And I remember that one of the many medical problems on the reservation is glaucoma. I think, I will make the shaman blind. Then I will have her being driven there by her niece who's also learning this kind of shamanism. She'd have to drive her there. Then I think, I can't have a blind crystal gazer. So the title is scrapped on my outline right there and it becomes *Listening Woman*, another form of shamanism. They have at least two levels of shamanism. There are diagnostic shaman, who tell you why you're sick, why you're unhappy, why you're drinking too much, what's wrong with you. And they have hand tremblers and listeners and crystal gazers, that I know of. So I think, well, I'll make her a listener.

And now I rewrite it and she, the listening woman, hears all this stuff. I have to have her alive because my Navajo cop has to interview her later on, to find out all this stuff the FBI won't understand. And that will lead him to the solution of the crime.

OK, so I have her, she's collected her information, she's going off to a little cul-de-sac where she can have quiet. And she listens. And when she comes back, she calls for her niece to come and get her and nobody comes. So she finds her stick and she taps her way back down to the hogan and I show her tapping her way right across the outstretched hand of her niece. And I go to bed thinking that's great. That's really exciting. And then I think, now her client is dead, her niece is dead, how does this poor old blind lady get back forty miles over the desert? Couldn't think of a way.

I think everybody who writes runs into these things that they can't solve. They think, well, inspiration will come. So I go ahead with it. I had a very astute editor at the time. She'll catch it and tell me, "Fix that." And if I couldn't think of a way to fix it, she'd tell me how to fix it. So I leave it. And I'm ashamed to report to mystery readers out there, that book's been in print now about thirty years and nobody, no reader yet, has given a second thought to how that poor old woman got home.

So now I am beginning to have suspicions about the value of an outline, because none of this was in the outline.

I come to chapter two. In chapter two, my plan was to introduce a protagonist, a Navajo cop named Joe Leaphorn. I was going to have him meet the gruesome George, the villain. And I was going to have Leaphorn try to arrest him, but the villain tries to kill Leaphorn and escapes. That's going to be chapter two. I start writing it. Leaphorn is sitting in his patrol car beside the empty highway. It's twilight. He sees a car coming. The whole thing is internal monologue, and he doesn't have much to think about. Again, it's dull. So I create another guy and have him be a sheep thief, a young guy who has escaped from jail, and Leaphorn's gone out and re-arrested him and he's in the car and now we have some repartee between these two. And it turns out that the kid is kind of a witty guy and it goes pretty good. So here comes a car, speeding. Leaphorn turns on his lights, stops the guy, gets out of his car, walks back toward the car.

Now I think, I've got to have a biography for this bad guy. Got to give him some life. Where'd he come from, all that stuff. The only thing I can think would be a pet dog riding in the back of the sedan. So I make it a dog, and I put the dog in a cage, one of these traveling things, and I make it a battle-trained guard dog and away we go. I'm thinking if I don't need the dog, out he goes. Delete dog. Right? But if any of you have read this book you're going to wonder, and I wonder, how could I have possibly written the thing without the dog? I mean every time I needed help, there was the dog.

I could go on. There are five or six wonderful examples of how an outline would have been nothing but a handicap to me. But I think maybe that's enough.

I do want to recommend to you developing a good memory and a deep knowledge of the wonderful benefits of plagiarism.

"When you sit down to write every day, don't write an hour or two hours. Get certain productivity done that day. Get two pages done or 250 words or 500 words done toward your book. If you can do four pages a day you can knock a book out in sixty days."

–Bud Gardner

ALAN JACOBSON, AUTHOR
False Accusations and *The Hunted*

When I first looked into the Maui Writers Conference, I realized it could be the proverbial key I needed to unlock the doors that stood in the way of furthering my writing career. I needed an agent; I needed guidance; and, most of all, I needed a publisher. By attending the conference, I felt I was positioning myself to obtain all three.

I decided to approach it like other business opportunities I'd had over the years. In the weeks leading up to the conference, I talked to people who had attended conferences, pored through 'how to' books, printed marketing materials, and sketched out a plan of action. First on my list was to purchase a Manuscript Resume for each of my completed novels. The resume included a three line pitch, or concept summary of the book, biographical info on myself, and a one-page story synopsis. This was then distributed, ahead of time, to all the participating agents and editors for their review. After submitting the resume, I used numerous resources to research the backgrounds of each of the agents and editors to determine which of them handled the type of fiction I wrote. In doing so, I figured I would be able to focus my energies.

With the above information in hand, I hit the shores of Maui in full stride. I purchased as many face-to-face agent/editor consultations as possible. To me, being able to sit across the table from the people who could make my career was an enormous opportunity. Where else—how else—could I have these professionals' undivided attention for fifteen minutes? Their time was mine, and I used it to my best advantage; in some cases, it was for them to read writing samples I'd brought with me. In others, it was for them to get to know me as a person and as a writer.

Though nine agents wanted to read my manuscripts, there was one agent I had thus far been unable to meet with: Jillian Manus, the keynote speaker. I waited two hours in line to sign up for a consultation with her, but my persistence was not wasted. Not only did I get Jillian's last appointment on the last day of the conference, but she loved my writing. A week later, I had a contract for representation on my desk.

Jillian subsequently negotiated a two-book deal with Simon & Schuster. Foreign rights for my first thriller, *False Accusations*, were sold to seven countries. Audio rights for False Accusations were also sold and I went on a twenty-one-city book tour. Appearances on CNN and numerous newscasts and radio shows followed, concluding with my most significant appearance of all: on the *USA Today* best seller list. I have similar aspirations for my second book, *The Hunted*, due out in January 2001.

Though I don't surf, I feel as if I've been riding a huge wave that originated on the shores of Maui. And if I have anything to say about it, I intend for it to keep building, with many more books and contracts to go before that wave crests.

"I think your style comes out of your attitude, what kind of person you are. That's your sound on paper."

–Elmore Leonard

Jackie Collins

The Glamorous World of a Blockbuster Author

There's nothing more exciting than writing. I love what I do. I've been doing it for over twenty years and there's still nothing I like doing better so I know what it's like for all of you. It's a passion. A lot of people get into the business and they don't have the passion, and they wonder why they never make it. It's because they're copying what other people do and they don't really have it in their hearts. You have to write what you know, and you have to write the way you know it.

I never talk about my sex life or my money. I write about other people's.

John Saul and I were talking earlier today and I asked him how long his finished manuscripts were. And he said, "Well, you know, the one I did the other day, it was too long. It was 650 typed pages." And I said, "Oh my God, I write a thousand pages. I never deliver a manuscript with less than a thousand pages." So basically you could put three Danielle Steeles into one Jackie Collins which is why she does two books a year and I do one every eighteen months. So you have to have a routine, otherwise you would never get that amount of work done. I like to fall out of bed in the morning and go straight to my desk and write a couple of sentences before I even have coffee or get dressed or anything. It gets me revved up for the day. A good trick is to leave off halfway through a sentence. Then you can go get dressed and have your coffee and you're not making that great excuse. I find writers have this great excuse: getting-to-the-desk syndrome. It's not writer's block. It's, "Oh God, I should defrost the fridge, take the dog for a walk. I've got all these things I must do before I get to my desk and write." But if you try that trick–get up and start immediately–it really works.

I was about fourteen when I started to write books. I would get a fabulous idea and I would write a book. I would get three-quarters of the way through and never finish it. So then I would have another great idea and I would go do that. I think people do that because they have a fear of failing. They never finish anything because if you don't finish it, you don't have to give it to somebody who's going to say, "Oh no, this stinks, goodbye."

I was finally encouraged by somebody who said to me, "What do you do?" And I said, "I'm a writer." And they said, "Let me see what you've written." And I showed them a book that I was writing called *The World Is Full of Married Men*, which was quite a provocative title. And they read it and they said, "You know, this is terrific. Why don't you finish it?" And I said, "Finish it? Why would I finish it?" Finally I did, only because this person encouraged me to do so. So I think we all need encouragement.

When I finished *The World is Full of Married Men*, I thought, what am I going to do with this book? I don't have an agent. I don't know what to do. I'm a school dropout. I'm sure all the grammar is wrong and everything is wrong. I was an avid reader. I read so many books and I thought, I love reading so much, I'm going to look at these books and see who the publisher is of most of the books that I buy. And it turned out to be a publisher in England called W.H. Allen. And I thought, well, if I like what they publish, they might like what I write. So I sent a manuscript with a letter and everything and then I got a kind of letter back from them about a month later, and apparently the secretary had received the manuscript. She had read it. She had passed it up to an editor. The editor read it. She passed it to another editor. And it had slowly risen in the publishing house until it reached the managing director who was Jeffrey Simmons. He called me up and he said, "I'd like to meet you." And I said, "I would love to meet you." I went in very excited, and as I walked in the door I looked at this man sitting there. My husband was with me at the time and he kind of kicked me because he knew I'm apt to say whatever comes to mind. I saw this man and I said, Oh my God, I've seen him across the gambling table so many times! But I never said that to him. I just said, "Oh, I'm thrilled you like the book." And they were the ones to publish it.

Usually I come up with a title and one main character and from the title and the character the book evolves. Another reason that I've never had writer's block in sixteen books is the fact that I don't know what's going to happen from day to day. I don't have an outline. I don't have a plan. I just have this character. And I like to think that when I finish a book–this is probably why my books are so long because this person's life is just going on and on and on–when I finish a book I think I could pick up that book anytime and continue it. These characters have their own lives that really exist for me. And my characters are very true to me.

I got the idea for *Hollywood Wives* just sitting around at Hollywood parties, seeing women who were married to very famous men, and the women ruled Hollywood. They made all the social arrangements and a lot of business deals are done socially. And so the women had the power. There was this one particular woman who was married to this very famous television star and they were getting a divorce. Everybody used to kiss this woman's ass, right? And then all of a sudden, she's getting a divorce and everybody's saying, "I never liked her." I was amazed by this, and I thought "Hollywood Wives!"

Another woman, married to a movie star, had a girl come to her door and say to the woman, "I'm pregnant by your husband." The woman was furious. The woman was so upset and she said, "Well you'd better have an abortion," and she forced this poor girl to have an abortion. When the husband came home, she said, "We're going somewhere tomorrow, darling. I've got an appointment for you." He said, "Where are we going?" And she said, "It's a surprise." This is a true story! She took him to the doctor and made him have a vasectomy! And I thought, *another* Hollywood wife story!

I've written sixteen books and to me they're all completely different. I write about Hollywood. I write about gangsters. I have this thing about the San Angelo family. I write about Las Vegas. A lot of people say, find a genre and just stick to that. I don't. I think I do a lot of different things but the press and the media categorize writers. There was a question earlier about getting publicity. I've been lucky enough to become known as the Hollywood expert, and that gets me on TV shows. And then I immediately talk about my book. They can ask me anything and I turn it around to the book.

There's a very interesting show in Los Angeles, *The Connie Martin Show*, and she taught me the main trick. She said, "Don't talk about your book, talk about the main character and get everyone who's listening so interested in that character that they're going to go out and buy the book. I tried it and boy did it work. I didn't look like I was so flagrantly plugging the book, which of course is what I was doing.

The most important thing is to write every day. If you can just write a page a day, you'll get that book finished within a year and that's very important. And then find a publisher that you think is going to like you. Or an agent. Write, and don't worry about rejection. And write what you know.

One of the things I'm really proud about is the fact that I get kids reading my books who don't read books. They like the excitement of my books. I get good reviews in *the Wall Street Journal*. Terrible in *People Magazine*. If I ever listened to reviews, I'd have stopped writing after my first book. But I get these letters from these kids who just go, "Hey! You really got me into reading, and now I'm going to read this and I'm going to read that," and then they go on to read more serious projects. So that's something I'm really proud of.

The difficulty about writing sex scenes is that when you've written sixteen books, what are you going to possibly write that's new? I try to write really great married sex because I find that's lacking in books. You never get great married sex in books. You always have the husband messing around, the wife is divorcing him, the husband has a mistress, the wife has a lover, and so when I have a married couple, I love writing sex. I think it's fun. Some male writers write as if they were gynecologists. We all know that's true and they think this is terribly sexy but it's a complete turn-off as opposed to a turn-on. And I think as a woman I try to make the sex in my book very erotic, very sensual, and fun. And the three things mix really well together.

The amount of research I do depends on what I'm writing. If I'm writing my Hollywood novels I don't need to do any. I just go to the parties and see what's going on and people call me every day and I know everything. I know where everybody is buried in Hollywood and the stories about Hollywood are so bizarre, that when I write about it I have to tone them down. It's true! In *Lovers and Gamblers*, I had this rock star who had this kind of interesting sexual escapade with twins on a boat. And everybody said, "Uh! You've gone too far this time! Twins on a boat! I mean, you know, this couldn't happen." And this actually was a real life rock star and it was triplets.

Exacting literary revenge is really fun. That's the best kind of revenge. There was this one particular woman in England who was a critic. Not a critic, exactly, she had a page every week where she would just write about anything she wanted to write about and she had this fixation with me and she would write these terrible things about me. So finally, one day, she kind of attacked my family and I thought, "She's gone far enough." So I sketched her immediately into a book, making it clear who it was. And, in case it wasn't made clear, there's a press magazine in England and they gleefully jumped on it and named her. So it was the ultimate revenge. She's never mentioned me since, strangely enough.

When I'm writing, I want to keep myself interested. So I will create a particular scene of characters' situations. And then I'll reach almost like a climax of that situation but it's not completely there and I'll end the chapter. I know I've got that exciting thing to come back to. And I really don't know what's going to happen next. So then I'll go up to a character that I've left hanging. And so I do have this kind of thing in my books of writing a lot of different characters and leaving them hanging at the end of every chapter, and not resolving everything until the end of the book. So it does make you keep on wanting to read. People say to me that they wish I would write more books. Unfortunately I can't write any quicker because I do write these huge books. But books cost so much. You've got to give people value for their money.

cℛ

"The purpose of reducing your premise into a simple, twenty-five-word "what if" is to help you focus and define your project so you can best communicate it to yourself and to others in a succinct, clear format. Until you have defined the basic idea, there is no way to pinpoint the proper starting point, nor will you know if your idea will sustain an entire novel. Thinking through your "what if" will make you focus on the basic story line, and give you something concrete to return to if your story gets off track."

–John Saul

Michael Eberhardt

The Legal Thriller

I think all of us know that the most important thing when you're writing any type of book, whether it's fiction or non-fiction, is the idea. I happened to come up with my idea based upon a case I had worked on that began in 1982.

In 1982, I was asked to represent an individual named Steven Jackson who was accused of murdering an individual named Julie Church. He was a young black man and she was a white woman and right away, in northern Los Angeles County, that automatically creates problems and controversy. Even worse, the prosecution was basing its case on Mr. Jackson without any direct evidence that this woman was, in fact, dead. It was what's referred to in legal terms as a "no body murder case." There is no body. This was somewhat unheard of in California at the time. I'd only even read about one such case in law school; it had occurred in 1955. For me it was a rare opportunity that I went at with vigor because it was one of those cases that comes along once in a lifetime. This happened in a small community of approximately a hundred thousand people. The prosecution had one heck of a problem in that when they charged Mr. Jackson with the crime, the young lady had only been missing one week.

When I took the case I immediately realized that was their major problem so I did something that no defense attorney ever does. We're known for dragging things out, but I decided to get this thing to trial as soon as possible because the less time she was missing, the more likely she was still alive. The prosecution had just the opposite problem. They didn't expect that somebody would try and push it through. So we went to trial almost immediately and the prosecution, realizing their problem, spent over nine months selecting the jury. It did this because they were hoping one of two things would occur. Number one, they'd either find the body, which they were actively looking for, or, the longer she was missing the more likely she was dead. To make a long story short, after twenty-three months the case ended with an acquittal.

But it's not the case itself that's important here; it's what it did to a community. Every day these people would get up and read about this case. And it became somewhat of a soap opera for them, just like the O.J. Simpson case. To add to the problem, about every two weeks they would come up with skeletal remains. Is this the woman who's been missing? And this was happening at least once a month. They had three full-time detectives going into cesspools and digging up mine shafts trying to find this young lady. And they were totally unsuccessful.

At the conclusion of the trial, I was approached by several true-crime writers who wanted me to collaborate with them on writing about the case. And quite frankly, I'd had my fill of this case. I had spent two years on it, working sixteen-hour days, seven days a week. I wasn't lucky enough to have seven or eight other attorneys working side-by-side with me. I wanted to have nothing to do with it, so I turned down all proposals, including TV.

I wanted to get on with my life. Even after the trial, after he was found not guilty, every time a body would be discovered I would get calls again, reporters would be approaching me and wanting me to comment. I found myself totally forgetting what had taken place during those two years. So instead of always referring to the file that was contained in twenty-nine boxes, I wrote an outline so I wouldn't get embarrassed every time somebody asked me a question.

That was my first mistake, because once I started doing that, I thought well, maybe this wouldn't be so bad. I didn't have the revulsion toward the case that I had before. Rather than just do the notes, I decided to go ahead and do a nonfiction account as best as I could.

I got only about fifty pages before I decided that the only thing that was really interesting about this case was the no body murder aspect to it. What captivated the community was the fact that it took so long and that they were living with this case from day to day. I also found when I was writing this nonfiction account of it that I was, perhaps, breaching some confidences that were part of the job, but I wasn't enthusiastic enough to go out and get releases or anything of that nature. Plus, I decided that the high desert community isn't all that interesting. And my characters weren't all that interesting. So I started to play with the idea of, what if I do this to this particular plot point, and what if I do this to this particular character? All of a sudden I found myself in an attorney's dream. I could change the facts of the case. I didn't have to work within the confines of a police report. I was in heaven.

Then the bug caught hold. I found myself getting up at four in the morning and writing before I went to work, and then writing after I got home from court. Within two or three months I ended up with four hundred pages on a legal pad, hand written, and I didn't know what I was going to do with it, but it was sure fun. I gave it to my secretary who loved it and I said, "OK, type it up and I'll see what I can do with it."

John Tullius and I went to high school together. I knew that he was a writer, so I called him one day and I said, "Hey, John, you won't believe it. I wrote four hundred pages of this fictionalized account of this case that I worked on, so help me out. Let's get this thing published." Well the phone call lasted probably ten minutes. Five minutes of it he was probably on the floor laughing because I didn't hear too much from him during the call. I thought if I took the time to write four hundred pages, then everybody in the world would be clamoring at my door. Anyway, John said, "No, I'm in the middle of something, Mike, uh, put it in your closet. Just forget about it and do what you do best." I did extract a promise from him that, when he was done with that project he would give it a read. And he did. I guess he liked what he read. John and I then worked a collaborative effort on these four hundred pages that I had written up. And then he helped me not only with the prose but also with the pacing and the plot. But I think what enticed John the most was the idea. And I had a very unique idea. I felt I had one up on every other mystery going and that was, you don't know whether or not that person's dead. And then you can decide who did it. So I felt that was my unique contribution.

We sent *Body of a Crime* off to John's agent. I got a phone call back and the agent basically said, "No thank you. It doesn't even have potential." It just didn't do anything for her. So I shelved it, but not before word got out that I had this project going. An acquaintance told me, "Hey, I've worked in New York before. Let me take a look at it." About a week later, I got a phone call back from this person saying, "You're meeting with this agent this afternoon or this evening for dinner. He's here from New York. His name is Peter Miller."

Peter saw a lot of promise in the manuscript and he made John and I commit to finish the book within a month. And we did. Then we sent it off to Peter. And I'll never forget, we had three or four houses interested in the book that John and I had basically decided to put in the round can. Within two or three days, the offers doubled. Then Peter called us on the phone and said, "OK, we've got three houses interested. Now I want a title and a one-page synopsis of your next book." And I remember John and I said, "Next book? Are you kidding? This is it! This is all you're getting out of us." But we did it.

Within a half hour we came up with a title, wrote a one-page synopsis, faxed it to Peter and within two days that was part of the package that sold for a mid-six figure price. He almost doubled what was offered us based on the one-page proposal. The problem was, John and I had to live up to that one-page proposal. We actually had to write a book based upon something that just came off the top of our heads.

I'm sure I am lucky, but quite frankly, a lot of the luck I think was the original idea that I worked on. And because I'm an attorney, all the courtroom scenes were accurate. Fiction requires you to be just as accurate as nonfiction.

∝

"Write a big book. Not necessarily big in length, but big in subjects–big stakes, big losses, big gains, big outcomes. The stakes must be high for the characters and the losses catastrophic. The characters must be larger than life, capable of more than most of us can aspire to. More hate, more love, more guts, more brains, more lust, more charity, more cruelty, more saintliness. Remember, character is plot."

–Bryce Courtenay

Deborah Iida, Author
Middle Son

There is inherent chaos when raising three young children, even in the calmest of families, and this sense of imbalance struck at my core. It was then, in that swirl of early motherhood, I decided to find a quiet corner in my life in which to write a novel. It's not that I had any idea of where to begin, for while I had all my life been a consummate reader, I had never had any educational training in what it might take to craft a book. Not once had I even attempted a short story or a character sketch. Nevertheless I began to write with pen and paper and the beginnings of *Middle Son* emerged.

In that search for balance I was craving, I chose a story that revolved around three boys, while in reality I was the mother of three girls. Before long I felt very much the mother of six.

Tentatively I began to mention to a few people that I was working on a novel, and one afternoon a friend arrived at my front door with the gift of an electric typewriter in her arms. Now I could type my emerging manuscript. Two years passed and that same friend again showed up, this time with a computer.

Meanwhile, my daughters were growing older and easier to handle than my characters. Often I found myself chasing after those boys I'd invented, trying to make sense of what they'd just done. In this way *Middle Son* continued to take shape, and one day I looked up from my computer and decided the book was finished. But now what? I didn't know a single author or agent or editor. And Maui is a long way from New York.

About then my husband saw an article in our local newspaper announcing the first Maui Writers Conference and suggested I go. The cost daunted me, but I'd worked hard and decided to drive to the far side of the island and attend.

For several days I attended workshops and presentations. Now I had names for the techniques I'd instinctively employed when writing my novel and ideas about how to better hone my work. On the final morning the conference director awarded prizes for submitted manuscripts, and I watched as joyful winners were called to the stage. Only the top prize remained, and when the director began to read from the winning manuscript, the words were mine.

In those tumbling days that followed, I decided upon an agent. Algonquin Books accepted *Middle Son* for publication, and I held the book in my hands. My family drove me to the airport the night I left for my mainland book tour. My husband pulled up to the curb, my daughters called out their final good-byes, and, incredibly, out I stepped.

"I wrote a novel this last year which is just about to come out. It was really a challenge for me. It was really hard to do, because it turns out–and you might want to take notes at this point–you need characters and a plot. You talk about a shock! It was right in the contract, though, where the author agrees to provide both characters and a plot. Author further agrees the plot does not consist of just booger jokes strung together. I was really worried about that, because at first I had no plot. I had some characters. And the characters were just standing around, going, 'What are we supposed to do?' 'I don't know. Maybe we'll find out in the next chapter.'"

–Dave Barry

Richard
Paul
Evans

Merry Christmas

Two weeks ago I was sitting in prison, Utah State Prison, preparing to speak to some particularly hard women inmates, and those in the penal system know that the women are harder than the men. As I sat there looking out at them, I had an idea. They asked me to come and be of inspiration to these women—some of them murderers, some of them drug dealers. What would I say to them?

I got an idea. What would happen if I read to them my children's book, a book I wrote to express my love to my daughters, as a father, knowing full well that most of these women had been abused as children? Their own fathers had abused many of them. I wondered what would happen, so I decided to take the chance. I read the book and I wasn't prepared for what would happen. Six of the inmates stood up and ran out of the room and came back with rolls of toilet paper, which they passed up and down the rows. One of the women shouted out, "We love you." It was really a pretty incredible experience.

There are certain things that connect with all of us. Someone once asked my wife what I do for a living, and she said I make people cry. But I do not write books to make people cry. I write books to remind people of their humanity and their responsibility to humanity, and this does not make me very popular with critics.

At the outset of my career, when *The Christmas Box* was the number one book in the nation, I received a phone call from a reporter from *USA Today*. She said, "I want to prepare you for something. You realize that you will not be very popular with critics; in fact, many of them will hate you."

I thought those were very strong words. I said, "Why would anyone hate me?"

She said, "Because you write about things that invoke emotion, and many of my colleagues are emotionally dead. Just prepare yourself." And sure enough, that is what happened. I tend to polarize critics, but I don't write for them. I write what comes through me.

Seven years ago I sat down to write a story for my daughters. I was not a writer by profession. I was a dad. I just wanted to write something that would express my love to my two little girls. I thought if I put it into book form, it was something they could read every year, and someday they might understand the depth of a father's feeling. And this is where the miracle began. Because as I began to write this story, the story began to write itself. It would wake me up in the middle of the night, or early in the morning. Once I pulled off the freeway and wrote an entire chapter on the back of bills and envelopes and whatever paper I could get my hands on in the car, and it went on this way for about five weeks. It was really peculiar because this story did not come in any linear sense, like from chapter one to chapter two. Instead, it came like a jigsaw puzzle. I had pieces here and there, but I really wasn't sure what the story was about until one very incredible morning.

One morning, at four o'clock, the story woke me up, and I went out to the kitchen table and began to write. In just a few sentences I was overcome with emotion, as I understood for the first time that this story was about the pain my mother felt over losing a child. And that moment I had a very profound experience. I felt that I was not in the room alone. I believed I was with my sister, Sue. My sister died when I was two years old. I said out loud, "Sue, you've given me this story for Mom," and instantly it came to my mind in the same way the story had come to my mind, "Dedicate this book to me." At this point I still had no intentions of publishing my story, but I knew I needed to share it with more than just my two daughters.

So I went out to a local Kinko's Copy Center and made up twenty copies. I came back and I gave the first copy to my wife and asked her to read it and tell me what she thought of my book, not realizing at the time what an intimidating thing this is to do to a wife. Because I either have to be a good writer or she has to be a good liar. So she tried to put it off, and I said, "Honey, just read the first three pages. If you don't like the book, you don't have to read it." So she started to read, and read, and read, and around midnight I noticed that there were tears streaming down her cheeks. She finished the book and set it aside, and said nothing. Of course I'm filled with anticipation. I said, "Honey, what did you think?" She fell on the couch and she began to cry. When she gained her composure, she said something very illustrative of what had happened. She said, "Rick, where did you get that story?" And then I told her about that morning. She said, "It makes me want to be a better mother."

A few nights later, on Christmas Eve, I had the privilege of giving that book to my own mother and telling her that I understood that after all these years she still hurt after the loss of my sister. She wept as I gave it to her. It opened up something in her that I had never seen before because my mother would never talk about my sister. It freed her.

I also gave the book to my brothers, and that was it. I felt very successful. I had set out to make two copies. I now had twenty in print. But the next day I received a phone call from one of my brothers. I come from a large family, with seven boys, so I expected something like, "Rick, I want you to know you have very poor punctuation." Instead he said, "Your book has changed my life." The next day I received a similar phone call, and the next day, and the next day. Three weeks later a woman called and said, "Mr. Evans, I want to tell you what your story means to me," and I asked, "Who are you?" She gave me her name and I said, "Where did you get my book?" She said from so and so. I asked, "Who's that?" And I realized the book had passed beyond my realm of family and friends.

Out of curiosity, I took a notepad and started to track down those copies, and as near as I could tell, in the four weeks since I had handed out those twenty copies, they had been read more than 160 times. A few weeks after that I received a phone call from a local bookstore. The clerk had been going down the white pages, calling all the R. Evans. And there are a few of us. So by the time she got to me, she just said, "Hello Mr. Evans. Did you write a Christmas story?" I said, "Yes." She said, "Oh, good. Where do we order it?" And I said, "You can't order it. It has never been published." And she was quiet for a moment, and she said, "But we've had ten orders for that book this week." And that's pretty good for any book, but for a Christmas book in February, that's unheard of. So she said, "Maybe you should publish this book." And I thought, "Maybe I should."

So at this point I started to send copies out to all the local publishers who wasted little time in sending me rejection slips. Wow! I've since talked to all the people who wrote me rejection slips. It's been delicious! But I was still receiving some requests, so I decided I would self-publish the book. Not knowing anything about the industry, I went out and typeset and designed the book, and printed up 9,000 books. I didn't realize 9,000 books was a lot of books. I thought you should be able to sell 9,000 of anything. So we had a garage full of books, and found that the bookstores didn't want the book either, for the same reason the publishers didn't want the book.

I needed some help. The printer felt sorry for me because he had taken all of my money and so he gave me the name of a distributor, and I remember the day I called this local distributor, I said, "Listen, I'm really new at this. Are you glad that I called or am I glad that you answered?" He said, "We reject ninety percent of what the publishers bring to us. Who's your publisher?" I knew by this point that it was bad to be self-published. But I told him some of the stories, and I talked him into reading the book. I took it down to him on a Friday afternoon, and the next Monday I called back, and said, "Listen, did you get a chance to read my book?" He said, "I did, and I hate to admit it because I'm a man, but I cried. Then my wife read it and she cried. She wants to give your book out for Christmas. We think you're going to do very well with your book. In fact, we would like to distribute it." I said, "Great, how many copies do you need?" He said, "We think you might sell as many as 3,000 copies." I asked, "Is that good?" He said, "Oh, yeah, that's what a popular local author sells. Nobody knows who *you* are."

So I thought, the way those twenty copies had affected so many people, just think what 3,000 copies will do. And besides, I'll have Christmas presents for the rest of my life. So we got them into bookstores, and by mid-November of '93, we had sold 3,000 copies, and the distributor was really excited. He said, "This is incredible. No one sells this many copies. We haven't even hit the Christmas season yet." He said, "You may have to reprint." So I said, "Well, how many should I print?" And he said, "Well, no one knows that."

And so I prayed about it. I learned at a young age about the power of prayer. And I received a very strong impression. "Print 20,000 more copies." And I thought, "bad inspiration." Nobody does that. But the inspiration remained. I actually wrote this in my journal. Common sense told me to print a few thousand copies more, and I had books left over, so I compromised, somewhere between inspiration and common sense, and I printed 10,000 more books. On December 10, 1993, we sold out of those first 9,000 books. The next day the 10,000 books were delivered to the warehouse, and three days later I get a phone call from a distributor asking, "Rick, where are your books?" I asked, "Didn't you get the 10,000?" He said, "We've sold them already."

By this point we were selling more than 3,000 books every single day along the Wasatch Front. This started an interesting phenomenon, because if you get 3,000 women looking for the same book, and it's not in the bookstore, they start calling a lot of bookstores, and they are clogging up the bookstores' phone lines in Salt Lake City. They were complaining, and the bookstores were complaining.

Now I had bought some radio commercials, which I now could not use because I had no books. So I thought, I'm going to use these ads and tell people that the book is sold out. I learned a really valuable marketing lesson that you might want to use sometime. If you want to sell a book, tell people that they can't have it. At this point, everyone had to have the book. We actually heard of two women in a shopping mall who got into a fistfight over the last copy of the book at a Walden's. We sold out before Christmas.

We decided that we would take the book national. We didn't know this was impossible. All we knew was that people wanted the book and we had no publisher. So we took it national, and soon found that it was nearly impossible, and we ran into some very difficult times. At one point, we thought we had lost everything. But the first of December of 1994, through some pretty incredible grace, we had shipped a quarter of a million copies. Now the president of Harper Collins Publishing asked me, "How could you sell a quarter of a million copies and the press hasn't noticed you?" I said, "It's because being self-published is like competing in the Olympics without a country. They make you run outside of the stadium."

But we got our first big break. *People Magazine* decided they would do a story on the *The Christmas Box*. The next day was an exciting day. I remember coming back from speaking at a junior high school, which is worse than speaking at a prison, and my secretary called on the cell phone and she said, "Rick, go home. NBC just called. You're on *The Today Show* tomorrow morning with Katie Couric. They've already booked your flight."

We packed up and went, and it started a national phenomenon, as people lined up outside of bookstores all across America. And we were only at the time in one out of five bookstores in America. So it started the same phenomenon that had happened in Salt Lake City. But we sold so many copies out of those bookstores that we managed by Christmas to hit number two on the *New York Times* best seller list. At this point, the publishers decided they really did want the book after all. Hollywood was a little bit more aggressive. I was receiving about three movie offers a day. Everyone from Steven Spielberg to Oliver Stone–I still think Oliver Stone's version of *The Christmas Box* would have been really interesting. I had already sold the rights to a local company who produced a television movie with CBS, which you might have seen, starring Maureen O'Hara and Richard Thomas, that went on to be the number one TV movie of 1995.

At this time it went back to New York, and this is every author's dream. I am meeting with the publishers of every major publishing house in New York. I remember the head of Random House got more and more excited as the sales people told him what this book had accomplished, and at one point, he pounded the table and he said, "Mr. Evans, what is it that is keeping you from signing with Random House right now?" And his aide turned to him and said, "About twenty-five other publishers." The book went into an auction that went on for three and half days, at the end of which Simon & Schuster bought it for $4.25 million.

At this point, we did something that was very unconventional. And I use that word kindly, because I was told it was stupid. We brought out both the hard cover and the paperback book simultaneously. We were told if we did this we would split the sales. It wasn't to make more money. I knew it would cost me money. I wanted the book to be available to every American, I wanted it to be available at $4.95, and so we brought out both books. And I felt strongly impressed that this was the right thing to do. And by Christmas Eve of 1995, we saw the wisdom as *The Christmas Box* became the only book in history to simultaneously hit number one on the *New York Times* hardcover and paperback best seller lists.

Since that time, this book has spread to more than forty countries worldwide. It's in seventeen languages. It's been a best seller in Japan for two years, which really surprises me since they don't have Christmas in Japan. And one of the highlights of the '95 season is that as I returned home from a book tour, we received a phone call from the White House and were invited to go back and spend a couple of days with the Clintons, which is really a remarkable experience, even for a Utah Republican.

The next April, Simon & Schuster released my second novel, *Timepiece*. I learned a really interesting lesson about society. We worship success but we hate the successful. The media loves to build people to destroy them. They love the excitement of a rising star, and then they love to shoot them down, and this is what happened. The day my second novel was released, I received a phone call early in the morning from Laurie Liss, my agent, who does not hide things from me. She said, "Rick, I just read the nastiest review I have ever read." She said, "With these people, it's personal." That was kind of the way things went and it was a tough tour.

This book that we brought out after selling three million copies in basically six weeks of *The Christmas Box*, we sold only a quarter of a million copies, which is nothing to cry over, but we had much higher expectations. The book fell off the *New York Times* best seller list after only about five weeks.

It looked like I was a one-book wonder. And that was painful. It was one of those tours where people had heard about the thousands of people who came to my book signings–so they rented an entire cathedral in Florida, and five people came. I was in Indiana and only six elderly women came to the signing. I remember sitting there, they had bodyguards for me, and I remember a bodyguard saying to me, "Can I do something for you?" And it's like, "Yes, if she gets too close with the cane, take her out." It was hard, it was really hard. And the criticism stung.

I wasn't used to this and it hurt. And it was personal. But we kept going. I believed in the book. And we convinced Simon & Schuster that the release was wrong, that everything had happened to me so quickly that no one knew my name, but that if we released it at Christmas time people would make the connection–and it would help if they made the book look like

The Christmas Box. And they did. And we outsold it in the second release. It started to sell, and it sold 300,000 copies that next fall, bringing the sales up to more than a half million copies. And since that time, it has sold more than a million copies. So this book that was a failure went on and we are very glad that we persevered.

The next book came out; it was called *The Letter*. *The Letter* came out, tenuous, no one knew what would happen, and it came out number eight. I was just hoping to hit the top ten with the *New York Times*. It bounced around for awhile, and then it started to climb as I developed a core following, and by Christmas of '97 I had the number four and number five book in the nation, and the *New York Times* christened me "The King of Christmas Fiction."

Since that time, it has been a very interesting road. I've learned a lot on that road. I think I've learned some things that could be helpful to you, and I would like to share them with you.

First thing I would like you to remember is to be your own best advocate. If you don't do it, no one else will. A defining moment for me, and you're going to have defining moments, was at the Rocky Mountain Book Festival. This was early in '94, I didn't have much money, and I'm promoting this book on a shoestring. I had bought space at a show and while I was sitting there in my booth, no one was coming by. No one wanted to see my book, and I thought, "Well, how come no one's here?" That worries everyone. It's a big show. And so I walked around and I found out where everyone was. Everyone was going to see the famous authors. They had a whole row of authors and they had their escorts behind them, and people would get in line to get free books autographed by the authors. And as soon as they finished, they would get back in line, and wait for the next string of authors. And I thought, "This is disastrous. I needed this show. I needed to talk to these book sellers and I can't meet them."

And then I noticed up by the table there was an empty seat. And I looked at it for a while, and I thought, no, I couldn't do that. I started to walk away and I thought, "If I don't care more about this book than anyone else, then why does it deserve to succeed?" I turned around, and I walked up there and I sat down in that empty seat. As soon as I did, one of the organizers spotted me and when she got to me, I looked up and said, "I'm sorry I'm late." It stunned her. She said, "May I get you some water?" The next year my book at that time was actually the number one book on the *New York Times* best seller list when I went back to that show, and I was their premier author. And the same woman was there. And I said, "Do you remember me?" And she said, "yes." And I said, "Thank you for not throwing me out last year." She said, "What did it hurt?"

Be your book's best advocate. Believe in your book, believe in your writing. Just because you have some rejections doesn't mean your book isn't worthy. Jack Canfield can tell you a lot about rejections. He has even more slips than I do. I think he has framed them by now. But you keep going if you believe in it.

The second thing I've learned is to have a website. Websites are wonderful and I have had such good dialogue. The exciting thing is you get this really fresh dialogue. The way I start my day, I go into work, and I open up my website and I get to read all the letters, all the e-mail that people sent me overnight after reading my latest book, usually *The Locket*. And it's great because it is instantaneous. They're usually still crying when they type in, and they tell you very wonderful personal things; it's a great way to start the day. It's a great way to interact. And this is something you want to do. You want to know your readers. You want to develop a core following. You want to know their names. If any of you come to get books signed afterward, I will give you a card and ask you if you want to be on my mailing list, to create a relationship with you. Do this with your readers. I've seen some authors, they don't sell that many books, but they have such a core following that they do really well because they have a relationship. It's almost like a big family that follows their books. It's a smart thing to do.

Three. Care about your readers. Care about them, love them. A book is a very intimate experience. I've met people who felt like at times they held onto my book because they felt like I was their only friend. I was at a book signing, it was at the end of '95, and I was tired of book signings, the book signings were too big, I had carpal tunnel, and they set up a book signing in a Wal-Mart ten days before Christmas. It's a dangerous place to be! And so I go to the signings; sure enough, people have already been lined up for two hours to get signed copies, and it goes around the building, and I go up there and I start signing books and thinking, this isn't fun. And I'm going through it, and suddenly a woman walks up outside the ropes and she sits and stares at me for a while, and then she shouts at me. She yelled, "I don't have time to wait in your line, Mr. Evans." I looked up at her, and everyone in the line turned around and looked at this peculiar woman, and there's something really different about her eyes. And then she said, "I just wanted to tell you that my little girl was hit by a car Thursday and killed. And I've read your book every day since then. It's the only thing that is keeping me going."

You don't know. A woman walked through the line carrying a camera, she just walked through, and I signed her book, and she started leaving. I said, "Ma'am, you have a camera. Did you want a picture?" She said, "Would that be all right?" I said, "I would love to have your picture," and I started talking to her. This woman had driven from three states away to come to my book signing. She had taken her vacation and her savings to come meet me, and she was willing to do all that for that short amount of time. You better appreciate that. You're not human if you don't appreciate that. And you better make it the best experience. I can't tell you how many times people say to me, "Thank you for being nice to me," because they have had a bad experience with authors. I'm grateful. I do not forget the times when no one came to my book signings. I remember sitting there for hours with no one coming by, and trying to talk people into coming. I never forget that.

I had another experience. A man came through and he got up to me and couldn't speak. He was very emotional. I said, "Would you like to talk for a moment?" and he nodded his head. And he came by and he said, "My wife died a couple of weeks ago and her last request was to have me read your book to her, and she died as I read it to her." You don't know. You don't know what they're carrying. You don't know how much you owe them. So assume that you owe them a lot. I'm grateful to be able to be a writer, to be employed, and that's possible because of good people who buy my books, and I think my readers are the best people in the world.

If you're writing because you want to be rich, you probably never will be. If you're writing because you want to be a best seller, you don't deserve to be. You write because what you want to write matters, and if what you write affects just two people in a powerful way, then it was worth it. I want you to remember this. If two little girls had read *The Christmas Box* and had understood that their father loved them, it would have been enough. If my mother was the only one who felt healed by my little book, it would have been okay. It would have been enough. It's reason enough to go ahead. So do your best and touch as many lights as you can. Go ahead and change the world.

❧

"I'm always looking for characters. I'm always looking for something I don't expect. Flawed characters are always more interesting. When I'm looking for a concept for a character, I always start with my relatives."

–Craig Lesley

Ernest J. Gaines

Behind *A Lesson Before Dying*

I was teaching at the University of Southwestern Louisiana in 1983 or 1984 when I came up with the idea of *A Lesson Before Dying*. The original idea was that the action of this novel would occur in the early 1980s. I wrote a letter to the warden at Angola State Prison in Louisiana informing him that I was a teacher at USL and an author. I said I had a novel in mind about a prisoner on death row, and would he, the warden, mind my asking him a few questions. Question number one: Would it be possible for someone to make a visit to an inmate on death row when the visitor was not kin to the condemned man, not a minister of religion, and not his legal adviser?

About a week later I received a letter from the warden's office informing me that he would not be able to guarantee that. I wrote a second letter, assuring the warden that I had no intention of visiting Angola on a regular basis, but that I was writing a novel and was wondering if it were possible that a teacher, for example, visit a condemned man.

Well, the warden's office never did answer my second letter and maybe that was a blessing in disguise. Being in residence on any university campus, you are constantly asked "How is the writing coming along?" and "When can we expect the next book?" etc. *A Gathering of Old Men* had been published in '83 so between 1983 and 1985 I was between books. When a colleague of mine at USL asked me what was I doing, I told him I had a novel in mind and told him the results of my letters to the warden. I gave him a general plot of the novel: It was about a young man at the wrong place and wrong time when a murder is committed. Paul knew of a case that I might be interested in reading, concerning a seventeen-year-old boy sentenced to be executed in the electric chair in Louisiana. The chair failed the first time and the youth was returned to his cell to await and see what the government would do next. Paul said the two cases were different but that I might benefit by reading his case. This particular trial that Paul spoke of happened in 1946 or 1947.

The case he spoke of happened only a few miles from where we were teaching. Though the two cases were quite different, I used some of the same material. For example, both young men were involved in killing a white man. Though the young man in Paul's case reportedly confessed to the crime, my young man claimed he was innocent. No witnesses for the defense were called in either case. Both young men were black and illiterate. Only white men served on both juries. This was the 1940s, so there were no women, and, of course, no blacks on juries.

After reading all the material Paul gave me and gathering more he recommended, I asked myself, why not take my story back to the '40s? I had written about that period in other books. If the story took place in the '40s, I could use the plantation as home to my characters. I knew the plantation well. I lived there the first fifteen and a half years of my life. I knew the work other people did on the plantation. I knew the crop that grew there, when it was planted, when it was harvested. I knew the people who lived there, what they ate, the clothes they wore, even knew all their religious songs. I had been a member of the church, the same place I had attended my first six years of school. I could use the church school that I attended as a child. The same church where my folks had worshipped on Sundays. I could use the small town, the courthouse, the jail. I read everything Paul gave me and all that he recommended because the young man was still on death row, to be executed later. The case went all the way to the Supreme Court but eventually lost by a decision of five to four, and the young man would be executed exactly one year and one week from the first time he was put into the chair. The case received much publicity even for the '40s in the deep South. All the publicity was not enough to save this young man's life.

But even with all the information that Paul had given me, I still needed more. Because I teach creative writing at a university and because I teach at night, we have a chance to draw people from outside the university and I always get lawyers as students. I've had one or more lawyers in every class since I started teaching at the university in 1981. Some lawyers have become good narrative writers. One of my students had a condemned man on death row and I would ask him questions about the reaction of someone who knows he's going to die on a certain date. I could always tell when my student had visited his client. He was much older than this young man and he had gotten very close to him and when he would come to my class for a visit I would tell by his wisdom that he had gotten too close, he had gotten too emotionally involved. He knew it, too, but he could not do anything about it.

He helped me in many ways. He brought me pictures of the state prison, cell blocks, pictures of the electric chair—it was called Gruesome Gertie. I asked him more questions. I asked him what kind of wood the chair was made of, how much did the chair weigh, how wide and thick were the straps that went around the arms and legs. He gave me as much information as he could and I kept pictures on my desk, especially when writing the last two chapters.

Another colleague of mine at USL knew someone whose father-in-law was sheriff of a small town. When we arrived at his house I was introduced to the sheriff, his wife, and to another man. The sheriff's wife served coffee. I was served last. And I noticed how much her hands shook when she served me. I was certain she had never served coffee to another black man in the house. But after all, I had written *The Autobiography of Miss Jane Pittman*, and I also knew her daughter-in-law, so she had to make somewhat of a Southern hospitality gesture toward me.

The sheriff and the other man wanted to know where I came from, did I like the South, and how long had I been teaching at USL. I told him I was born about sixty miles from where we sat and my people had lived in the same parish for 100 years and that I had been teaching at USL for about five years and I liked it very much. That relaxed them a bit and we finished our coffee. I asked the sheriff the same question that I proposed to the warden in my letter. Could someone who was not a close relative, who is not a minister of religion, who's not a legal adviser visit someone on death row? The sheriff told me that it would be entirely up to the discretion of the sheriff.

That bit of information was vital. Now I had to find a reason to pressure my sheriff into allowing a visit to a prisoner by someone the sheriff may not like. As usual, my colleagues at the university would ask how the novel was going and when I would tell them I was still trying to get everything straight in my mind, they would always come up with suggestions. One fellow who considered himself a writer, too, had an idea how to pressure the sheriff into letting someone visit. Find something on the sheriff that the sheriff did not want people to know about. I told him that was blackmail and I didn't want any of that. He told me he had another idea. The sheriff's wife had had an abortion in Paris and you know how Southerners feel about that. I told him I didn't care for that idea, either. He said, WWell, the sheriff's wife could have had a relationship with a black man and your character threatened to tell. My God, that would make him let him come there." And I said, "More than likely my character will get killed before we ever got to that jail." I said, "No thanks."

So as I said before, the original idea of the novel was that a young man named Grant who was living in California would come back to Louisville one summer to visit his aunt and eventually get to visit Jefferson, the prisoner. That was the original reason for the questions. If someone was not kin, a religious minister or a legal adviser, I'm sure the warden or sheriff would not have wanted an outsider, especially someone from the North, interfering with that business. It was not until I decided that the story could take place in the '40s that I decided to make Grant a teacher who had gone away for his education and now had come back to teach on the same plantation where he was born, raised, and where all of his people had lived for at least seven generations. Still, because he was educated, one of the smart ones, I had to find a way to assure he could visit Jefferson in the local jail, because I wanted my story told from that first-person point of view.

My colleague at USL had given me an idea of how to solve my problem when he mentioned the sheriff's wife several times. I would not cause her to ever have an abortion or a black lover, but I'll put her in a position where she could definitely help solve my problem. My maternal grandmother had worked at the big house on that plantation for many years. I knew other women who had done the same. I had worked in the yard at the big house on several occasions, collecting eggs where the chickens had laid them in the grass, and gathering fruit from the trees. Now suppose I made the sheriff's wife remember a family like that, where my grandmother had worked all those years. Suppose another older black woman had worked there just as long, serving two generations of the sheriff's wife's ancestors. Couldn't they put enough pressure on her so she could pressure her husband to let Grant visit Jefferson? That, I thought, was a much better reason to get the sheriff to accept Grant than what my colleague had suggested.

Thus, I created Tante Lou, Grant's aunt, and Miss Emma, Jefferson's godmother, who would apply pressure.

Once I decided the story would take place in the late '40s, not the '80s, and that Grant would have been educated and returned to the plantation where he had grown up, it added another dimension to the story. I didn't want just a simple story of a black prisoner in jail waiting to be executed. That has been done many times before. To make my story different I had to do something else. I had to make Grant a prisoner as well. In a way. Grant teaches in a parish. He hates teaching, he hates the South. But this is the 1940s and professions for blacks are extremely, extremely limited. He could be a teacher to black children. He could be an underpaid barber, but he could not be an attorney. He could not be a banker, a doctor, or a politician. And certainly he could not vote.

Grant wants to run away. He knows that he is a poor teacher and he's probably hurting his students as much as he's helping them. He wants to run away, but he has an aunt, Tante Lou, and just as she and Miss Emma exert pressure on the sheriff, they do the same to Grant to keep him in the South.

All characters are created for reasons, or they should not be in the book. Tante Lou and Miss Emma were definitely created to exert pressure. They're the two who drive *A Lesson Before Dying*.

As I said earlier, I always had attorneys in my class. In 1986 one of those students, a young woman who was an attorney, asked me if I would like to meet a lawyer who had defended the young man that Paul Nolan had told me about. I told her I certainly would. She brought the older man to my home. He was a Cajun fellow, probably in his seventies, thin and frail. My student and I made coffee and she had brought some cookies and we sat out on the porch. It was this man who told me about the traveling electric chair.

I'd heard about it, read about it, but I had not spoken to anyone who knew about it firsthand. He also told me about the generator that accompanied the chair. I should mention here that there is no traveling electric chair in Louisiana anymore. Lethal injection is the method of execution in the state today. But let's get back to the '40s, when it did travel from one parish to the other. At that time execution was administered in the parish in which the crime was committed, not at a state prison as it is done today. The attorney told me about the chair, the generator and the public truck that delivered it the morning or the night before an execution.

He said the time of execution in a particular parish was between noon and three on Friday. He told me that the generator had to be in working order when it was time. And he told me that you could hear the generator at least two city blocks away from the jail. He had witnessed the execution of the young man who had been sent to the chair a year earlier, when the chair failed. He, this attorney, had taken the case all the way to the Supreme Court in Washington, arguing that this was cruel and unusual punishment to send this young man back to the chair. But he failed by a vote of five to four. He could remember the year, the week, the day, the exact hour, forty years later when he's telling me the story. Suddenly he stopped talking and brought his hands up to his face. My student moved closer to him and held him. And he lay his head on her shoulder, weeping.

Students are always asking me, "Do you know the ending of your novel when you start writing?" I always use the analogy of getting on a train in San Francisco to go to New York. It could take me three or four days to get there. I know some facts: I'm leaving San Francisco to go to New York to visit some friends. And I know some of the states I'll travel through and some of the things I'll see and do. I know I'll go to the dining car, I'll go to the club car for a drink, I'll read a book that I've brought along. I'll get so many hours of sleep. Now these are things that I know. What I don't know is how the weather is going to be the entire trip. I don't know who will get on the train, where they will sit, how they will be dressed. I don't know all the valleys and the hills that I'll cross. I don't know about all the different colors of nature–the color of leaves on trees, the color of the different crops in the different fields. I don't know all the turning and twisting of the rails or when the train will make a sudden stop. In other words, I can't anticipate everything that will happen on the trip. Sometimes I don't get to New York at all, but end up in Philadelphia. When I first started writing *A Lesson Before Dying*, I knew Jefferson would be sentenced to die, because this was Louisiana in the '40s and he had been on the premises where a white man had been killed. He had been caught with a white man's liquor in his hand, a white man's money in his pocket. That meant he was guilty according to Louisiana law. But will he be executed? I did not know.

But after the attorney described a truck delivering that electric chair and the generator, and the noise it made that could be heard two city blocks away, and that the time of execution was on a Friday between noon and three, I knew then that I had another new ending for that Jefferson execution. I wanted you, the reader, to see the public truck delivering that chair, and that generator, in the early foggy morning in the small Louisiana town. And I wanted all to hear the generator and know what it was all about.

Getting back to that train trip from San Francisco to New York—or maybe Philadelphia—two things that I had not anticipated when I began the novel, and which would be important roles in the novel, are the radio and the notebook. After I had gone so far into the novel and Jefferson still refused to communicate with anyone, I knew I had to find some way to make him talk.

On that plantation where I lived as a child, on Saturday nights the people in one or two of the houses in the quarters would give house fairs. There would be food, beer, there'd be music. In one of his visits to the jail, Grant mentions the music at one of the house fairs to Jefferson. When Jefferson shows a sign of interest, Grant promises to get him a radio so he could always have music in his cell anytime he wished. As I said, the idea of the radio came up only by chance, but it was the first turning point in the story of communication. From that moment on, there was some, if limited, communication between the two of them. Still Jefferson refused to open up completely to anyone—Grant or his godmother or Miss Emma, or the minister of that church. So we know a little about Jefferson, what's inside of him, what he's really thinking about, what he thinks about life, but I felt we had to know him better. Once I decided he would be executed, I knew he would not want to reveal his feelings to anyone, but he still had to. I did not want any last moment soliloquy on his way to be executed. I needed that information long before then. Thus, I created a notebook. Grant would bring him a notebook and a pencil, and tell him to write down anything he wishes. Anything. The least little thoughts. When Grant visits him again, after he has given him the notebook and sees that he has written and erased, Grant tells him not to erase. Never erase, but put down anything he wishes and the way he wishes to do it, which he does from then on.

Jefferson is illiterate. He has never written a letter in his life. He's barely able to write his elementary school assignments. He does not know whether to write above the lines or across the lines, so he does both. He does not erase. He does not capitalize. He uses no punctuation marks. He writes what comes into his mind. He writes at night when there is light because he doesn't want others to see him during the day. He writes the night before his execution because the sheriff has promised him that on that last night he can have all the light that he wants. He writes about people, about things, about love. And he asks questions about justice. And about God. All of this above and across the lines of his notebook without capitalization, without punctuation. Grant does not attend the execution. He cannot. He would not be strong enough to stand.

A young deputy brings Jefferson's notebook to Grant and tells him that Jefferson was the strongest man in that room when he came to die. The young deputy tells Grant that he is a wonderful, wonderful teacher, to have changed Jefferson so much. Grant hears this from outside the school. When he returns to his classroom, to his students, they're waiting for some news of Jefferson. Grant, cynical up to this moment, looks at his students, and he's crying.

Writing for me is discovery. If I knew everything when I started a novel, it would be very boring to write it. I do not know everything that is going to happen. I don't want to know everything. I want to find out, as you the reader finds out, what the story is going to be about. Let us say we do know the plot, what the story's about. We know the plot of *Hamlet*.

But we still read *Hamlet* because there's something there much more than plot. There's beauty of language. There's poetry. Symbols. Subplots. All kinds of little mysteries we had overlooked. Those are the things that happened on that train trip, from San Francisco to New York—or maybe Philadelphia. Not only that we don't know all the people who are going to get on the train, but we don't know what they can do to change our lives.

Oprah Winfrey asked me what I tried to do with my writing and I said something like this, "I try to create characters with character, to help develop my own character and maybe help the reader develop his. I don't know where all these characters come from. They hop on the train somewhere along the way and I deal with them as best I can."

"The best time to start a book is when you least expect to, or when you don't have time to. Don't take it seriously, just write it."

—Elmore Leonard

JAMES CLEMENS, AUTHOR
Wit'ch Fire, Wit'ch Storm,
and *Wit'ch War*

"Someday I'll write that novel...."
How many times during my life did I tell myself that? Ever since I first picked up a book, that was my dream. When I was younger, I even believed such a dream was possible. I scrawled daily in a notebook—short stories, journal entries, and the beginnings of countless novels. I loved the power of words to conjure other worlds, other peoples. I fantasized about writing the next great American novel.

But as one ages, we are taught to put aside such childish dreams and fantasies. We are instructed to pursue a career, raise a family, earn a living. And unfortunately, I listened.

I applied and was accepted into the Veterinary College of the University of Missouri. Here is my career, I told myself. I set aside my notebooks and journals, picked up a textbook and a stethoscope, and set out on my journey toward a doctorate in Veterinary medicine.

Though I loved medicine and working with animals, I still felt something was missing from my life. "Someday..." I would whisper to myself in the middle of the night. "Someday I'll write again." But my notebooks and pens continued to gather dust. As the years rolled by, the call to write grew more and more strident. Finally, I realized I was fooling myself. That voice would never die away. The only way to shut it up would be to obey its command.

After almost twenty years, I again collected my old notebooks and put pen to paper. Words came out in a huge flood. Story after story poured forth. Horrible, poorly-written stories! But who cared? I was writing again.

Over the next four years, I honed my skill: reading how-to books, attending on-line classes, and practicing, practicing, practicing. I spent years searching for a way to pull that voice out of my head and put it on paper.

In the summer 1996, I signed up for the Maui Writers Conference, ready to learn more about the writing business. During that summer I also began work on a fantasy series. I wrote the first 200 pages and decided to submit it to the conference's writing contest. What could it hurt?

So as Labor Day rolled around, I packed up my bags and dreams, and headed for the sunny shores of Maui. On the first day of the conference, at a meet-and-greet cocktail party, I spotted one of my idols: Terry Brooks, international best selling author of the Shannara fantasy series. I approached him and thanked him for writing such wonderful novels over the years.

He, in turn, glanced to my nametag and said. "Oh, I'm a fan of yours, too."

I didn't know what Terry Brooks was talking about, so I just laughed nervously as if I understood his joke (because that's what you do when you meet one of your childhood idols).

He responded matter-of-factly, "No, I'm serious. I was one of the judges for this year's contest. And here's my publisher. He'd like to talk to you." From that meeting, a three-book deal for my fantasy series was eventually struck. In that single weekend, my life changed. It was as if I had woken up after a long sleep. I was a novelist. Who would have guessed?

I write this to prove that childhood dreams can come true. And trust me, these words are not the stuff of fantasy.

"My four-year-old daughter came home one afternoon and she said, 'Dad, can I ask you a question?' And I said, 'Yeah, what's the question?' I thought it was going to be, you know, Winnie the Pooh or something. And she said, 'Dad, are you stable?' And I told her. I told her truthfully, I said, 'Spencer, no, Daddy is not stable. Daddy is a writer.'"

–David Baldacci

Julie Garwood

How Romantic

I will start by telling you something that I do that's so bizarre, and it wasn't until my fifth book that I realized I was doing it. I've always said I was creative. I've never said I was bright. I write three different endings to every single book, even the kids' books that I've done. I finish the first one and I think, what was I thinking? And then I rewrite it from a different angle, different perspective, and then I think, no, no, that's not it, and I write a third ending. I always send the first ending. Isn't that bizarre? My editor said it's my way of letting go of the characters. Well, I think it's my way of stopping myself from rewriting the book completely. I always think that I need to do more and more and more. So we're going to talk about romance today, and that's going to be fun. I hope.

I believe that the number one objective for this gathering should be to rekindle the enthusiasm we have for the writing. I've heard in the last six months a lot of whining about the marketplace for romance. I'm hearing that it's tough on all of us. That we can't open a magazine or talk to anyone in publishing without hearing about that shrinking mid-list, etc. We know that within romance the competition is enormous. We all should know that romance is not a protected genre. By that I mean we compete for the readers' money but also his or her time. And that's a precious commodity these days.

When a reader walks into a bookstore, ready to select a book to spend her money on, she sees thousands of choices. Our competition isn't just within the romance genre, we must compete with the Grishams, the Kings, and all those Chicken Soups, too. Well, guess what? Romance is definitely holding its own. Some of us manage to write some good books. The Energizer Bunny looks like a slacker next to a romance writer. It isn't surprising that our books hold their own in the marketplace. Why? Because they're good. They're uplifting novels with strong characters, appealing settings, and compelling plots. There is a vast reading public who wants what we can give them. Books that raise their spirits, make them think, give them knowledge or a new idea, take them away to another time and place, make them laugh, make them feel.

It all began when that first man etched those picture stories on his cave wall and his next-door neighbor came by to take a look. And by the way, that was the birth of the first critic as well. It continued with the medieval troubadours who traveled the land encountering wondrous tales. And the bards of old brought crowds to gather to make them laugh and cry at the exploit of lovers. And it will continue as long as there are people interested in the knowledge and the experiences of other people. We're part of that noble tradition.

Want some cold hard facts about romance? Well, it makes up half of the paperback market today and a very large share of the hard cover. And it generates over a billion dollars a year in revenue. Pretty impressive, huh? Having said that, I've got to admit I never thought I was going to end up a romance writer when I went back to college. Writing was just for pleasure. But looking back, I realize I had the romance affliction pretty early on. I just didn't know it was a career path.

This is a true story. When I was in college I was given a final exam in ancient history. We had to compare the philosophies of Plato and Socrates. Well, I didn't want to just compare and contrast the philosophies. I wanted my essay to have plot, dialogue and setting. And I wanted to show what Socrates and Plato were really feeling as they argued their points. I created a woman to moderate the debate. A lovely, intelligent, spirited woman who, of course, knew far more than both the philosophers did, and who, of course, captivated them and took their breath away. Well, I imagine I took my instructor's breath away, too. He'd never received a paper with dialogue before, but he gave me an "A" for sheer enthusiasm.

Anyway, now that I've given you my commercial for why you should be writing romance, I'll welcome you to "Love 101." Close your eyes for a minute and let your mind wander a bit. Love is in the air. Imagine yourself with the man or woman of your dreams. You're in the ultimate romantic setting, like Maui. We're here to talk about romance and that's why I say we're here to talk about happiness. Your interpretation of the word may be totally different from that of the person sitting next to you. I'm here to show you how to add romance to your writing, and that's easier said than done. I operate under the theory that love is what happens while you're busy going about the business of living. You don't set out in the morning, saying, I think I'll fall in love today. No, you just go about your life. Events bring you together with other people and then something happens and you find yourself drawn to one special person. The senses perk up, the hormones kick in. And without thinking, you catch yourself thinking or daydreaming about what he or she is doing at that very moment. And you're checking your watch or your calendar to calculate how long it's going to be before you see her again.

Romance–listen to the larger picture and before you know it, it runs the show. Love definitely makes the world go around. And it's everywhere. It's in our books, in our movies, in our songs and our commercials: everywhere. Love is the most fundamental and yet the most complex of emotions since the beginning of man and, therefore, it's going to appeal to a reader like no other subject. It's one of the best devices you can use to draw the reader to your character. Romance can be a bit player, or it can add humanity to your story, or it can become the story. Shakespeare warned us, "the course of true love never runs smooth." And writers for centuries have capitalized on that fact.

Anyone who rejects romance as trivial, or unsuitable for serious writing, is missing an opportunity to reach and connect with a massive audience. So let's take a look at how we add romance to what we write.

First of all, we need to fit it into a larger framework of dramatic fiction, or simply what we call telling a good story. Every good work of fiction can be defined by its premise, its theme. It's the core of the story, that central idea that the plot illustrates or proves. For example, *To Kill A Mockingbird*, which happens to be one of my favorites. I think its premise is that human dignity will not be destroyed by prejudice or ignorance. All the action and all the sub-plots of that novel reinforce that idea. Same thing goes for romance. The theme, then, determines what scenes we include in our story. And the majority of what we read in one way or another includes the romance.

There are stories in which the romance is just one of the supporting elements of the premise. Like in a really good mystery, for example, with the theme of "good guy will always outsmart the bad guy," you might add a romance as a secondary plot that reinforces that idea. The victim's wife might fall for the dashing detective, for instance.

Then there's the story in which love is the theme. The theme of *The Notebook* is that true love endures. It will outlast the fullness of time and distance and illness, even death. On the other hand, in a novel like *Anna Karenina*, the premise is that elicit love destroys. Both of these novels are romances of a sort, but they deliver two completely different messages.

When you're dealing with love as a theme, the variations are literally limitless. The first job of a dramatic story is to determine the premise. Following that, the most important factor is character, character, character. It's the essential element. It's your foundation. The action of the story is the tool you use to reveal that character. When it comes to writing relationships, the same idea applies. Showing a reaction to what's happening can be much more effective at exposing the feelings of the character than if you simply declare it. For example, a scene where a hero finds the object of his affection in some sort of peril. Now you could say he was real worried about her, or you could express his thoughts through actions—have him running through a spray of bullets, screaming her name. As in everything else you write, you show, don't tell. That certainly applies to romance.

So how do you write romance? You write it like you write anything else. You write it like you'd write intrigue, or horror, or humor. You use what you know. I'm not suggesting you have to reveal your innermost feelings or disclose your dark secrets or fantasies, but rather I'm suggesting you draw from your vast bank of experiences and observations. If you're writing intrigue, what intrigues you? If you're writing horror, what scares you? If you're writing romance, what do you remember about the first time you ever fell in love? What tugs at your heartstrings and makes your knees go weak? That will define romance for you.

After you've defined it, how do you apply it to your writing and communicate it in your story? Once again, you draw from what you know. You let your own voice shine through. If I were to give each one of you the beginning of a scene right now and ask each of you to write the story, I bet I'd have as many interpretations as there are people in this room. That's because we all have a unique voice and a unique view of the world. It's who we are that we bring to that writing. I call it our vision. I'm a big believer in visions. Knowledge of trends is good and it does pay to keep your eyes and ears open. Gather advice, tips, and techniques from those who have succeeded, but then proceed. I'm not telling you to buck the trends; I just don't think it's a good idea to chase them. The readers love Danielle Steele. Look at the numbers. But we have a Danielle Steele. Publishers are looking for a new, fresh, vibrant voice. So it's important that you let your way of looking at love and relationships come through in the writing.

So where do you find your vision? Well if you're like me, you find it everywhere. In the people you meet, the places you go, the things you do, and the human dramas that are played out in front of you. If there is a story inside of you that you're dying to tell, don't be dissuaded by what other authors before you have done. Or are doing. Don't let their visions dictate yours. Write your own story and write it from the heart.

My own perspective on writing romance is a relatively simple one. I believe a romance is a story about feelings. It's about a relationship that undergoes conflict, change, and resolution. Sometimes the relationship is the primary conflict and sometimes the relationship is secondary to another plot line. But there is always this underlying question: Are they going to end up together? If we were to examine the huge number of short stories, novels, plays, and screenplays, over time we'd find a large percentage of them fit into this very broad category. Writers like Austin, Bronte, Tolstoy, even Shakespeare, were writing romances. And today there are other great writers who are giving us wonderful stories destined to become classics. There are countless categories of romances–gothic, historical, romantic suspense, contemporary romance– but they all have one common thread that connects them. They're all about intimate relationship. If they're good, they'll draw the reader or the viewer in and make him feel for those characters. There aren't any blueprints for you to follow. You're going to have to come up with your own version. But if you'll draw from your own observations and feelings, your words are more likely to ring true and you'll find your writing will have a stronger voice.

I am going to give you some suggestions that have worked for me. So here we go.

Number one, have a basic comprehension of the differences between men and women. I always recommend to writers that they read a book called *Men Are From Mars, Women Are From Venus,* by John Gray. There is a difference between us, of course, and the way we think. Doesn't have anything to do with intelligence, creativity, or superiority. It's more to do with perception. I really believe that there's some validity to the whole idea of women's intuition. Women seem more attuned to vibes and the way people relate to one another. I'm sure it's all part of nature's big plan. We have needed that nurturing instinct if you go back through history. Why men and women are so different is a complex question that the psychologists will argue about forever. And I know there are a lot of answers ranging from biology to cultural conditioning.

Dr. Gray says men value power and achievement. Their sense of self is defined by their ability to get results, to accomplish things. They're more interested in objects than people. Women, on the other hand, value love, beauty, communications, relationships. And they spend a great deal of time helping, supporting, and nurturing. Their sense of self is defined by their feeling and the quality in their relationships. Men and women communicate but we're not always on the same page. And that's a real important thing to remember when you're writing a romance. And it makes it kind of fun, too. I think men take words a little more at face value, whereas women will be looking for that hidden meaning behind the words and will pay attention to the way people express themselves.

I just finished a scene with the hero and a heroine of a book I'm writing. He wants to marry her, but she has obligations and can't. She can't think about settling down to a traditional life, even though that is her dream. She says to him, "You don't understand. I can never have Annie Drummond's house." Now Annie Drummond was a character they'd met earlier. She was a woman with a lovely home, loving husband, a baby on the way, a truly idealistic life in the eyes of our heroine. So what our heroine is trying to convey is, "I can't have that kind of life because of the responsibilities in the way." But his answer to her is, "You want Annie Drummond's house? Mine's bigger." She says the figurative; he hears the literal. They're on two different wavelengths.

In my books I like happy endings. There are some wonderful writers who can just tear your heart out with tragedy. They're wonderful, but I just happen to like the happy resolutions. While I put my heroes and heroines through all sorts of trials and tribulations, in the end, they will be rewarded in triumph.

Next, since I'm the boss, I'm going to create heroes and heroines I like. Each of them may be different in personality but they will have character traits I think are important. If he's a medieval warrior, I'll make him honorable, loyal, and just. And then I'll put armor on him and show his might in battle, but never against a woman, of course. He's going to think he's invincible. But the reader, and the heroine, are going to see his Achilles' heel and like him anyway. She, on the other hand, is going to be vulnerable, but she will also be determined and resourceful. She's going to be strong and intelligent and if she isn't, I'm not going to like her and I guarantee if I don't like her, the reader won't either. The hero, by the way, is not going to save the heroine. She's going to save herself, but they will form a partnership that will last over time.

Though the majority of my readers are women, I hear from quite a lot of men, too. I think it's because I like to write from both the male and the female points of view in my books. I love to get inside the heads of the characters and show how a man and a woman can have two completely different reactions to the same situation. I believe it's that counterpoint, that friction that arises when males and females try to connect, that creates a sexual tension. But the true heart-melting scenes, I think, are the ones that are more subtle. For example, a scene where one character has that moment of realization of how deep his feelings go, or how important she is to him. When a hero recognizes he doesn't want to live without her, or the heroine realizes he's become the center of her universe—that, to me, is real romance.

I also believe true romance is in the heart, and it's best depicted by showing what's going on in the mind of the character and not necessarily in describing scenes of great physical passion. I've received thousands of letters from readers. They tell me they like reading about the physical attraction that arises between the hero and the heroine, but I would say that ninety-nine percent of them tell me that what they like most is the tremendous emotional bond that develops between the two and holds them together. So in essence, what they're telling me is what I find romantic, they find romantic. There are so many moments like this in books and plays and movies. Moments where the truth just marches up and smacks the character between the eyes.

I want my readers to know that there is going to be a happily ever after. I get many requests for sequels. While I don't write pure sequels, I have written books where there's a tie-in to a previous book and characters. Sometimes it's fun just to get a glimpse at them and see that things did, in fact, work out.

The hero of my book doesn't have to have a chiseled physique and handsome big features. But the heroine has to think he does. And the heroine doesn't have to be a dazzling beauty. But I guarantee you, the hero will think she is. That's why, for the most part, if I talk about how beautiful she is, it's usually through his eyes. And vice versa.

I can't stress enough how important it is that you bring your own voice to the writing. It's going to set your work apart. Because each one of us has a unique way even of falling in love and the things that excite us and make our knees go weak are different from everybody else.

I happen to think humor is sexy. I know I have a rather warped sense of humor and it's inevitable that it's going to show up in my writing. When people ask me where it comes from I answer that I really didn't have a chance. I grew up in a large Irish Catholic family and in our family nobody could take anything seriously. It was loud, chaotic, and lots of fun. So another quality I like to include in the romances is humor. They may get into sticky situations and one of them may absolutely send the other to wits end, but they'll be able to laugh. Their love won't be so somber and sentimental that we can't have some fun with them. They say, and I believe it, that you can tell the couples who are going to last by how much laughter there is in their relationship.

When I was beginning my career and had sold a couple of books, I attended a conference and I was told by an editor that you should never push humor in historical romances. They won't sell. As it has turned out, that's the one thing I hear most about, and the one that gratifies me the most, and that is that the reader laughed when she was reading my book. Hopefully, she was laughing at the book.

❧

"The first self-appraisal you need to make is: Am I more of an artist when I write, or more of a craftsman? Once you figure that out, the next several years of your life should be dedicated to doing better what you already do well, and learning to do the other half which you know little about."

–Bob Mayer

Elizabeth George

Building Your Fictional Landscape

First of all, what is landscape? Why have it at all? Landscape is the entire environment in which a novel or a short story takes place. Sometimes we think of it as the setting of the story. The purpose of having a setting is to evoke atmosphere, to make it very clear to the reader what type of novel the reader is reading. More specifically, it creates a situation in which you, the writer, invite the reader to engage in details, and a detailed examination of a place.

So when I'm starting out with a landscape, the first thing I do is to go to that landscape. And I'm always trying to deal in the specific rather than in the generic. So let me talk first about the landscape of a place. The landscape of place is the broad vista into which you're setting your story. I write what I call The Big Tapestry Novels. My books are crime novels, they are suspense novels, they're mystery novels, they're whatever you want to call them. But to me, they are tapestry novels.

From the very beginning of my time as a writer, I set out to write the tapestry novel–a novel that was rich in detail, rich in character, and one which evoked place. So it's this broad vista into which I set my novels. And if you think of novels that you're familiar with, you'll get an idea of what I mean. For example, in John Steinbeck's *The Grapes of Wrath*, the landscape is the dust bowl and then the area in central California to which the people escaping the dust bowl came as migrant workers. That's landscape. But landscape can be as undramatic, let's say, as the Los Altos foothills up in northern California, which is where Wallace Stegner set his novel, *All the Little Live Things*. And what's interesting about that particular book for me as a reader was that I didn't know anything about where he was setting his novels. I grew up in the San Francisco Bay area in a town called Mountain View, which is right next door to the Los Altos foothills. And as I was reading *All the Little Live Things*, I thought, God this is amazing. This sounds exactly like the Los Altos foothills. And I then flipped to the back to read the author bio and saw that he taught at Stanford. He evoked the Los Altos hills so well that despite the fact that there are foothills all over the continent, I knew exactly what set of foothills he was talking about.

The purpose of including this in a novel is that it adds to verisimilitude. When we write books, what we're trying to do is invite the reader into a land with us and we're asking the reader to suspend their disbelief and to believe that our setting, our story, is real. Including landscape in a novel adds to that verisimilitude. If you can make the land real, you're one step closer to making the novel real. If you ask the reader to own the landscape, you're allowing the reader to own the story and to become part of it. So this promotes connection and emotion on the part of the reader.

Consider this: Have you ever gone someplace because you read about it in a novel? Have you ever taken a vacation somewhere because a novel was set there? I've done that. I went to the Island of Corfu because when I was in high school I loved the work of Mary Stewart, the British novelist. And Mary Stewart always evoked place amazingly well. I went to the Island of Skye because Mary Stewart set a book in Skye. There are many places that I've gone because I read about it and it sounded so compelling. If you are writing your landscape and you're doing it skillfully, you actually put the reader into it. It's a total experience in a novel, it can't be addressed in a single paragraph, its elements are interwoven throughout the entire book. It's not dismissed in a simple bow to the setting; it's omnipresent. That's what landscape is.

OK, so what are the elements you have to work with in landscape? Well, first of all you've got the land itself. You have what grows on the land and what does not grow on the land. You have the shape of the land and you have its texture. You have what's built upon the land.

I write about England. England is a very small country but it has a tremendous variety of landscapes that I can use. And no matter where I am in England, the buildings are all constructed of different materials. If you're in the south of England, you're not going to see the same type of buildings or the same kind of construction as you will in the north of England. The sky is different everywhere. That's part of the landscape. Clouds are different. Stars are different. The weather of a given day is part of the landscape. The marks that a culture leaves upon the land are part of the landscape. And that doesn't make any difference even if you're dealing with an old culture. In England, the land has been inhabited for 250,000 years by one group or another, so there's a tremendous expanse of time that I can work with in this landscape. And the McDonald's cup that's being blown down the street is also part of the current landscape. There's a difference in wildlife from that place to another place. The point is that the emerging landscape should stimulate the reader's senses.

Let's say that you're writing a children's book. And you're saying, "Well I don't need to do this landscape stuff because this is just a children's book and kids don't care about that. They just want to get involved in a good yarn." And I would say that's not the case; that there are hundreds and hundreds and thousands of people who go to Prince Edward Island up in Canada because of the *Anne of Green Gables* books. I know because I did it. I was there and everybody else was there, looking at the lake of shining waters, and the Green Gables house and the haunted wood and everything. That is the only reason that most people go to Prince Edward Island. And that's a children's book. The same thing with Laura Ingalls Wilder. The Little House books that ended up as the big television series. One of the beauties of her books was this tremendous evocation of place, because people who read the books know that they start in the Little House in the Big Woods. And they go from the Big Woods to Plum Creek to the Prairie, and all of those places are very carefully explained and exposed by Laura Ingalls Wilder. And it's the same thing with science fiction books. I'm not a great reader of science fiction but I will never, ever forget the sand worm in *Dune*. And the body suits and that planet that Frank Herbert created. Yorkshire as James Herriot renders it; Victorian London as Charles Dickens renders it; America's southwest as Tony Hillerman renders it—all of these are part of the landscape.

A secondary thing to remember when you're creating landscape is that you have to be able to feel something about the place where you've decided to set your book. If you can't feel it, you can't write it.

The second kind of landscape that is equally important is the landscape of person, because people also have their landscapes. They have exterior landscapes and they have interior landscapes. It's our duty as writers to make sure that the reader understands and experiences those landscapes as well. A person's exterior landscape is real obvious. It's the way the character looks. It's how he dresses. But it's also the individual setting in which he moves. His house, his bedroom, his apartment, his office, whatever. And the purpose of developing an exterior landscape for a character is that it adds to the characterization. You're trying to create a believable character. If you add to the characterization you promote a connection between the reader and the character. We bring the character to life that way. The important elements are the telling details. The character's cracked front tooth, the unusual piece of jewelry that the character wears, the shape of an ear, the political button, the bumper sticker on the car, the stuff hanging on walls. My character always wears T-shirts. She's sort of a slob. And so what I do is, I do the bumper stickers but I do them with T-shirts. So the first T-shirt I think she ever wore was a T-shirt that said, "Cock Robin Deserved It." And one time a button fell out of her purse, like a little political button, but I would now put it on a T-shirt, and it said, "Chicken Little Was Right." It's that kind of stuff that tells you what the character is like.

We have the exterior landscape of person and now we're ready to move into the interior landscape of person, because that's probably the most important landscape that we can give our characters, because this is the landscape of their emotion. This is the landscape of their psyche, and the landscape of their soul. The interior landscape of character gives the character life by exploring the character's wants and needs, by allowing the character to have reflections and speculations. And the purpose of the interior landscape is to give characterization to evoke reader's sympathy, to give depth to the novel and dignity to the character. So how do you create an interior landscape of character? How do we do it? There's only one way to do it. It's the worst way but it has to be done. And that is that we create our characters before we write our novel.

Now a lot of times, people think that novel writing is about sitting down and getting in touch with the cosmos. And we just sit there and let our hands drift over the keys, and maybe what happens if we're really lucky is a book comes out of that. And that probably works really well for somebody but it doesn't work for me. Because I'm trying to have a book that is as evocative as possible, a book that deals with the place and that deals with people.

To develop the character's exterior landscape, I have to create that character first. So how do I do it? I start out with the name of the character. Names of characters are extremely important. One time I named a working-class English woman Peggy Moon. The name just didn't work. Once I changed her name to Jeannie Cooper, I could write about her. I didn't have any difficulty with that.

I begin with the name of the character. Who is this person? I have a generic list of stuff about that character that I am going to develop, that I'm going to write about. I put that generic list next to my computer and I start writing about the character. I write about the character's background and the character's family and the character's emotions and the character's sexuality and the character's agenda in the novel.

The most important part of what I believe that I do in creating characters is to give every character a core need in life. Every person sitting in this room has a core need. And some of us know what our core needs are, and some of us don't know what our core needs are. When I was teaching in the Writing Retreat last week, after my students and I talked for a while I said, what do you think my core need is? And they got it immediately. I was a little humiliated that I was that obvious. But everybody has a core need and your characters need to have it. The core need can be the need to be real. The need to be spontaneous. The need to do his or her duty. The need to be competent and perfect. The need to be loved. The need for forgiveness. It could be anything. You can make it whatever you want but your characters need to have that because in our lives we all operate from that core need. The subtext of our behavior is always our core need and our attempts to meet that core need.

Once you have a core need then your character's landscape has to include a pathological maneuver. And the pathological maneuver is what your character does when his core need is not being met. In, for example, the play *Macbeth*, what you have is a man whose core need, I believe, was that he had to prove himself a man. The only problem was that he had misidentified what it was to be a man. He had defined manhood for himself in the only way he could never possibly succeed. I think this is a play about manhood. Because he has defined manhood in the only way he can't possibly ever be a man, he's continually stressed out. He's continually defeated and defeated and defeated. So what's his pathology? Well, Shakespeare shows us his pathology through his obsessive thoughts. The man is caught up in the obsessive thoughts, one after another. And ultimately the whole thing leads to his downfall. So what we have is a core need for manhood, and a pathological maneuver when the core need isn't met. And that's what you have to have in your characters and that's what gives the characters life.

So that's what landscape is all about. It's about the place where something occurs, it's about the people who are in the place, and when these things work together, then what you have is a tapestry that makes it all very, very real for the reader. That's what I try to do with my writing. And that's what I would hope we all try to do as well.

"I never think about how commercial something eventually will be. I sit down and I write whatever moves me and I tell whatever story that I feel I have to tell."

–Joe Eszterhas

SUSAN MCCARTHY, AUTHOR
Lay That Trumpet in Our Hands

Any writer worth her thesaurus remembers the moment when someone who mattered said, "Hey, you can write!" My memory is from fifth grade: Mrs. Gladys Wilson, and the sweet agony of wrestling my poem, "Where the River Goes," into life–paring down words, puring down rhythms, peeling back jabber to get to the gist. At age twelve, I saw clear through the looking glass into the light of a larger Self.

At thirteen, the mirror cracked. Puberty reflected a face, a self, flawed beyond belief. Clarity flew out the window. But, hey, I was clever with words. I confess I rode writing like a prized pony through high school, preened and pranced my way through college, and honestly won the wry advice, "Hey, you should write advertising."

And, I did. In my first job as an agency receptionist, I wrote radio spots on spec and hopped to a bigger desk. In the twenty years that followed, I skipped to Atlanta, and jumped to San Francisco, trotting out headlines, taglines, :30 storyboards, :60 spots. I strapped cleverness to my hips like a pair of six guns and dazzled clients with my dog and pony. Hey, I could copywrite!

At the Maui Writers' Conference, I heard other writers, collected craft in a green palm-frond bowl: plotting from Ernest J. Gaines, tension from Liz Engstrom, editing from Don McQuinn, and from Bryce Courtenay, bum glue! ("Glue your bum to the chair and write!") In the keynote, Mitch Albom's *Tuesdays with Morrie* reminded me of my own Friday phone calls with my father. My novel was to have been a gift for Dad's seventy-fifth birthday. Like Morrie, he died too soon; the book clearly his gift to me.

After Maui, I listened harder and wrote better, over and again. In April '99, Lane Zachary became my agent. In August, at the Maui Writers' Retreat, Elizabeth George helped put the sheen on my seventh draft. In December, Bantam Dell purchased *Lay That Trumpet In Our Hands* at auction, with a generous two-book contract.

I confess this not to impress, but to inspire that self within yourself that your Mrs. Wilson recognized long ago. You can write. You can also choose—to ride that talent like a trick pony or to transcribe the whispers of your very soul. Either way, hey, don't scrimp on the bum glue!

"Some writers balk at the thought that there are formulas to writing. But really all we're listing are the ingredients. A Caesar salad contains such and such. However, two different people cooking from the same recipe don't produce the same dish. The one who is more creative and innovative will concoct something that transcends formula."

–Raymond Obstfeld

David Guterson

The Role of the Storyteller

It's nice to be in a gathering of writers, artists, and friends of artists who share similar concerns and confront similar challenges. That sense of kinship, of a shared exploration of craft, art, profession–whatever you want to call it–is what makes a conference such as this worthwhile in the first place. Otherwise, we may as well sit at home going quietly about our work, which also isn't a bad idea, by the way.

In fact, I don't know if this story is apocryphal or true but apparently at one point Dylan Thomas came to a podium such as this. Thomas often was drunk in his talks and readings and he was drunk on this occasion. He knew full well that the house was full of writers. He came up to the stage, bent to the microphone and said, "How many people here are writers?" Everybody raised their hand. He said, "Go home and write," and walked off the stage.

I want to talk about craft this morning and about vision and purpose. I want to focus on the first part, on the creating, because I believe that without a thorough devotion to that, you've got nothing to sell and you can sit and pitch all you want. But, of course, the real work is the work itself and when the work is good it paves the way for everything else to happen.

I also want to refer back to something Dr. Paul Pearsall said last night when he asked the question, "Why do you write? Is it to sell a thousand books or to save a thousand souls?" It's a question we all ought to be asking ourselves. What is our vision? What is our purpose? Why do we go about this work? I also believe, however, that large questions of vision and purpose for writers are subsumed by a much more literal question which is, Do we have the craft? Do we have the artistry? Do we have the bag of tools required to achieve our vision and purpose as writers?

First of all, what is craft? It's used loosely and could mean a lot of things. I think first of all, craft is certainly a noun, a kind of facility or skill, an adeptness or adroitness, a mechanical ability. But it's also a verb. That is, it's something we do. We craft stories, novels, screenplays, and poems, which is a way of saying that we give them shape by applying our skills to their creation. A partial list of the elements that might be included in the writer's craft are things like word choice, sentence rhythm, dialogue, symbolism, point of view—and the obvious ones like thought, character, and setting—and the mechanics of rendering a scene. Our job is to put all those elements of craft together and to become polished and proficient at their use.

There's something a bit mechanical about it, as if we are building a house, an edifice, of some sort. We're a plumber, an electrician, a carpenter, a stone mason, an architect, building this edifice called the story. I'm not sure that that's entirely useful as a way of thinking about what we're doing because certainly the opposite metaphor is equally true. We might equally think of ourselves as sculptors who start with an amorphous rock. Our job is to tear away at it until something beautiful emerges. There are a number of useful metaphors for what we do as fiction writers but all of them include craft. And it's important to take craft seriously.

That said, it's important to point out that craft is hollow and of little use if it isn't in the service of some larger vision.

It's one thing to have gained a certain facility and adroitness when it comes to storytelling, but it's another for that facility and adroitness to serve a larger vision. Craft is not an end in itself. It's a vehicle, a set of skills employed toward a particular purpose. Maybe that's obvious. But here's something less obvious. The development of your craft as a writer is contingent upon your personal vision as a writer and, in extension, contingent on your vision as a human being. There is a connection between who you are as a person, who you are as a writer, the developments of your proficiency, your technical ability as a writer. This is so because the development of craft is difficult work by definition. And only a sound vision, a sound idea of your purpose, can sustain and motivate you in pursuit of it.

But things like money, fame, achieving best seller status, those things, from my point of view, are ultimately hollow aims, ephemeral, transitory, have nothing to do with what's really important while we're here on this planet, and ultimately can't sustain you in the long run in your effort to develop your craft. You need something deeper, more serious, more fundamental, more human, more important than those superficial things to ensure that you're fully developed as a writer.

I like to think of stories as meaningful, purposeful expressions of the human spirit, rather than as mere entertainment, as vehicles for an author's ego or bank account. Or even as solely artistic utterances of the soul. I might be wrong. But it seems to me that stories matter, that they deeply matter, and that they have always played an enormously important role, not only in the lives of human beings but also in the lives of cultures. I remain convinced that stories *do* something; that, like politics and religion, they're central to our lives and to our visions of ourselves. It's in these stories that the central sustaining myths of civilization are transmitted from one generation to the next. It's via stories that we find out who we are or who we might be at our best and worst.

It's through stories that the central dilemmas both of the human condition and of our particular historical condition are brought to our attention in ways that prompt our thoughts and actions. No other form of human expression is quite as powerful as a story. The narrative seems so deeply imbedded in us as to suggest that it is coded in the structure of the brain like language itself. Something so deeply rooted, perhaps, that it's part of the definition of the species. We've always told stories and it's difficult for me to imagine humanity without them. We would cease to be who we are altogether and our unifying myths would wither.

As a public high school teacher for ten years in the '80s and early '90s I came face to face on a daily basis with the power of stories. I think of books like Harper Lee's *To Kill A Mockingbird*, which year after year is read by thousands of young people in classrooms across this country, and which year after year alters forever their inner lives and permanently shapes their values. I think of Orwell's *1984*, how Orwell heightened our collective consciousness about the dangers facing us in such a way that hopefully these dangers may be warded off. For me, as an English teacher, the list goes on. Books like *Lord of the Flies* and *A Separate Peace*, Shakespeare's *Hamlet*, *The Invisible Man, Native Son*–these are all stories that we've placed in our curricula precisely because they do the work of shaping the hearts and minds of young people, inspiring them to be more thoughtful, more sensitive than they would be without these stories.

I think this is largely what we do in English classes. We don't merely present literature for analysis or part of history, but we also present it to fend off the cultural chaos that might ensue without stories. I took my job as an English teacher seriously, like judges, pastors, presidents. My job was to preserve and transmit those central and timeless human values that have always sustained us as human beings. And it seemed to me there was no better tool available for this purpose than well-told, well-crafted stories.

Here on Maui it's difficult for me to really grasp the true condition of humanity at the latter end of the twentieth century. I arrived here on Tuesday and the real world dropped away. We're here among successful, well-fed people pursuing their pleasures. All of them are engaged in this pursuit for the time that we are here. But it's not the real world. The fact is, the real world is full of hunger and suffering and disease and calamity and hardships and warfare. These are the facts of the human condition, undeniable. We can temporarily turn away from them, but they are real. And they are as desperately real today as they have ever been—perhaps more so. Now given that, looking in an honest way at the perennial state of humanity, what is the role of the writer? Why do we write? What is our function, given this sort of a reality?

To answer that question, it's helpful for me to imagine humanity as a small tribe. It's hard for me to know my place as a writer in the culture at large when the culture is so immense and complex. But when I think of it as a much smaller unit of people and me as one of the members of it, then it's easier for me to grasp my role. So I imagine myself as part of a small tribe. Allegorically speaking, the tribe is weary. It's winter, the people are cold and starving, many have died, others are sick. There's no food to be had. The days are dark. Cruel enemies are closing in. The sun has set. The wind has come up. The cries of the children can be heard. And so, in desperation, the tribe gathers around the warmth of a fire that will shortly go out, for there's little fuel to be had. And what happens at this fire on this dark night in the tribe's life as they're assailed on all sides by enemies?

The tribe turns to the chief in hopes that this person will speak true words that will allow the tribe to continue. This is what we hope for from our politicians. This is why politics is so essential to our lives; we just hope that somebody will stand up and utter something that will allow us to go on with the work of being who we are. And when that person is done speaking, another silence falls across the tribe. And another person rises to speak, and this is whoever holds the spirit of the tribe, the spirit keeper. And again, we hope from this person who holds our religious instincts, our religious impulses in their palm, we hope that this person will say something that will allow us to continue with the work of being who we are. And when that person is done, another silence falls and some innocent young voice speaks up from beyond the plains with the darkness of the world at everybody's back, and that small innocent voice says, "Tell us a story."

It always happens at a campfire. It's the most natural thing in the world. When people are gathered around the fire, sooner or later a story is told, and this is the moment at which you are called upon to do something. The moment when you are called upon to be the best storyteller that you can be. This is why you work hard all the days of your life, to be ready for this moment. So you have the full bag of tricks at your disposal and you've paid attention to your tribe's long, long history of storytelling so that you can utter essential myths in this desperate moment. You are now called upon. Everybody turns to you, the tribe storyteller, and not just to be swept away, not just to be transported out of troubled times by the sheer force of a well-told story–although they want that. But more importantly, they turn to you because without stories–stories that inspire those who hear them to carry on with the work of sustaining what's best in human beings–without stories there is no tribe. So that is our work, our vital work as writers–to tell the stories that will allow our survival. It's nothing less than that. It's a very sacred task, one that we must take seriously.

Now I do not mean to suggest that we should denigrate entertainment. When the tribe gathers around to hear a story, the storyteller's primary task is to entertain. Without it, people fall asleep, they leave, they're not interested. And they're not drawn into that special world of the story, which allows the current world, the present world, to disappear, so all of the current troubles of the tribe no longer exist. That is, in fact, what you're trying to do in creating stories: to create a world in which the reader is so deeply drawn that the real world ceases to exist. You can only do that if you entertain.

Now, of course, if your only meaning is to entertain, if that's all you do for the members of the tribe in this moment, then you really haven't done your job. You distracted them from the horrors of their current condition for an hour or two, the duration of the story, but when it's over they're back where they were. They're back in the present world full of calamities and trouble and in no better condition to face what they must face. But if, in the midst of this entertainment, the central sustaining myths of your culture are presented in such a way that the people are inspired, then when they leave the campfire and the next day dawns, they are prepared to continue living by those values that have made them a people in the first place. So entertainment is the primary vehicle, not to be denigrated, because it is a vehicle for something deeper. It has a function beyond itself. It is a vehicle for achieving something far beyond entertainment.

Now that brings us back to craft. Because without craft, none of what I said has any chance of occurring. That is, you don't have a good story to tell around the fire unless you've worked on your craft. From this perspective, it's easy to see that the writer with a clear vision of his or her role in the tribe will be enormously motivated and disciplined in the pursuit of craft. Because everything is at stake. The survival of the tribe is at stake—every time you sit down to write. And so your devotion to the acquisition of craft becomes monk-like. And the feeling you have is that of an acolyte who has taken vows, enters a monastery, and is now devoted with every fiber of your being to achieving mastery. Without this kind of zealous devotion, craft cannot be mastered. So, motivation is everything. Being properly motivated to achieve craft mastery is everything. A good question to ask yourself when you sit down to write every day is, "Why am I doing this?" If the answer is an honorable one, it becomes much easier to practice your craft because every potentially wearying detail has a reason, a good reason behind it. You put on your shoes so you can go to the barn, so it's important to know how to tie your laces. In the barn you sort through your tools for a scrub brush. You scrub the bucket then work the hand pump. Eventually there is water and you fill the bucket with it. And you fill the bucket so that people might drink—something that wouldn't have been possible if you'd never learned to tie your shoes. So when tying your laces seems tiresome, remember that no one else will be able to drink unless you get those laces tied. And the same thing is true for storytellers when you're flogging through the wearying day-to-day details of learning your craft.

Now I want to add another principal beyond discipline and motivation in the pursuit of one's craft. I want to add the idea that all components of craft need to be tied together by a central unifying principle. That the various aspects of the writer's craft need to be used in concert and in the service of a larger goal. In the case of storytelling this is all we've seen. That is, your choices about what you're going to do with plot and character and sentence structure and so on, are always contingent on a clear vision of your story's meaning, or at least of the territory of the human condition that you're seeking to explore in your story. When you have a clear sense of theme you have a pearl at the center of an oyster around which all components of craft can revolve. The theme is the organizing principle for all your choices about craft.

I want to give you an example of this and one that isn't often, I think, addressed fully enough: the question of point of view. I think a lot of people are aware that when you set out to write a story you have a choice whether you're going to write it in third person or first person or sometimes the second person. You've got a lot of other elements to think about, too, but my point is that it's not an arbitrary decision. That is, you don't say to yourself, Well, I think I'll work in third person, limited to a single character's point of view, because I *want* to. I think you say to yourself, I choose third person, limited to a single character's point of view, because I *have* to, given what my theme is. If you think of a story like Shirley Jackson's "The Lottery," you see that Jackson had no choice but a very distant anonymous narration with no allegiance to the point of view of any particular character because of her theme, the nature of community. She needed to address this entire community and its ethos, its horrifying ethos. And so she needed to be detached from it and present it in a very objective, distant way.

Take another story at the opposite end of the spectrum like J.D. Salinger's *Catcher in the Rye*, which is a first person story where the narrator is entirely unreliable, that is, we don't know whether to believe anything he reports about himself and his journey. There was no other possible point of view from which this story could be told. That is, this story would not be what it is without this particular narrator, without his particular point of view. Now I don't think either Jackson or Salinger decided in some arbitrary way to choose the point they chose. I think they knew what themes they were trying to develop and chose a point of view appropriately.

And that's only one component of craft, the point of view. There are a lot of other things. There are dialogue and sentence structure and plot and character, all of which must work in concert in the service of some larger theme. So for me theme is the starting place. When you know what your theme is, you can begin to select aspects of craft that will increase around your sense of theme and work in concert organically in the service of this larger whole. Just as character is fate, character and action are tied together, so that what somebody does is a function of who they are. The two are inextricably bound. So point of view is inextricably bound to scene. You already know this. You know that who tells the story matters enormously. If the story is told from another point of view, it's a different story altogether.

In the story of this talk this morning, I have one perspective and you have another. And each of you has a different perspective on what happens. For you, you are the hero of this story. For me, I am the hero of this story. It's a different story for each of us depending on the point of view from which it's told. It's not inconsequential and it's not arbitrary. Like every other aspect of craft you have developed, you must come to the place where you have a great facility with every possible point of view, so your bag of tricks is large enough to encompass whatever present purpose you might have. It's practice. It's taking a short story and saying, in this short story I'm going to use this point of view and I'm going to learn how to use it. So ten years from now when I set out to write a novel and I need this point of view I know how to use it because I practiced it. Basic. It's like anything else.

To me the best sort of comparison would be something like what the martial artist does. Practice, practice, practice. This kick, this punch, and so on, so that when that moment comes, once in a lifetime, that kick, that punch is available. And that's what you're doing in developing your craft. You are making a whole panorama of abilities, talents, and skills available so that you can use them when the time comes.

I want to use a one-word example about this, what some people call voice. I would rather narrow it down to something less vague, like word choice or prose rhythm. And I really think this is also a choice that has to do with your sense of theme. When you know what your essential theme is, I think you know more about what particular voice, or syntax, or word choice, or sentence rhythm you want to use. You want to elicit certain emotional responses in your reader.

Now sometimes people feel as if, "I discovered what my voice is and I'm stuck with it. That Faulkner wrote *Go Down Moses* because he's Faulkner. And Austen wrote *Pride and Prejudice* because she's Austen. It's not as if you can choose your voice. Your voice is something you're stuck with for better or for worse." I'm not sure I entirely agree with that. If you read *Pride and Prejudice* and *Mansfield Park* back to back, you see two very different voices at work. *Pride and Prejudice* is full of wit and irony; *Mansfield Park* isn't. It's a book that is much more serious in tone. And its seriousness is appropriate to Austen's dramatic ambitions in *Mansfield Park*. It's a novel about the triumph of virtue over beauty. It's much less satirical than *Pride and Prejudice*. You're not stuck with only one voice because you know that within your own soul there's a whole range of possible voices. You know that you are subject to moods. You know that you have a great variety of persona that you're comfortable with. You don't have one voice. You have many voices. And you can choose from among those voices for the purposes of your current work.

You have this massive feeling and all of these considerations regarding your current work. Point of view, voice, theme, and sometimes you begin to feel that you're lost. And you start to experience all your thoughts about your work as a kind of confusion, and it paralyzes you. You want to begin. You want to do the work but you're not really quite sure what you're doing. You sit down every day full of confusion. What am I doing? Why am I doing this? Is this going right? I'm not sure. I'd better join a group. I'd better go to a conference. I'd better get somebody else to validate what I'm doing and tell me that it's right, because I'm confused. That perception, that quality of thought that has to do with confusion is entirely appropriate and entirely normal and not to be ignored. Because what you're being prompted to do is work through that confusion until it goes away. Do whatever it takes. But you've got to get to the point where that confusion begins to resolve itself into clarity.

It's part of the writer's experience, the quality of the writer's life to feel confused about what you're doing. And what you want is first, to ask yourself, what is my theme? And what is it I'm trying to say? Why am I writing this book? What is this book about? What am I exploring? What aspect of the human condition is it that I want to illuminate? And once you've determined that, then you begin to make your choices. What plot best serves this theme? What characters best serve this theme? What point of view best serves this theme? And that's an organizing principle for your confusion. It's really what the pre-writing work is about. I think you need to do a lot of that kind of thinking before you even get started. Some of the answers will occur in a very gratifying and mysterious way.

There is absolutely no substitute for practice and a lot of years. To go back to an earlier metaphor, you need to scrub the monastery bricks each day, carry water, meditate, and don't waste your time thinking about things like success and money and fame because then you're not thinking about your work. You're thinking about things that you really can't control.

The only way to be successful is to dedicate yourself to the work. As soon as you stop working and start thinking about being successful, you're wasting your time. There is only one way. Disciplined work.

A conference like this is a wonderful opportunity in a variety of ways. I see from the schedule that there are some excellent possibilities for you in the days to come. There are workshops that are very much hands-on about craft. There's also a bookstore next door, full of guidebooks and manuals that you will find helpful. There are all sorts of people here who are masters, who have been doing this for a long time, who know how to do it. And they're here for you; that's why they came. You should take advantage of that as well. A writers conference allows for an intense commitment to the development of one's writing life, and it temporarily exempts us from the obligations of the life left behind. Now is a good time to reconfirm your commitment to learning your craft. It's the highest expression of your creative urgings, which have no life in the world without it.

For me, craft is the keynote to be struck at a writing conference, the first and harmonically fundamental tone of our scale as writers, and the quality that makes us truly writers. Without craft, we're only talking about writing or about the business of writing ad nauseam. With it, we truly become the keepers of our cultures and central myths, the adroit, able, skilled practitioners of the high art of storytelling.

◌

"Good ideas all have one thing in common. Chill factor. When an idea's one line is given, you get a little chill, little goose bumps that say 'ooh, that's sort of enticing.'"

–Mike Sack

Susan Isaacs

Writing for Fun and Profit

I was at an author lunch once and after the meal people came over to chat with us. From the rear of the room came a woman, a formidable woman with shoulder pads the size of first and second base, and she came through the crowd up to me–you know, it's kind of scary–and she said, "Susan!" So I said, "Yes?" She said, "You give me so much confidence!" So I started warming to her and then she said, "You know, if you can do it, anybody can."

Well, maybe that's true, I don't know. Before 1978, which was the year I became a living American novelist, I went from being an editorial assistant to a senior editor at *Seventeen* and up to that point the highlight of my career was a rewrite of the article, "How to Say No To a Boy." A concept that quite frankly, had never occurred to me until my managing editor suggested the assignment. After *Seventeen* I did a bit of free-lancing and political speech writing for depressed Democrats. But since the '70s, when *Compromising Positions* was published, I've had a couple of thoughts on the subject of writing and I thought this would be a terrific opportunity to discuss my aesthetic sensibility as well as my creative philosophy. Are you ready? All right.

Here is the message of great solemnity and consequence that I want to impart: Have fun. "Yeah, sure," you say, "have fun. Being an accountant or a dentist or a technical writer doesn't get you a seat at the Round Table. And a free-lance writer for *Pet Food News* is hardly a cause for boundless mirth. Fun is for weekends. *You* may be sitting on Long Island making up stories but, *we're* in the *real* world, the *tough* world. It's hard to get a book published. Life is not a movie starring Steve Martin and Eddie Murphy." I know.

Let me tell you my story. I dropped out of Queens College in the mid-60's, mere moments before they could invite me to leave. Up to that point my work consisted of babysitting, some temporary secretarial work, and being a wrapper in a shoe store. My only responsibility was to put the shoeboxes into bags when the cashier was giving the customer change, and then say, "Thank you." Anyway, I was fired after three days. They said I didn't wrap fast enough. And the shoe store manager, who looked like a weasel with an Errol Flynn mustache, said my thank-you's weren't up to the shoe store standards.

So there I was out of college and broke. Did I go out and have fun? Not initially. I did the proper thing, the smart thing. I went through the want ads looking for jobs for good prospects and, ah-ha! I finally found something from an employment agency. It said, "Take our free aptitude test. Become a computer programmer." Naturally, it being 1966, I didn't know a computer from a hot rock but it sounded like a promising field. I immediately envisioned myself in a white lab coat with a clipboard and saying something like "48.658, Mr. Goldfarb." You know, in a precise but perky voice. I'm sure it's obvious to you that I was not cut out for this growth field. It was also made obvious to me when, after I took the test, the woman from the employment agency came out of her cubicle and said, "You failed." I said, "I failed?" "Listen," she said. "All we got is an opening as an assistant in the reader-mail department of *Seventeen* magazine. The girls they take are usually from the Seven Sisters School, but it says on your application you were on your college newspaper. The position's been open for months. Maybe they're desperate."

Well, indeed, they were and so was I. So I took the job but, boy, did I have misgivings. First of all, it paid seventy-five bucks a week. Now you say, "Oh, seventy-five bucks in 1966 is like $478 million a week now." But the truth was, it was a miserably low salary even then. And second, it wasn't a growth industry. It was a magazine, and I don't mean *Atlantic Monthly*. It taught adolescent females how to make gargantuan carnations out of crepe paper. So did I say at this point, "Hey this sounds like a giddy, mindless place—just the sort of place I'd love"? Definitely not at the beginning. I was uncomfortable there because it was frivolous. It wasn't adult. It wasn't serious. And most of all, it was fun. That was the scary part. Anything that could be that pleasurable could not be worthwhile. I was wasting my time, frittering away my life, not getting ahead. There I was with a congenial group of mostly women, talking over coffee, churning out answers to readers' letters from the idiotic, "Dear *Seventeen*: How does the model on page 174 get her eyes so blue?" to the actual heart-breaking, "Dear *Seventeen*: How do you know if you're pregnant?"

In any case, after a few months I began writing a book review column. But something felt wrong to me. I was actually getting paid for what I liked. Reading books and writing. I mean, I'd always been able to throw a few sentences together and form a paragraph. But I was never one of those adorably precocious sensitive little creatures who entered her every thought into a journal at age eight. Writing, like reading, like talking to my friends, was something both natural and pleasurable. The fact that I could write didn't mean I was a genuine writer. It just meant I never got less than a B on an English paper. Writers were like Joyce Carol Oates, gaunt and haunted-looking. Or glamour pusses like Jackie Collins. Not Susan Isaacs who took the subway home to Queens every night.

Clearly this writing business was not the proper way to make a living, not for me anyway. Too bad I was having such a grand time. Now I'm not saying that every day at *Seventeen* was the equivalent of cocktails with Noel Coward. And when it got too silly, I got them to let me write about some substantive matters, like the eighteen-year-old vote issue. But I found

I was doing work that was natural to me in an agreeable atmosphere.

Maybe that should be the definition of fun: doing what is natural, what is real, the old, "this above all, to thine own self be true." Because when you're doing what is true, what is honest to your nature, you feel right. Think about it. If your great love is gossip and fashion, is it going to do you or anyone else any good to prove how sincere you are by writing a novel about a botanist working to save endangered species? If you only start to come alive with a computer when the commuter train descends into the tunnel to the center of the city, why should you let yourself get stuck writing tongue-in-cheek essays about being a suburban housewife for your local newspaper?

Look, I know the business of writing isn't easy. After I left *Seventeen*, I tried my hand at free-lancing and in six years I had two articles published. So was I having fun? Did the sixty-two rejections to my query letters leave me laughing? No, of course not. Very few of us, I think, think we're entitled to have more than a few hours of fun a week. Why do we think that? I could quote from the Protestant ethic and the spirit of capitalism, or talk about Jewish guilt and no doubt come out with something for the Catholics and the Muslims and the Buddhists as well. But the bottom line is, when you're not having fun, when you're not fulfilled, you certainly won't make your mark on the world and you probably won't be doing anyone any good. You'll be living life in safe half- or quarter-measures. If you become a copy editor when you really want to be a TV reviewer, what will become of you after five or ten or forty years of changing colons to semi-colons? If you become a financial writer only because you got "A"s in Economics, chances are you won't be tap dancing down Wall Street. You'll be shuffling along, looking at your watch, waiting for your time to end.

Follow what interests you. Follow what makes you come alive. Much of life is prosaic and some of it is tragic. So why not have fun as often as you can? Ask yourself, what do I want? I'm not talking about those predictable yuppie egocentric-type goals. If all you yearn for in life is to see your name in the Liz Smith column and own a red Porsche, then you're truly lost. But discovering the real answer to "What do I want?" will satisfy you, strengthen you and enrich you. It will make you a more significant human being and a more valuable member of society. And a better writer.

Now let's fast forward. I've written two screenplays that have actually been made into film. I've gotten married. I've had one baby, left *Seventeen*, had another baby. I'm living in a split level house on Long Island. In between carpools and Hadassah meetings, the thought occurs to me that I should write a novel. A character comes to me. A suburban housewife who wants to solve a murder. A periodontist has been killed—because, I thought, who better deserves to die? So what do I do with that? I fight the urge to write like crazy. Because who am I to write a novel? What if I try and I can't? What if I do, what if I actually do it and it's no good? I remember reading a book review during that period, when the reviewer referred to the "delicate, almost sublime balance between structure and content." Look, I knew what content was. It was the stuff in the book. But at that point I wasn't exactly sure about structure. And if I didn't know what structure was, how could I possibly write a novel? How could I presume?

Well, I presumed. I presumed because I couldn't avoid it. I tried to find a fiction course and found one but then I couldn't get a babysitter for six o'clock on a Monday night. And I tried to get a job in publishing three days a week because I wanted to be with my kids, but only full-time jobs were available. I spent a year fighting what I desperately wanted to do because I was afraid. But finally I was able to whip up enough courage to buy a "how to" book and box of typing paper.

Cut to six months later. I'm halfway through my first novel, *Compromising Positions*. It's a mystery. Why did I start with a mystery? Well, it didn't seem as terrifying as writing a real novel. No one would say, "Who does she think she is, Virginia Woolf?" And I love mysteries. I read them all the time. They're fun. Anyway, at this point, I turn to my husband and say, "I'm scared." And he wanted to know why. I said, "I'm scared because I love this writing so much. I'm having more fun writing this book than anything else. Oh, well, almost anything, dear. What if no one likes it?" And he said, "So you'll write another one."

Slow dissolve, seven years later. I've had three novels published, I've written a screenplay of *Compromising Positions* that's been made into a reasonably successful movie. I'm doing what I love doing. And then what happens? I am pursued by an eager, intense, politically correct, incorrigibly adorable television actress. "I want you," she said, "to create the quintessential feminist situation comedy." I should have known, but what did I do? Me, the great reader and movie lover, the person who thinks the ideal situation comedy is *Our Miss Brooks*. I take a meeting with this actress and her two exhaustingly sincere producers. They say, "We want searing social satire, incisive characterizations, oh yeah, we want warmth, too. We want your original thinking, Susan. Well, we do have a vague idea, you know, about a career woman who marries a divorced man who has custody of five or six kids." I told them, "Look. I love children. My own. My children's friends. But living with them was enough. I didn't want to write about them. Thanks, anyway." And they said, "The kids are just the backdrop. We want adult comedy, not just laughs. We want to say something."

What they really wanted to say is, write us a white *Cosby* and make us rich. But instead they used all the right buzzwords and I let myself be had. Because I should have known, I should have known from the second I walked into this actress' all white living room and was offered a too-full cup of coffee and my hands started shaking. Then I got a knot in my stomach. I'm not talking about nervousness. Right before I went on *The Today Show* to talk about *Red, White and Blue* last year, I had my usual five minutes of the big quease. You know, nerves are normal. But a knot in your stomach, the sense of wrongness, of malaise, that let-me-outta-here feeling, is not. So what happened is that I allowed myself, never much of a TV fan, to be manipulated into writing a sitcom about a woman who marries a man with five children and, alas, they were children who were seen *and* heard. I conceived my heroine as an upper class woman whose family had gone bust right after she finished prep school so she had to go out to work. They said, "Make her more average." I wanted professions for my characters that were visual, intrinsically interesting and would allow them to come into contact with other people. I made her a society decorator, and him the owner of a restaurant in Little Italy. Now this was before *Designing Women*, and the restaurant at *Frank's Place* and the coffee house in *Friends*, etc. So what happened? They shook their heads. "No. Find something more, more what people who watch ABC can identify with." They said, "It has to play in Peoria." I said, "Listen, Peoria gets it." They shook their heads. I was the one who didn't get it. So freeze frame. I was stuck, working with people I didn't like, creating characters who bored me, writing a situation comedy in which the situation was the now, and the comedy was forced. It turned out to be the lousiest piece of writing I ever did. And that's because it wasn't true. It wasn't natural. From that first meeting when that anorexic actress walked in, straight from her exercise class, sweating and eating some grainy gook that stuck to her teeth, I said to myself, "This isn't fun." And it wasn't.

Maybe you're thinking, Yeah, fun. Easy for her to say. She does fun work. Well, yeah. Fun, challenging, and I'll use that over-worked word, creative. But fun doesn't mean being silly or mindless. My novel *Shining Through* was set against the background of World War II in Nazi Germany. *Red, White and Blue* is about an East Coast journalist and a Western FBI agent up against a radical paramilitary group in Wyoming. But the characters I created were fun for me. They were good-natured, even humorous people who found themselves in perilous situations. And that kind of creation was fun. Look, sitting in front of a computer every day for three years working on a novel is never a Mardi Gras. It can be lonely, exhausting, disheartening, and very often tedious. But so can being a soap opera writer or shoe columnist for *Women's Wear Daily*, or head of the London bureau of *The Washington Post*. No job is relentlessly thrilling, endlessly rewarding, including writing novels.

Some of the most miserable people I know are writers who write for big bucks or to please the critics. They shut out the sound of their own true voices in order to hear applause. But what good does their dishonesty do in the long run? Their work won't be remembered. There are too many overblown, sloppily written, badly edited, glitzy novels and utterly predictable, unthrilling thrillers. And there are too many minutely observed, monumentally boring works of fiction like generic *New Yorker* short stories. All present tense, all long on exquisite language and short on character and on plot. What have these writers done to themselves? They've abandoned their truth, their art, their voice, their own pleasure. They provide a product in return, receive some compensation in the form of checks or quietly deferential reviews.

I want something better than that for my life. And so should you. Profit will follow fun. Profit will not follow if you write what your fiction workshop leader likes. It will not come if you're writing something that you think some agent or editor or producer might buy. Profit will come, maybe, if you write what you were dying to read. That's what I do. I write the book that I most desperately want to read that nobody else is writing. Will it work? I don't know. Because creating fiction is a gift or something you either have at birth or you develop by age seven.

The only way to know whether or not you've been given this gift is if you don't feel it inside you. It has to be there on the printed page. It's to write. It's not to write a chapter. It's not to write three chapters and an outline. Then you're a chapterist.

To be a novelist you have to write the whole book. Listen, remember when your mother said, Do this, or eat that, you'll be a better person for it? Listen to me. I'm a Jewish mother. Have fun, work hard, write about what you want to write about, and you know what? You will be a better person for it.

❧

"The secret to writing a successful sex scene is in the after-glow. This is the greatest opportunity for revealing character there is, yet most writers fail to take advantage of it. If you do a superb job with your characters' thoughts, emotions, conversation and actions in the afterglow, you don't even need the sex part."

–Elizabeth Engstrom

KITTA REEDS, AUTHOR
Sit Back and Sell: The Zen Way

It took me four years and thirty-nine rejections, but because my friends wouldn't let me give up, I sold my book. The
first time I went to a writer's conference, I thought I'd hit the
jackpot. My nonfiction entry won a small prize, and as I stepped
onto the stage to receive the certificate, they read the title of
my article—"Zen and the Art of Proposal Writing"—and this
500-voice roar of a laugh came at me across the footlights.
During the break, an agent asked me if I'd thought of expand-
ing my article into something larger.

"Something larger?" "Based on the audience reaction
alone," he said, "I think it could be a good book." "A book?"
"Yes, a short book." "A short book?" Dear lord, I thought.
I've got a New York agent interested in my writing and all I
can do is echo what he's saying.

As he kept talking, I began to think maybe I could write
this book. I began adding ideas, and we stood there nodding
and laughing and planning the book. The agent tried hard, but
at the end of Year One, we had a stack of letters saying the
proposal was very solid, "but not quite right for our list."

In Year Two, my daughter did a Tarot reading to answer my question, "Will this agent ever sell my book?" The cards said I should not rely solely on this agent. Selling a book was like a giving birth to a baby, she said. I needed to push and keep pushing. The agent and I parted company, and I set out to sell the book on my own. A sleek friend who works in marketing had sold her book without an agent and assured me I could certainly do it, too. I found it a grim business, however, subtitled Wasting Stamps.

In Year Three, I attracted the interest of a publishing house so small you didn't need an agent, because they paid too little to attract agents. When they finally said they "liked it very much, but," I whined to my friend Gene, who told me about the time *The New Yorker* used the same words to turn down one of his short stories. Gene called the editor to ask, "If you liked it so much, why aren't you going to publish it?" "We liked it, Gene," said the editor, "but we didn't love it." Gene urged me to keep sending out the book proposal. 'Keep it in play to the nth degree," he said. "Hang around bus stations: Hey mister, wanna see a book proposal?"

In Year Four, when I sent my manuscript resume to the MWC Manuscript Marketplace, things speeded up immensely. Seventeen agents and editors loved it. I chose a team of agents, Linda Mead and Nancy Ellis-Bell. Within a month–before I even arrived at the conference–we had a deal with Crown Publishing. *Sit Back and Sell: The Zen Way* will be published in 2001.

"Does each scene move the plot forward? Is there a balance of action scenes and lower-paced scenes? Is there internal as well as external conflict? Is the reader made to wait for something exciting to happen? Does the character have a secret? Is time running out?"

– Susan Wiggs

Ridley Pearson

What Research Tells Me

In 1990 while researching *Probable Cause* I had the opportunity to tour the Salinas Crime Lab. Before we even got through the front door we went through a little cold room, where the lab folks had framed several of their forensics trophies they were really proud of, and one was a little tiny black burned match.

They'd had a series of fifteen vacant-structure arsons. It was really a serious case. They had been trying to close in on somebody who was responsible for burning down fifteen vacant houses over about an eighteen-month period. The sixteenth of those fires killed a person. That house wasn't vacant. The person who committed the arson thought it was vacant but there was a human being in the house and it burned the person alive. So now they had an arson homicide and fifteen vacant-structure fires.

Typically, vacant-construction fires are started by kids, juveniles. So they had all the snitches they could muster looking for who was responsible and they had a lead, they had a name. During the course of the investigation this guy who was seventeen would turn eighteen, and was no longer a minor and that also became significant. The cops put this seventeen-year-old kid under surveillance because you have to have enough probable cause to get in there and start looking. They didn't have that with a seventeen-year-old. So they put him under surveillance for over a year.

After the homicide, the vacant-structure fires stopped. Whoever was doing this was smart enough to know he was in deep trouble and better not keep torching places. But forensic science had come along so far that the people in the lab could determine the area of origin for a fire, and they could determine what accelerant caused a fire. In fact, they can not only determine that it's gasoline, but they can determine that it was, say, unleaded gasoline. They can determine that it was unleaded gasoline manufactured by Shell Oil Company, and they can determine that it was unleaded gasoline manufactured and refined by Shell Oil between August 31, 1999, and October 31, 1999, because every single batch that comes out of every single refinery is fingerprinted and sent to the FBI for chemical analysis. So they knew that the same guy set all these fires because they kept seeing the same accelerant used at all the fires. And they wanted to get into this kid's house to find that gasoline.

The kid ran a red light. All of you criminals in this room, don't run red lights. He not only ran a red light, but when the cops chased him through the red light he ran, and that was important, because when they finally pulled him over, they had him for a felony: attempting to escape arrest. They kicked in the door to his house, kicked in his garage—no gasoline. After two years of investigation, they were no further along than they had been.

But at the Salinas Crime Lab, there was a very creative and inventive lab tech. And in the inventory of what they did find was a Folgers's coffee can on this guy's dresser half filled with used matchbooks. At that arson homicide they had found in that area of origin a small black match. And for the next three months, lab technicians in Salinas took the feathered ends of this fragile burned match and attempted to fit it back into the tear tabs of each of those matchbooks. Three months into it, they had an exact match.

Those are the stories that, pardon the pun, set me on fire. And eight years later I would write a book about arson because I was so excited about that. It would turn out that in my work on the book on arson a different accelerant came up and I never even got to use the match story.

But the match story started me going on a book that eight years later I would finally get to. Research doesn't necessarily mean spring pressure on the trigger mechanism. It means knowing what you are talking about. It also means knowing when to leave something out; you're never going to be able to put all of it in. If you do, it will be a boring book because the story is going to give way to the technology and the research in it. And people want to know first and foremost about people. Readers want somebody to like. They want someone to care about and someone to believe in.

About the fourth novel, I started using my research almost more for the character than for the technology or the procedures. When I go to interview a cop or an FBI agent or an ATF agent, I spend half that hour finding out about their job and how it works and am I getting this right in my outline. But the thing I'm really interested in is where did they go to school, when did they meet their wife, where did their interest in this come from, why did they spend eighteen hours a day making $18,000 a year? That's the stuff that intrigues me. And what I try to bring to readers is that character stuff that builds these people and makes them so rich and so real.

The people need to be real, and so do the places. Readers will never forgive you if you goof up their hometown. You get more e-mail, more letters about this than anything—"It's not a one-way street; I live on it!" Day after day you will get this stuff, no matter how hard you do your research. My first novel, I had no money, I was paid about enough to buy a microwave oven. The result was that I took eighty books out of the local library to write a book about espionage involving chemical weapons with a chase across Canada. I have never been a spy. I knew nothing about chemical weapons and I had never been to Canada. That book was published. It took me eighty books in the library to get it done. You get your research done where you need to get it done, but if you don't do it right, you'll hear about it.

And by the way, one of those books was an atlas and a map, so when I was doing the chase in Montreal, I could know that the street was one way and that it dead-ended into this circle and you could only take a right. So when people from Montreal read the book, they go, "He was here all right!" It reads true. I wasn't there, but that's all right. Sometimes when we do research we chase the facts first. Keep in mind, however, that they are the least important. I think people are the most important, places are really important, and facts are fun.

I visited a nuclear research facility, thinking maybe there was a story there, and I was toured through the whole facility–purple water and bubbling vats–and I thought, uh-huh. Never used any of that. But on the way in–it seems like I am always getting all my best stuff on the way in to these interviews–the government, in all its wisdom, gives you a thirty-minute lecture on how wonderful and safe nuclear energy is to our society. One of the wonderful facts is, not only is radium used on your watch face so you can see the hands at night, but Band-Aids are sterilized using low-level radiation. They package them first, they make them sterile second. I went, "Wow, that's cool!" And wrote that into a book. *Booklist* reviewed the book and, while I'm not sure they liked the book, the one line they cited in the whole book was the part about Band-Aids.

I went to the West Edmonton Mall for a book called *The Seizing of Yankee Green Mall.* I told them that I was writing an article for the travel magazine for United Airlines. In fact I was writing a spec article for them, but what I was really going to do was to figure how I could blow up the mall, and in all my wisdom I went into Peggy's Yarn Shop and said, "Peggy, if you were going to blow up this wing of the mall…." She showed me to the door. But I continued wandering around the West Edmonton Mall for about three days, and eventually had my meeting with head of security. Now this mall is a small city; 250,000 people go in and out its doors each week. There are

700 shops in the West Edmonton Mall, there's a thirteen-acre water park, there's an indoor triple-loop roller coaster, there are 114 restaurants, and the whole thing occupies eleven football fields–you can imagine security for this place. It is something fairly significant. And I wanted to talk to this guy. So I sat down and he said, "Are you enjoying your stay here in West Edmonton?"

"Oh, yes."

"Do you enjoy the mall?"

"Yes," I said. "Let me tell you what I have been doing."

And he said, "No, let me tell you, Ridley." And he pulls out a notebook. They had had me followed for three days at the West Edmonton Mall because I was asking everybody about blowing up the mall. So they had put an undercover officer on me and I had been followed for three days without knowing it.

In writing your book, the longer you stay with accurate detail, the more convincing the story, and that's why I use research so much. We're trying to write stories that suspend reader's disbelief. There is no better way than by telling the truth. That will always suspend disbelief. Almost always. So what I do and the reason I use research in these books is so that when you are reading it, you believe it.

Nonetheless, the characters are everything in books, absolutely everything. The stories are written about the characters, and how the story affects the character's lives is what the reader cares about. I post all my scenes up on a wall like a screenwriter. I outline on the bottom of each card what's happening to the characters in the book. The top of the card is the plot, the story line; the bottom is where the characters are going. You have arcs–that this character is starting to regret and he's going toward jealousy and he's going from jealousy to being madly in love, so when I get there in the book, I've built the reader up so that now you are going to believe this guy would be that jealous. So part of my plotting is plotting where and how the characters go. I think, and this is just my own editorial comment, that techno-thrillers give too much power to research. I don't really care about the muzzle velocity of the magnum weapon. There are people who do, and those books sell like mad, but that's not what I do. I gain enough research knowledge to tell you all that, but I leave it all out.

And this brings us back to the *Yankee Green Mall*. I spent eight years writing before I had one cent for writing. For those of you out there who are still struggling, if you think you are struggling, I wrote more than ten screenplays–none of them were produced or published–and six drafts, or 3,000 pages, of a novel that we submitted to twenty-three publishers, probably including Kinko's, who wouldn't even copy it, and it was never published.

I started a second novel. I wrote it four times, that was probably 2,000 pages worth of rewrites. It was submitted, and purchased. I bought a yellow pad and a new Bic pen for my first big meeting with my New York editor. I was so excited. And he called up and we talked about the book, and he said, "Ridley, I only have two problems with this book," and I thought, "I spent the money on the ledger and the pen." He said, "That's the premise and the ending." Great guy. I started the book all over, from the first sentence, and wrote it four more times, and it was published as *Never Look Back*, my first novel, and that was the one he gave me enough to buy a microwave oven for.

But when I was up there at the West Edmonton Mall in those eight years of struggling, not making it, I had already done every job there is, including being a house cleaner at a hospital, cleaning up bone chips off the emergency room floor. So I knew all about janitors. And when I was at the West Edmonton Mall I knew to follow the janitors. The janitors can get into any place, because as a janitor at the hospital I had access to everything. So I followed the janitors and, sure enough, one of these guys opened a secure door and I just walked in behind him and cruised around.

Well, this was one of the things that the security guy said: "And what were you doing in the catacombs?" How did he know that, how did he know that I had sneaked in there? He knew because they had buried heat sensors in the cement walls of the mall. There were so many cameras to monitor, they couldn't monitor all of them. So they had these little flip screens–we've all seen them on security things–it's like a five-second rotation. But you can miss things on those. So they had sensors to tell the guys looking at these flip screens, "Somebody just entered secure area forty-four." And they can punch in forty-four and pull up a guy in a blue blazer with his note pad. And that was me. So in the book I put in that they had installed heat sensors in the walls, and the editor called me up and said, "There is just one really unbelievable element in the whole book, and that's these heat sensors in the wall. Lose the heat sensors!" And I said, "That's the only fact in the whole book!" He said, "I don't care. Nobody is going to believe it. Lose them." So we lost them.

I do all my paper research–the library work, now the Internet–first. I use Lexis-Nexis, the legal search company. In one day I can now do what used to take me three or four weeks in the library. I call Lexis-Nexis and for a fee I tell them some key words. Like "illegal alien container" for the book that just came out, *The First Victim.* They faxed me within an hour the titles of eighty or ninety articles from around the world that deal with illegal aliens and shipping containers. I then circle the six or seven articles that I like of those titles and within about twenty minutes, those are faxed to me in full text versions and I've got research from Peru, India, Venezuela–wherever it happened–on my desk, and I'm off and flying.

I had heard about illegal organ harvesting and donating, and I thought, even if this is not true, it would be an amazing novel. And I called up Lexis-Nexis and said, "I need to know if this is true. Find out about illegal organ donating and illegal organ harvesting." We got eighty-five articles from around the world. It's true. It's happening. I even found out there was a cafe in Cairo where if you went in on Tuesday with $3,500 cash, on Friday they would have an organ, a kidney matching your blood type, ready to be put into you. It was that easy. And so I wrote a book about that, *The Angel Maker,* but when I went out on tour everybody said, "Yeah, but this is fiction." And I said, "No, not fiction."

So, for the first novel I took eighty books out of the library. For the next novel, *Blood of the Albatross,* I went to Seattle.

It seemed like the closest, big, interesting city that I could set a story in. And I had interviews set up through the FBI's information officer, which they all have. Any of you can get in the same way I get in. You call up any of these government organizations and say I want to speak to either your public relations or your information officer. And those people will arrange interviews for you. Anyway, I went to Seattle with about 200 bucks to my name and headed over to the FBI. I arrive. I'm so excited. It's the only $200 I have. This is my big chance to see the FBI. The night before they've had a shootout with a hundred FBI officers and six white supremacists. Now when you go into a cop shop, it is never like *Hill Street Blues*. It looks more like an IBM place. I mean, people sitting around, typing things. When I went into the cop shop on this day, it *was* like *Hill Street Blues*. It was as busy as I've ever seen any place. This was FBI headquarters in Seattle. People were coming and going. People were upset. There were nerves. There had been a massive shootout. I went in to talk to my guy, and he said, "Sorry, I can't give you the afternoon as I promised. I can give you twenty minutes." And I went, "Oh!" and pulled out my tape recorder. And he said, "Ridley, we don't do tape recorders at the FBI," and I went, "Oh!" and had an interview with him that netted absolutely no information.

This guy's name was Joe Smith with the FBI. No kidding. He turned out to be a great friend and has helped me for years now. When I finished *Blood of the Albatross* I thanked Joe Smith profusely in the book's acknowledgements for all the incredible time and energy and knowledge he had bestowed upon me and sent him five autographed copies. Well, the next time I called Joe Smith, it was "Ridley, how are you! When are you coming over again?" And I told him and he said, "Well, bring that tape recorder!" And I did.

I would come back to Joe Smith for *Undercurrents* and I would end up writing in *Undercurrents* a subplot about the currents in Puget Sound. A body washes up on shore, and I wondered if the police could track it back to where it went in. I did a ton of research with the University of Washington Oceanography Science Division, and we found out, yes, you can, in a place like Puget Sound. At that time there was a giant working model of Puget Sound in the Pacific Science Center, and we went there with these little wax balls made to different densities because I had spoken to the medical examiner about how bodies rot in water and their buoyancy. And we put our little wax balls into this working model of Puget Sound and the last one popped up right where it was supposed to, so we knew where it had gone in. And I wrote that into the novel.

Well, several years would pass and the prosecuting attorney of Skagit County in Washington was reading *Undercurrents* as entertainment at night—when a body popped up in Beauman's Bay, Washington, and he claimed that because he was reading *Undercurrents* he didn't trust his detectives' assessment, which was "Accidental Death by Propeller." So he sent his two homicide cops down to Scott's Bookstore in Mount Vernon to buy *Undercurrents*. And I got a call from Scott's Bookstore, where I had toured, saying, "You're not going to believe this, but two cops just came in here and bought *Undercurrents*." They had bought *Undercurrents* because I had acknowledged, and you always want to acknowledge if they will let you, the people who help you.

One of the people I had acknowledged was oceanographer Dr. Alyn Duxbury from the University of Washington. The homicide cops looked him up and said, "Ridley writes this subplot in this book. Is it fiction or is it fact? Is he just blowing smoke at us or is this for real?" And Duxbury said, "Oh, no, we did this. This is completely for real." And he said, "Can you do it again?" They brought Duxbury up to Skagit County, he got out his computer working models, and he told them where the body had gone in. It had gone in, he believed, beneath Deception Point Pass Bridge. The bottom line is, they put away the husband of this woman for throwing her off the bridge. He was sent up for thirty-one years.

I have been telling this story on tour for years, and I told it again this summer when I was out for *The First Victim* because Dr. Duxbury was in the audience, and I wanted to acknowledge him. He came up to me afterward and said, "Ridley, we're now up to two." The Navy had been reading *Un-*

dercurrents, and they found a suitcase floating in Puget Sound that contained body parts, and because of *Undercurrents* they went back to Dr. Duxbury and he did his plotting again and they got that person. So we've now solved two homicides from a piece of fiction.

At the end of that interview, the prosecuting attorney said, "So, Ridley, you've helped me with your fiction. Thank you. And if there's ever anything I can do," and I cut him off. I didn't even let him finish. I said, "There is. Could you introduce me to so and so?" He said, "I know him personally. Not a problem."

I was pretty jazzed up. I had a couple of best sellers under my belt and I was going in to see a senior policeman I had always wanted to see. I flew over to Seattle; I didn't drive this time. Went up to the fifth floor of the Public Safety Building where they buzz you through a door into homicide. I had written one book about Lou Boldt, who is a character in *Undercurrents*, and I was starting to work on the organ story, and if it was going to be set in Seattle I figured it had to have Lou Boldt. So now I actually had three books with Lou Boldt in it, and I was going in to meet this senior guy. Well, the door is buzzed, and it opens up, and I'm standing face to face with Lou Boldt. It was the most eerie thing; this guy I had described for years in my writing is standing there looking down at me and introducing himself. He knew a little something about me. Instead of taking me to his office, he took me to "the Box," the interrogation room. And he sat me down in the interrogation room and my half-hour interview with him ran to ninety minutes. At the end of it I said, "You know, if I've been sort of goo-goo and gaa-gaaing at you for the last ninety minutes, it's because you bear an uncanny resemblance to my lead character, Lou Boldt." And this sly little grin formed on his face and he said, "Ridley, I've read all your books. I know I'm Lou Boldt."

About the third time I met with this gentleman–we had gotten to be friends now–he was helping me with yet another book, and I said, "How's the wife?" And this fifty-five-year-old guy who had seen hell and gone every day of his life in his job, tears up and says, "I lost her to cancer a month ago." That's where you get your character research done. So in my series now of Boldt books, about the third or fourth book in, Boldt's wife gets cancer. And in it, she survives. And that was to give him something back that real life wouldn't give him.

Readers, however, aren't as forgiving. And every reader who sent me a letter said, "How dare you give Liz cancer just so she can die and Boldt can marry Daphne!" These are characters in the book, and I thought, how far from the truth can we get?

I'm never afraid to ask these guys. I'm never afraid to call up and say, "I'm just a Joe Schmo novelist, but I'd rather do it right than do it stereotyped. Can you give me a half hour?" And you know what? They always say yes. Because they don't want to be stereotyped. So I would say to you: just ask.

In doing your research and putting it into your books, make them want more. Make them want the next book and the research in that book. Don't overdo it; the story, the characters, the place, is way more important. Another thing to keep in mind is that as novelists, we can't write the way it really happens. In real life the investigations I use in my books took eighteen months or two years or three years, and in my novels they take eight weeks. I compress them so you are compelled to turn the page and the story moves faster.

My secret is this: I put in a fact and a fact and a fact and I make up a fact. And when I do that, you don't know which one has been made up. And I do that because I have to move the story. I don't do it in every novel. If I can write a novel without making something up, especially in the fact end, I do, but if I need a machine that the lab is using to determine something that is absolutely impossible to determine, I will make up the machine. And because I have been so accurate in the book up to that point, I will have people from labs come up to me and say, "Geez, I never knew the radio spectrophemeters actually existed yet."

And I say, "Not yet. It's coming."

"Failure exists, but failure is not what happens when you try and don't succeed. Failure in its pure form is what happens when you die without ever having tried anything."

–Bud Gardner

Nicholas Sparks

A Writer's Life

I never grew up thinking I was going to be a writer. I know a lot of people who have been successful in this profession grew up thinking that. For me, it was absolutely the furthest thing from my mind. When I was growing up, I was really involved in athletics and school in general and writing just kind of came on a whim.

When I was a freshman in college, I was a full scholarship athlete. Track and field was probably the most important thing in my life. I was running eighty, ninety, a hundred miles a week and I got injured, and it was an injury that needed time to heal. So I went home after that freshman year and I was recuperating. If you're a runner and somebody says, "You can't do this anymore at all," and this is something you've been doing for two or three hours a day, you go bananas. So there I was, going bananas and my mom got tired of it. She finally turned to me and she said, "Don't just pout, do something." And I said, "Like what?" And she said, "Well I don't know. Write a book." I said, "OK."

No joke. I was nineteen years old. I pulled out an old typewriter, set it on the kitchen table, and six weeks later I was the proud creator of my first novel. It was a horror novel, by the way. Really interesting with fascinating characters and a really intriguing setting, and everything was great about this book, except for the writing, which sort of doomed its success. So I set that book aside.

What I realized, though, was that I actually liked to write. I found a tremendous sense of completion in setting out and completing this goal, so I went back to college for my sophomore year and had to choose my major. Knowing how much I enjoyed writing, I decided to major in business finance. And proceeded not to write a single thing for the next two and a half, three years. Halfway through my senior year in college, I was taking a very light load. I only needed four classes to graduate and I thought, "I'm going to write myself a different book. I think I should write a murder mystery, like Agatha Christie." I wrote out half a book and then March rolled along and I decided I was going to go off with my friends to spring break, so I rolled down to Florida and I met a girl. It was *her*. And, well, I met her, went googly-eyed, and writing took a back seat to flirting and correspondence and getting to know this beautiful young gal. And so I didn't finish that book. We got married the following year.

After I graduated, I intended to go to law school but I didn't get in anywhere. I got wait-listed at one place, though, and so I wrote them a nice letter asking, "Why did I get wait-listed?" I got a nice letter back from them and they said, essentially, as a business major we don't believe you have acquired the writing skills that will be necessary to be a success in law." I said, "OK." So I got married and bumbled from job to job.

In the process I remembered this half book that I'd written, so I decided to go back and finish it. Just like the first one, it's still in the attic. So I bumbled through all these different types of jobs and then my son was born when I was in my mid-twenties, and at that time my wife came to me with some really solid advice. Advice that I'll never forget. She said to me, "Honey, get a job." So I did. I got a job selling pharmaceuticals.

In the process of all this I co-wrote a book with a good friend named Billy Mills. Anybody know Billy Mills? Few people do. Billy Mills was an Olympic gold medalist. He's the only American ever to win the 10,000-meter run in Tokyo. He's the only American ever to win that event and they made a movie about fifteen years ago about his life, starring Robbie Benson. It was called *Running Brave*. Bill approached me to help him write this little book. I dated his daughter for four years and he's the godfather of my children, so that's how I got that job. We put together this little book and it was published by a small place in California and eventually picked up by Random House, and it was my first taste of writing success. Except for one little thing, and that was that when Random House picked up the book they only had one criteria to publish this nationally and that was, they had to take my name off.

When I was twenty-eight I had an epiphany. Does anybody remember the television show, *Cheers*? Everybody does. *Cheers* ended a twelve-year run when I was twenty-eight years old. And I remember that night, after the last show was over, I turned off the television and I stayed awake all night long. *Cheers* had started when I was a high school sophomore. From the time *Cheers* started to the time it ended, so many things in my life had changed. I'd graduated high school, gone to college, moved across the country, gotten married, had two children, bought a house, even got a job. When I was sixteen years old I had a lot of dreams that I wanted to accomplish. When you're sixteen you think the world is out there for your taking. Then I found out it's hard. And by the time I was twenty-eight, I realized, yeah, I'm working, I got my house, I got the wife, I got the kids, but at the same time, looking toward the future meant buying pork chops on Thursday for dinner on Sunday. And that really wasn't what I was looking for. So I said to myself, I'm never going to let another twelve-year period pass in my life where I don't have any dreams left. So I decided then and there that I was going to do something again. I'm going to write. I can do this while I work. I'm not going to give up anything except maybe some free time. The book that came out when I was twenty-eight years old was *The Note-book*.

Let me tell you a little bit about *The Notebook*, which is a story of unconditional, everlasting love. It was inspired by my wife's grandparents. They were very much in love throughout their entire life. When my wife and I got married, they lived about forty-five minutes away from where we were getting married. However, they were under doctor's orders not to travel—even to the wedding. They were just not well enough to travel. They were heartbroken. And my wife was heartbroken about it. So the day after the wedding, after you're tired and you're stressed and you've done all this stuff and you're just wiped out, my wife nudged me in the morning. She said, "Get up. We've got something to do." So that morning I got up, I put on my tuxedo and my wife put on her wedding dress. We grabbed a piece of wedding cake and a video and we popped out to visit the grandparents—kind of brought a little wedding to them. It was really nice; we pinned their corsages on them and took pictures with them and we spent the rest of the afternoon with them. And that was the first time I spent long hours with them and got to see how much they meant to each other.

I remember marveling that these two people, after sixty years of marriage, were treating each other exactly the same as my wife and I were treating each other after twelve hours of marriage. What a wonderful lesson to learn! It was probably the best gift we received for our wedding. And so when I was twenty-eight and the time came to write a book I knew exactly what little story I wanted to write. I worked out the plot in my head, got everything that I needed and I said, OK. Time to sit down and start the book. So I started the book in July of 1994 and finished it up in January. When I finished the novel in its first draft, the book was 80,000 words long. The book that's out there on the shelf is 47,000 words. I cut and I cut and I cut, until I got something that I felt was very tightly written.

I cut the stuff for a reason. It wasn't very good. Let me give you an example. There's a scene on page ten where Noah—he's the protagonist—is holding a book of poetry. He'd carried this book by Walt Whitman throughout the war. In the original draft I went on for about four pages. I had this great scene where Noah was carrying this book in the war and he brought it into battle and lost the book behind enemy lines. He got back and realized it was gone and had to go out and almost get shot, and he got back and got in trouble. Four pages and it was very, very tightly written, good exciting stuff. But I read it and said, you know, this is a love story. This really is kind of tangential to that. So I cut it from four pages down to three and then I went from three pages to two and I felt pretty good. I read it and I said, wow, this is really much, much tighter. I'm very pleased. But you know I still think it's a little long. So I went from two pages down to one. Read it. It's still a little long. It went from four paragraphs to three, three to two, two to one. And then I was really proud of it because I went four pages down to a paragraph. It's still just a little long. So I went from four sentences to three, three to two, two to one, and this four-page section, this whole war time experience of Noah and his book, was summed up in a single line: "The book had once taken a bullet for him." Which pretty well captured it all anyway. So I finished this book and I was pretty pleased with it.

I went to a bookstore and I got a book called *How to Get a Literary Agent*. I wrote seventeen drafts of my query letter in two weeks. It's the most important page that you'll ever write if you don't have an agent. It's a sales pitch, and always keep that in mind. So I worked really hard on mine, shipped out twenty-five queries, and a week later I got a call from a literary agent. So I ship out my book and four days later, she calls and says, "I'd really like to work with you on this." I tell you, I felt so good about myself! Over the course of the next two months, the other twenty-four came back and they all said no. So I had this one agent who was working with me. But she still hadn't sent me the official agency agreement. So I thought, "Well, I guess it's time to run the interview." So I called her up and I said, "So, you're a literary agent. Do you mind if I ask you a few questions?" She said, "No." I said, "Well, um, well, how old are you?" She says, "Twenty-seven." "Well, how long have you been a literary agent?" She said, "Eight, nine months."

I said, "Oh! Have you ever sold a novel before?" "No." I said, "OK, you're hired!" That was how I got my agent. We worked on this manuscript and we edited, edited, edited and she calls me in October and she says, "You know, publishing shuts down in November and December. If we want to move on this thing before the end of the year we've got to do it now." So I shipped twenty-five copies of my book to New York on Wednesday and told myself not to call my agent for six weeks. Well, on Friday night she calls me and she says, "You know? I think we might have something big." Big! Wow! Big! My wife is out walking the dogs around the block and the kids around the block so I go running out to my wife and I say, "You know, I was just talking to my agent and uh, and uh, she said uh, we might have something big." And my wife, she said, "Well what does that mean?" And I said, "I don't know."

Before she hung up, my agent said, "Could you please be here on Monday because I think we're gonna get what's called a pre-emptive offer to buy your book, and I really need to be in contact with you." And I said, "Well, you know, I really can't. I'm a pharmaceutical rep. I've got this luncheon sched-uled, I can't back out on the luncheon at the last minute. It's for an entire office, but I'll check my voice mail every hour." So Monday morning I call at eight and there's nothing there. So I checked at nine o'clock. Nothing. Ten o'clock. Nothing. Eleven o'clock. Nothing. At noon I checked my voice mail again. There was a message from my agent! "Call me. It's important." So I called and she said, "We got a pre-emptive offer from Warner Books." I said, "And?" She said, "Warner Books would like to offer you $1 million. What do you think?" I'm like, "I think that's great!" I hang up the phone and I call my wife but she's not home. I call my brother and he's not home. I call my best friend and he's not home, either. And by then it's like, bustin' up and bubbling up inside and this nurse comes up the stairs and I said, "Stop! I just sold my book to Warner Books for a million dollars! Shhh! Don't tell anybody!"

Three days later I had to go to a pharmaceutical confer-ence in Hilton Head, South Carolina. Hilton Head was about four hours from where I lived and you're allowed to take your wife and your kids down for that, so we all loaded up in the car. I'm kind of still dizzy from this whole scheme of events and we're driving down to Hilton Head and we have to stop about two hours into the drive because the kids need a break. So we pull into this little McDonald's and I remember I decided I'm gonna go check the phone and so I go over there and I check my voice mail and there's a message from my agent. So I call and we get to talking for a little bit and she goes, "Oh, by the way, New Line Cinema wants to buy your book and make it into a movie." I'm standing there in my shorts and my flip flops and staring off–the kids are jumping through the balls and my wife's eating a cheeseburger and I'm thinking, this is a strange life I'm leading. She said, "Oh yeah, they love it! They're really into this project, blah, blah, blah. They want to make it big. What do you think?" "I think that's great!" So that was how we sold the movie. That was in October of 1995.

The book came out in October of 1996 and during that year all sorts of exciting things happened. I kept my job because even though I had earned that much money, I still have a wife and kids and want to plan for the future. And I didn't know if the book would sell once it hit the market. So I decided to keep my job.

But of all these exciting things that happened, I guess the most exciting thing was when I get a call from the Warner Books Publicity Department. They said, "Oh, Andrew Cohen from *48 Hours* picked up your book at the ABA–it was out in the early form, you know, advanced readers' copy–he read it, he loved it and he wants to do a show on you. What do you think?" "I think that's great! Ain't no better subject than me!" The very first thing I did was get strapped up to a cordless mike for sixteem hours with a camera two inches from my head, all day long, catching everything.

The very first week it was out, *The Notebook* hit the best seller list. And it proceeded to stay on the best seller list for the next fifty-six weeks. Now let me put that in perspective. In the last twenty-five years, there have been four novels that have spent more than one year consecutively on the *New York*

Times list. There have only been four. Hardcover. So this book really entered rarified air. *The Notebook* did something that was very, very rare. And very wonderful. Here's the amazing part about this. At a fifty-six-week run, not once in that entire fifty-six weeks did *The Notebook* ever go to number one, number two, or number three on the list. That sucks.

So I had to write another book. I had another book, *Message In A Bottle*. That book again, took six to eight months to write. *Message In A Bottle* was inspired by my father after the death of my mother. My mother and father had been married for twenty-six years and she died tragically in a horseback riding accident. She was alive one day and dead the next day. Just like that. We'd been over for a barbecue the night before. My father loved my mother very much and for a year and a half following my mother's death, my father wore black every day. Every day.

I began to wonder if my father would ever fall in love again, if it was even possible for my father to actually meet somebody new and fall in love. And that, in essence, is the theme of *Message In A Bottle*. In *The Notebook*, if the theme is unconditional, everlasting love, the theme of *Message* is a question. Is it possible to fall in love a second time after losing your one true love? In time my father did eventually meet somebody and he said he was in love with her. They seemed very happy when they were together and on the cusp of that, my father feel asleep at the wheel of his car and the car veered into a truck and my father died. Now if anybody's read *Message In A Bottle*, you'll see some similarities.

❧

"Horror reveals a hidden part of all of us. The dark side. The id. The Other, with a capital O. You need to acknowledge the darkness to acknowledge the light. You need the bad guy. It's yin and yang."

– Jay Bonansinga

BARRY SHANNON, AUTHOR
The Bold Stroke

I still can't believe it happened to me. I had always wanted to write but, like everyone else, by the time I finished work every day, all I wanted to do was hang out and indulge myself for working so hard. When I retired from the private investigative field at forty-three and moved to Maui, once again, all I wanted to do was hang out. After all, it's Maui. After a few years, however, my bliss began to be intruded upon by a parade of the most bizarre and unforgettable characters, phantoms from the past that wouldn't leave me alone, even though many of them were long dead. With the characters came the stories, the wild crazy stories that no one could make up. The '70s were a decade of wild and colorful times in San Francisco. Trying times, the saying went. Everyone was trying everything, and many were getting caught. I was privileged to work some of the most extraordinary cases. I didn't realize it at the time but I was not only gathering material, I was learning how to write on the job. From writing investigative reports, I learned the most important thing of all: It's the story, stupid.

Eventually, I began to write these stories down. Over a period of a couple of years the pile of paper mounted until I had several hundred pages. It was about this time that the first Maui Writers Conference was held at Kapalua. At that first conference I learned two very important things. Like many beginning writers, I had written my stories in first person, mostly because they happened to me. At the conference I learned the freedom of third person. The other thing I learned was how to pitch a story in one sentence. It had never occurred to me that it would be necessary, but of course it's imperative to be able to do so. It's not enough to write the great American novel, you've got to be able to sell it, in one sentence.

Ultimately, the most important things that I gained at the first MWC, and the other three that I attended, were contacts. At the first conference I met Elizabeth Engstrom who taught me the virtues of third person. Engstrom, a successful author and highly regarded creative writing teacher, returned to Maui the following year and taught her course, which I attended. In her five-day, twenty-hour intensive she presented enough material for a person at the right stage of their evolution as a writer to actually write a book. I was at that stage, and over the next year I took that pile of stories and wrote my first novel.

At another MWC I met the man who would become my agent and my manuscript was off to the Manhattan Triangle, where it disappeared from the face of the earth. Five years passed and I had actually forgotten about it. Then one Spring day the phone rang. "We would like to publish your book," the voice said.

At the MWC you will hear stories like that over and over again. Stories of amazing luck and incredible perseverance. That's the other thing that I always take away from the MWC: inspiration. Coming in contact with that intense field of as-sembled talent can change your life. It changed mine.

PART TWO:

NONFICTION

If fiction is a work of imagination, nonfiction is a work of information. If fiction depends on the interplay of character and the tug of story urging us to turn the page, then nonfiction relies on interesting facts built into a compelling argument. As tools for communicating information, nonfiction books are arguably the broadest category of letters–encompassing such diverse genres as memoir, journalism, travel writing, cookbooks, biography, history, and "how to"–virtually anything that is not fiction.

Nonfiction helps us re-codify old facts into new and revealing systems of thought, and mold new facts (products and ideas)–from quarks to computer chips, phyto-chemicals to Viagra–into a road map that will chart our future.

Accuracy is the cornerstone of nonfiction. Whether it be in a biography or a technical manual, credibility of information is the essential value that will keep well-researched books one step ahead of the often questionable data spouted by the electronic age.

–Joe Ortiz

"If you cannot become interested in serving your world, I suggest you will not find success as a writer. Serving your world is not just volunteering at a hospital or hospice. It's little things you can do. A kind word to somebody. When you go over a toll bridge, pay the toll for the person behind you. Pick up some litter. When you visit a bathroom, clean the sink up for the next person. We forget how smiling at someone can make a difference."

–Dan Millman

Mitch
Albom

A Year of Tuesdays

I want to tell you something today that I've never really talked about in public before. It has been a crazy two years since this little book came out. I want to give you an idea of what can happen when something you do for one reason is absorbed for a number of other reasons, and then things start happening that really twist you around as to why you started to write and why you wrote a book in the first place.

The last class of my old professor's life took place once a week in his house by a window in the study where he could watch a small hibiscus plant shed its pink leaves. Class met on Tuesdays after breakfast. The subject was the meaning of life. It was taught from experience.

No grades were given but there were oral exams each week and you were expected to respond to questions and pose questions of your own. You were also required to perform physical tasks now and then such as lifting the professor's head to a comfortable spot on the pillow or placing his glasses on the bridge of his nose. Kissing him goodbye earned you extra credit.

No books were required, yet many topics were covered, including love, work, community, family, aging, forgiveness, and finally, death.

The last lecture was brief, only a few words.

A funeral was held in lieu of graduation. Although no final exam was given, you were expected to produce one long paper on what was learned. That paper is presented here.

The last class of my old professor's life had only one student. I was the student.

I wrote that page in the basement of my house where I live in Michigan. It's not much of a basement. It's pretty small. There are no windows. Sometimes we get these funny smells because we live in a kind of wooded area and there's some kind of duct and creatures get in there and they die. And so every now and then we have to call this guy we know and he comes and he crawls into the vent; he's kind of like the groundskeeper from *Caddyshack* and he goes, "Oh, here it is!" And he comes out with a rodent or a muskrat or something and then the smell goes away. And it was in the basement that I began this book about my old professor, Morrie Schwartz.

Morrie had died about six weeks earlier from Lou Gehrig's disease. The idea to write the book began very innocently when I found out how in debt Morrie was for his medical bills. Because he chose to die at home instead of going to the hospital, insurance did not cover many of the things that were associated with his disease and he had built up this enormous bill. And so I got the idea to write this book simply to pay off his bills. That was it. I was a writer. That's all I knew how to do. He needed money, I came up with the idea for the book.

He never met the publishers of *Tuesdays with Morrie*. Never saw them face to face, never even spoke to them on the telephone. The only contact between Morrie and the people who published his book was a tape I had him make, just on a whim one time about two weeks before he died. I said, "You know what? I want these people to hear your voice. I want to have it with me and in their minds when we go through this whole publishing process." He said, "All right." So I took a tape recorder and I said, "Say something." And he began this message in one take, to the people at Doubleday. It began, "Oh, hello! Good people of Doubleday! Mitch and I are going to work on a project and I'll provide some words and he'll provide some music and it'll be a wonderful symphony together...." And he went on and on for a couple of seconds and then he said, "I won't be there to see the finished product, but wherever I am, I'll be watching."

And I can't tell you how helpful that tape came in during the course of my writing of this book. But it began with a notion to help somebody out, and we took all the advance money and paid his medical bills. And that's all it was supposed to be.

Now here's what happened after that. I finished the book. When it first came out, it didn't come out to any kind of expectations of several million copies. In fact it came out the way most books come out–quietly, in a very small press run of 25,000 copies. They figured they would sell some in Michigan and some in Boston and that would be it. They sent me out on a book tour. I was not welcome in most of the places I went. "What's a sportswriter writing about death for? We don't want a dying book about an old man! How about if he comes in and talks about the Pistons?"

I went to a radio station in St. Louis that was so small it was actually in the back of a woman's house. I went in to do this interview and she had the mikes taped onto gooseneck lamps. We started doing this interview in the back of her house and there was an open window in the room. I've done enough radio to know you don't broadcast with an open window. Five minutes into the interview–which was live–sure enough, someone outside the window started mowing the lawn.

The next day they sent me to Indianapolis, where we took whoever would take us. And the only place that would take us there in the morning was a heavy-metal rock 'n' roll morning show. I walked into the studio and it was pitch black except for those black lights, you know, like we used to have for our *Easy Rider* posters? And there was a DJ and the music was blaring and I thought, "Oh, I'm in the wrong place." But I saw my book out there on the counter and I said, "Well all right, maybe. Maybe there's a chance he read it." So I went in and he motioned me in to sit down. The music's blaring and he pulls down the mike and says, "Hey, that was Van Halen and now we have a really special guest! Mitch Ab-lom here wrote a booklet, *Tuesdays with Maurice*. So I suppose the first question everybody wants to know is, why Tuesday?" I'm a fairly glib guy but I just had no response to that.

This went on like this for a number of weeks. No response. I mean we heard from outlying areas. People were starting to buy the book, enjoying it, some were passing it on, but it was in so few places that it really didn't make much of a dent. And David, my agent, started to complain as agents are wont to do to the publisher, "What's going on? Why can't you publish more? How can you expect this book to do anything?" And it was in the middle of one of these awful arguments, where he was screaming at them and they were screaming at him in New York, you know, two people who were actually two blocks away from one another but they have to talk on the telephone to scream at one another about the effort that they're putting in, when all of a sudden a woman ran in from the publicity department and said, "Stop! Stop! Oprah called!" And David said, "Never mind." And the publisher said, "Never mind." And I went on *The Oprah Winfrey Show*. I was not a selection in her book club, but I did go on her program for eight minutes.

I didn't meet Oprah beforehand. They didn't introduce me to her or anything. They kept me on the side of the stage. They gave me a nice coffee mug with her name on it but that was as close as I got. And then they walked me out on stage. About twenty seconds before it was time to start the segment, she sat down, and said, "Hi Mitch!" As if she's known me her whole life. I said, "Hi, Oprah!" Because what do you do when Oprah says, Hi Mitch! You say, Hi Oprah back. And she said,

"Somebody get me my *Tuesdays with Morrie*; it's by my bed." Why she had a bed in the studio, I don't know, but someone came running in with a very dog-eared, used copy of my book and it had been all lined and underlined and yellow marked and everything. At one point she actually took the book and she said, "I love this little book!"

We finished my eight minutes. I walked off. I figured I got a coffee mug and I got an interview–this is a pretty good day. On my way out, someone stopped me and said, "The president of Oprah's company would like to see you on the top floor. Do you have a minute?" OK. Go upstairs, meet this guy, beautiful office. And I sat down and he said, "Oprah really wants to make a movie out of this. We'd like to buy the movie rights to this book." "OK." "How many copies you got out there now?" I said, "Well I think they're up to about 27,000."

He said, "What? Twenty-seven thousand?" I said, "Yeah, we started at 25,000 but we got 'em up two more." He said, "Are you crazy? Do you know what Oprah just did?" And I said, "No." He said, "She held up your book and said she loved it! You need at least 200,000 copies out there right now!" So I said, "If I call a phone number in New York, right now, and give you the phone, will you just say exactly what you said to whoever's on the other end of the line?" And he said, "Yes." I picked up the phone and I called Doubleday and I demanded to have Arlene Friedman get on the phone. I said, "Arlene? I'm in the office of Oprah Winfrey's president and he has something to say to you." I gave him the phone and sure enough he said, "If you don't have 200,000 copies in the stores by the time this show airs, you're gonna regret it." And I left there feeling like I really accomplished something!

And Doubleday printed another 5,000. Consequently, when the show came out, the book disappeared from the shelves. We went through one of those periods of time that authors will tell you about, with two or three weeks, when nobody could find the book anywhere. Eventually they got the book in and it started to move.

I got a phone call from my agent. Book's on the best seller list. Number twelve. Little book that was written to pay somebody's medical bills. Wow. Who could ask for anything more than this? Number twelve! We took the paper, we framed it. This was great! Number twelve! And then, couple more weeks, it's number nine. Great! And you keep thinking, well that's as far as it's gonna go. I mean it's a little book. I kept waiting for it to stop. It didn't stop. And then there were some more interview requests and more appearances. *USA Today* reviewed it and I did *The Today Show* and I did *Roseanne*. The book moves up five, four, and one day I get a call from my agent. He's in tears. In tears! The book is number one! He can't breathe. I ended up trying to calm him down. I said, "Relax! It's all right. Nobody died! This is a *good* thing!"

Well, nothing could be better than that. One week at number one! It stayed there. And I kept waiting for it to fall. It didn't fall. And now funny things started happening. First of all they were up to 500,000, 600,000 copies. Then 700,000 copies out there. And Christmas was coming and it was selling big and phone calls started coming in from the strangest people. Bo Derek. I'm gonna take that call, but I mean, why? Burt Bacharach. I finally got back to him and he said, "I really want to meet you. I really need to talk to you. Are you ever in Los Angeles?" So the next time my wife and I went to Los Angeles, he called and said, "You've got to come down to my house. I have a beach house here and please come down!" I said to Jenny, "You want to go see Burt Bacharach?" "OK." Went to Burt Bacharach's house!

Out on the beach he said, "The book changed my life. My therapist turned me on to it and it was really great. And by the way, I think it'd make a hell of a musical!" There was movie talk and phone calls from actors and Dustin Hoffman wanted to play Morrie and Adam Sandler called and wanted to play me, and have a career change, which really would have been a career change! And I said, Who? What? I kept waiting for it to fall. Disappear. These phone calls to stop. Didn't stop. And now there are over a million copies.

And it reminds me of one of those scenes from *Broadcast News*, where Albert Brooks is talking to William Hurt and all these wonderful things are happening to William Hurt's career despite the fact that he doesn't have all that much talent, and he said to Albert Brooks, "What do you do when your real life exceeds your wildest dreams?" And Albert Brooks says, "Keep it to yourself!" But when a book is a best seller like this it's not so easy to keep it to yourself. Everybody notices.

I began to notice some other changes among my friends or my colleagues—a lot of people who said, "What a wonderful thing this is you're doing to help out your old professor and now there's like, a million copies, huh? Hmmm. Are you gonna pick up the check?"

A lot of writers who I worked alongside of thought of me as a nice little sportswriter, and he's never going to sell that many books so he can be our friend. All of a sudden they weren't so friendly to me any more. Now it became a competitive thing. How many weeks are you on there? I even heard people say, "Humph! Wish I had found an old dying professor!" "Wish I had paid more attention in high school or college!" Literally. And that's not a fun thing to hear. And suddenly the perspective on why I did it was being turned around and somehow held against me.

One time I did a writers' conference and waiting outside the writers' conference—not this one, a different one—was Maria Shriver. It was up in Sun Valley, and she said, "Would you come over to the house tonight? Arnold and I would like to have you and your wife over to dinner. We want to talk to you about something." OK. Next thing I know we're at Arnold Schwarzenegger's house with Maria Shriver. And she wants to make a movie with a friend of hers; could I talk to Oprah Winfrey about her? I said, "Look, I don't have anything to do with this stuff." Next thing I knew, Arnold Schwarzenegger is saying, "You know you should write the movie for me."

And the book keeps selling. And it's 1.2 million, and 1.3 million and 1.4 and I keep waiting for it to stop. And it doesn't stop. And now the phone calls are getting really weird. My old school called and said, "We'd like you to endow a chair at $2.5 million." I hadn't even gotten a royalty check yet. The first money went to Morrie; I didn't have a penny! $2.5 million! And they said it in a way that if you turned them down you were doing something wrong. I got a request from people asking me to fly to Florida and appear at their father's retirement party because he read the book and he really loved it. And when I wrote a nice letter back saying, "Gee I just can't do that. It won't work with my schedule, but thank you for reading the book," I got an angry letter back from somebody saying, "Obviously you haven't learned anything from Morrie, because you didn't come." It flipped around on me. And the requests got really weird. CDs inspired by *Tuesdays with Morrie*. Could we make one? Day planners inspired by *Tuesdays with Morrie*. Calendars inspired by *Tuesdays with Morrie*. Refrigerator magnets!

And people would stop me in airports and say, "Can I talk to you for a second? My grandmother is dying of this or that." "Can I talk to you for a second? I just had someone die from cancer." "Could I talk to you for a second?" Left and right. I couldn't get through an airport without fifteen tragedy stories from the gate to where the taxi was. What do you do? How can you stop for everybody? And I kept looking at the sales, looking at the book, and waiting for it all to stop. It didn't stop: 1.7 million, 1.8 million. And now they're making a movie and they want me to come and talk to them. At one point, I'm sitting with the director and the writer and they're talking about Jack Lemmon and Hank Azaria, and one of the guys said, "Well the Mitch character. He doesn't really have the right arc." And I'm right there! I said, "I *am* Mitch! What character?"

And they talked about sequels. "Could you do a *Wednesdays with Morrie*? Or a *Thursdays with Morrie*? Weren't there some things you left out? How about *More Morrie*?"

What I did was try to go back and re-read the book I wrote. And try to remember what the whole thing was about in the first place. Because if you've read it or you're familiar with it, you know it deals with someone who had kind of lost his way.

And here I was in a situation, threatened with the exact same thing happening again. And so I re-read it and I revisited it and I was reminded of a few things. I was reminded of who Morrie was, when I first met him. Just this little old gray-haired professor. I walked into his room, first day of class when I was a freshman, and the first thing he said to me when he was calling roll was, "Mitchell Albom. Is it Mitch or Mitchell? Which do you prefer?" Nobody had ever asked me that before. They just took whatever name they had at the beginning of the year and that's who I was. You know, Mitch, Mitchell, Mitchie, M period, whatever. And so I said, "Mitch. My friends call me Mitch." And he said, "Well, Mitch it is. And Mitch?" I said, "Yeah?" He said, "I hope one day you'll think of me as your friend."

That was the first thing he said to me. And that began this four-year relationship that we had, where I took every class that he offered. My senior year I had run out of classes. We had to make one up just so I could stay with him. I majored in Sociology because of him. When I left, when I graduated, I bought him a briefcase with his initials on it. I gave it to him. He hugged me, he cried, which Morrie was wont to do, and he said, "You're one of the special ones, Mitch. Promise me you'll stay in touch." And I said, "Of course I'm gonna stay in touch." "No, promise me. Promise me." "OK, I promise I'll stay in touch." "Promise?" "I promise." "Promise! Let me hear you say it again." "I promise I'll stay in touch."

And then I proceeded to break that promise for every week and every month and every year for sixteen years, while I pursued a sportswriting career. I remember how I got caught up in my success. People tapped me on the back and said, "What a great job you're doing," and "Hey, you're making a lot of money," and "You got a nice house," and "Oooh, you know Michael Jordan," and "Oooh, you hang out with Larry Sanders," and "Oh, you get to go to all these great games and you win these awards. You're doin' great! You're doin' great!" People slapped me on the back and I was advancing. It's very easy, when that kind of stuff happens, to forget where you came from, the people who made you to that point.

And so I lost touch with him. I remembered how that had happened once. Lost touch with what it was supposed to be about. And I remembered how all during that time Morrie never lost touch with who he was. He never aspired to big, big things. It was enough that he taught a handful of kids every year, the same classes over and over. Thirty years. And at night he would visit with friends. He would start things in his community. Started a clinic for poor people who needed therapy in the community. It isn't just the rich people who need psychiatric help. He would go dancing at night, expressing his joy for life. He would go to this place in Cambridge where you could pay five bucks and go in and just dance any way you want. It was called Dance Free. He would go in there and do the rumba and the tango and they were playing rock music at the time but it didn't matter. He would grab a student and spin 'em around and they thought he was this crazy old man. He wasn't crazy. He loved life. And that's how he expressed himself. And when he started to lose his ability to walk, his breath was short, simple trips took a lot out of him. And he began this process of trying to find out what was going on with his body. Why was he tripping and stumbling?

And finally he sat in a neurologist's office on a nice summer day, a beautiful day like today, and the neurologist said to him, "Morrie, you have ALS." And Morrie said, "ALS? That's fatal." "Yeah," the neurologist said. He said, "Well, we can do something about it, right? I mean they have something now you can do about it?" "No." "Well, how long do I have?" "Maybe two years, maybe less." And I thought back to how Morrie left the office that day and stood on the steps of that building and saw that same beautiful vista that he had seen when he went in. People shopping, people riding bikes, people laughing, moving around, and this voice inside of him said, "Hey! Hey! What's going on? Isn't everybody supposed to stop now? Aren't all these laughing people not supposed to laugh anymore? Isn't everybody supposed to come running up to me and say, 'We heard the bad news. We're gonna be miserable with you all the days of your life.'"

The world doesn't work that way. And I remember how Morrie, on the steps of that building, made a very profound decision. He could be bitter, angry, for the rest of his days. Or he could try to find something positive in it. And because he was that kind of a person, and because he was a teacher, this is the route he chose. And so as his body decayed, and as he lost his ability to walk and he went from a cane to a wheelchair to being carried from bed to chair, and he lost his ability to brush his teeth, comb his hair, blow his own nose, wipe tears from his eyes, eat without his hand shaking, wipe his own rear end–as his body decayed into this rotten husk, he somehow managed to maintain a positive attitude, to contribute and to teach. To teach people what it was like to die. Because he thought, I can still contribute. Despite the melting of his body.

I finally was reunited with him after sixteen years, after accidentally flipping the remote control one night in my big house, in my comfortable life, on my very-big-screen TV and catching him doing an interview with Ted Koppel. And it was only through that accident that I happened to be reunited with my old professor, sixteen years later, who was now about to die.

I thought back to those circumstances. Why did that happen? What was in the cards that made me flip the remote control that night? What fate brought us back together? And I thought about how when I first pulled up to see him that first day, I was on a cell phone talking to ESPN. He was waiting for me in his driveway–because he didn't want me to even have to walk to his front door. He wanted to greet me right there. I was on a cell phone, talking to ESPN and because work mattered to me so much, I actually hit the brakes and continued my conversation on the cell phone while he was waiting–but I slipped down underneath the dashboard, pretending I was looking for my keys. Because at that point, work mattered more to me than anything–even a dying old man. I thought about how I was like that. And I thought about that moment that I found myself in right then, with the opportunity to be on a cell phone all day long if I wanted. Talking about movie deals, talking about refrigerator magnets. Talking about CDs inspired by, or sequels. And then I thought to the heart of the matter, the lessons that I learned sitting alongside Morrie's bed every one of those Tuesdays. And that was when it really hit home.

I thought about compassion. I thought how one time I watched with Morrie a television report, a news report from Bosnia. The war was going on and they were showing these atrocities and Morrie started to cry. I said, "Why are you crying?" He said, "This is just so terrible." I said, "I know, but you're not Bosnian. You've never been to Bosnia. You don't know anybody in Bosnia." And he said, "Mitch, when you start to die, you realize how we're all alike. How anyone who suffers is really your brother. It doesn't matter where they live, black or white, or poor or foreign, whatever, you have this amazing kinship with anyone who's suffering." That's how we really should be.

And I thought back to a story he told me about a mental hospital where he worked when he was a young researcher. And how this woman came out every morning she could and lay face down on the floor. Face down on the floor. And the orderlies would walk past her, leave her there. She was a nut. And eventually they would have to pick her up, scoop her, and put her back in bed. And Morrie watched this as a research assistant for weeks and he made notes, and finally one day he went over and he sat down on the floor. And he started to talk to her. She didn't respond. Next day he did the same thing. Sat down on the floor, started to talk to her. No response. Third day he sits down on the floor, starts to talk to her. She gets up, looks at him. Walks back and goes to her room on her own. And never did it again. And the lesson he told me was, sometimes people just need to be paid attention to. Sometimes they just need to be heard and need to know that someone cares.

I realized that when people stop me in the airport and I might be in a hurry to something that I think is very important, when someone says, "Can I talk to you about my grandmother who's dying from ALS?" Or, "I read your book. I read it to my sister just before she died from cancer." When that happens I know that I have to stop. I wasn't going to rush past those people. I was going to stop and change my life in that direction. Because they mattered. They always have.

I thought about money, when Morrie and I talked about it–how I brought him this article one time about Ted Turner who was trying to buy a network at that time, was trying to buy CBS. It was so important, how to buy CBS. And they said, "Why is it so important to you to buy CBS?" And he said, "I don't want my tombstone to read, 'He never owned a network.'" And I showed that to Morrie, who was trying to figure out what his tombstone really should read. And he said, "This guy Turner couldn't come up with anything better than that?"

And I thought about how people would wait outside Morrie's office trying to cheer him up and they'd say, "I'm going to go in and cheer him up. I'm going to tell him a funny story." And they'd go in and the door would close. And they'd come out an hour later with tears in their eyes and they'd say, they were crying about their divorce or about their job, or something like that. And they said, "I can't believe it! I went in there to cheer him up and after five minutes he's cheering me up! He's talking to me! He's talking, I'm telling my problems, I don't know what happened!"

I watched this happen so many times that finally I went into Morrie and I said, "I don't get it. If ever anyone has earned the right to say, 'Hey, let's talk about me, how about bringing the sympathy in my direction! Look at me here! I can't move!'" If ever anyone had earned that sympathy it was him. And I said, "Why don't you accept that?" And he looked at me as if I was from outer space and he said, "Mitch, why would I do that? That would just make me feel like I'm dying. Giving makes me feel like I'm living." That's a very profound sentence. It also rhymes. *Giving makes me feel like I'm living.*

Gee, I have a nice house now but I sure would like that one over there. Oh, I have that. Now I finally have that, there's one on a lake that I would like to have. If I could just have the one on the lake, I'd be happy. Oh, there's a bigger one across the way. I have a nice car now but there's one that goes really fast. I'd like to have that one. It's always the next thing, and the next thing, and the next thing. And more money, and the next job, and the next position. We always want to take. And what happens? We don't feel satisfied. We don't understand it. The reason you don't feel satisfied is because you're on the wrong side of the equation. It's giving that makes you feel like you're living. The taking never will. And you think about those scenes in movies where the patriarch or the matriarch is about to die and he has his family all gather around him, and they're listening for the last word. What's he going to say? Does he ever say, "Bring me the big screen television set. I just wanna touch it one more time." Of course not! It's preposterous! But think about it. If in that precious last moment when you're clinging to the only things that really matter, what you want are the people who you love around you, and you want to feel loved, you don't think about anything that you own. If in that last drop of sand from the hour glass that's the most important thing, what makes you think that all the other drops of the hour glass are different? They aren't. The giving is the living. The taking is not.

So I said no to every single merchandising opportunity for this book. There has never been and will never be, a calendar of *Tuesdays with Morrie*; a day planner of *Tuesdays with Morrie*; a refrigerator magnet, a CD, a reprint. There are no *Wednesdays with Morrie*, *Thursdays with Morrie*, *Fridays with Venus and Mars and Morrie*, none. One was all I did. I did it from the heart and that didn't need to change. I thought about forgiveness. I thought about these people, these friends of mine who were angry at me now because of this sudden shift in attitude about the success of this book. I was hurt. I said, "Don't they understand why I did this?" I was angry and I thought well maybe they're not my friends. And then I remembered Morrie telling me a story of a friend of his who had been very close with him. Very close. Then the friend had moved away. Norman, his name was. And a few years later, when Morrie's wife got sick, Norman, who knew his wife, didn't call. And when Morrie's wife got better he finally called and they said, "Gee, we're sorry we didn't call." And Morrie said, "It's all right." "Well no, we're really sorry." "It's all right. Don't worry about it." And every subsequent phone call, "We're sorry." "It's all right. Forget about it. It's over." But it wasn't over. A crack had developed in the friendship and that crack spread and eventually split the friendship apart.

I'm here to tell you that Morrie had a lot of reasons to cry. When your body can't move and you need to be carried to the toilet, you don't need a big excuse. But I never saw him cry as hard as he did when he finished this story. Tears from his soul. And he said, "Mitch, I found out last year that Norman died from cancer. I never had the chance to make it out there. I never had the chance to say, it didn't matter. Why did I let that nothing little incident separate us for all these years? All I want now is that he would be here. I could hold his hand and tell him how much he meant to me. And instead I let this nothing separate us." He looked me in the eye and he said, "Mitch, if there's anybody you're fighting with, anybody that you're upset over, a spat, a feud, someone you love, let it go. Let it go. If you're one hundred percent right and they're one hundred percent wrong, you say you're wrong. Because when you get to this point here, it's not going to matter who's right or wrong. All you'll care about is that they're there with you."

I thought about that and I said, I'm not going to be mad. I'm not going to lose these friends over a little thing like that. I'm not going to lose these people I value because they made a comment about a book or they were insensitive. I'm not going to go that route.

Finally, I thought about the last thing that Morrie really said to me. Two weeks before he died, a lesson that I've always said is the essence of this book. He asked me to come visit him in his grave after he died. I said, "Of course I will." He said, "Well, I don't mean with flowers. I want you to come when you have some time. I want you to bring a blanket and some sandwiches, plan on sticking around for a while. And I want you to talk to me at my grave." I said, "You want me to sit at a grave with some sandwiches and a blanket and talk to you?" He said, "Yeah."

To me that has always been the essence of this book. And the essence of everything I try to do. Because if you lead your life the way Morrie did, with people, making memories with people, giving of your time with people, then when you're gone, you're not one hundred percent gone. You live on. You're inside them. They can talk to you, at cemeteries or when they're driving late at night. When they picture your face. Because you took the time to put your voice inside them while you were here.

But if you work all day, if you're trying to make a big stock portfolio, if you're in front of the make-up mirror, or the gym, or buffin' up, working on yourself, yourself, yourself, yourself, then when you die, you better be prepared to be really dead. Because they're going to fight over your money, your body's going to rot in the ground, but that one thing that you had that made you distinctly you–your voice–you didn't share with anybody. You were too busy. So if you really want immortality, really want to put your chips against death, it's not in a network. It's not in a building. It's not in a sequel. It's not in a movie. It's not in a refrigerator magnet. It's not in another book on the best seller list. It's not in all the accomplishments that you can stack up. It's in every little act of kindness and open-heartedness that you show to somebody else.

And if you don't believe that, then why are you here in this room right now? You did not know Morrie Schwartz. You never met him. He wasn't famous. He wasn't on the Forbes 500 list, he never acted in a movie, and yet he touched me. One person. I wrote something, touched somebody else. They read it, they passed it on, touched somebody else, and somebody else and somebody else. The whole world is a potential classroom. And everybody has that power within them. And that to me was what this was always about.

So, having said no to all those things, now when people say, "Well, what are you going to do next?" I say, "I don't know." I have no agreements to do another book. Because I haven't come up with anything that's right from the heart again. But I will. Eventually. And I do know this: Although I don't know the "what" of it, I do know the "where." I'm gonna go right back to the basement with the little smelly animals.

Don't lose track of your heart. Do things for the right reasons. Right from your heart. Make it a labor of love. Good things will happen. They happened to me.

"The idea of research for a biography is to find unifying themes among seemingly contradictory events or actions. Keep your eyes open for ideas or events that changed the person's perspective, so you can monitor his or her emotional pulse. The points at which subjects' lives are most vivid to them are the points with which readers will identify most."

–Katherine Ramsland

Tad Bartimus

Are You Sure You Want to Finish Your Book?

I think the very first thing that a person who wants to write has to examine is their commitment to the project. Are you committed to the project? If you're committed to the project, then you have to look at what that means in terms of honesty and truth in the project.

Because to write any kind of a book you're going to have good stuff in it, and you're going to have bad stuff in it. If it's a "how-to" book, you'll have to know how not to do something, and in order to do that you have to give negative examples. If it's a memoir, bad things happen to people.

Usually people who want to write memoirs want to write about lessons they have learned in life and experiences they have. So you have to decide if you're going to be committed to writing a book, and the next thing you have to decide is how honest you're going to be in writing the book. And whether you really want to go to these places in your mind and on your path.

Don't waste your time writing a bad book that you're un-happy with if you're not committed to the project. It's real simple. It doesn't mean that you won't write a book at some point, it just means, are you ready to write it now? Are you qualified to write it now? Are you secure enough to write it now? Are you prepared to deal with the consequences of writing it now, professionally or personally, or both? Nobody ever asks this question of themselves when they think, "I'll write a book!" And then they get in the middle of it. It's like walking across a newly laid concrete sidewalk. You get halfway across and you look back, and those steps have suddenly solidified.

I decided that I would not presume to write about other people's emotions. I would not presume to write about what they did that did not pertain to their interactions with me. I would not psychoanalyze their motives. I would write only about my interaction with them from my point of view. In other words, I own that vision. They would disagree with me. Sometimes even if they were portrayed in a flattering light, they would disagree with the event.

When you're writing memoir, you're going to see it in your unique way. You also may not see it as it actually happened. If there is a car accident or something and police come around to interview witnesses, everybody saw it differently. Sometimes they saw things that didn't happen, sometimes they embellished, sometimes they missed something–everybody sees things in a different way. So when you're writing a personal reflective memoir, or even if you're writing about something that happened to you in your practice, and there were other people there, they will see it in a completely different way than you did.

We write in a kind of a vacuum but the work doesn't go out to the world in a vacuum. So it's your story, but it's not really your story. It's the story of every single person that was involved in what you're writing about. And they're going to see it in a different way, and you're going to have to be prepared for that. There are going to be hurt feelings, misunderstandings. You can circumvent this in a couple of ways if you want. You can mitigate it; you can share the written piece with them in advance and ask for their view of it. You can do this with a clear understanding that you will take their comment under advisement, but that doesn't mean that you're going to change your point of view. You can condition them throughout the process, by telling them what you're writing about and asking them how they remember it, as long as you can remain true to your own vision of how you are going to write it so that you don't spring it on them.

I made a very bad mistake with a story on my father. I didn't warn anybody that it was coming. And that was a tremendous mistake on my part. Somebody called me and told me it was in the New York Times, and I thought, "I'm screwed." Because I hadn't been brave enough to tell my mother. So prepare people for the things that are going to happen if you're intent about writing about them. You can also write in a way in which you don't name them, or if you're writing a memoir, you can change the names.

When you're a writer, the more you put out, the more floats back to you because we all have universal issues. I recommend that you have a writing partner, one writing partner that you trust implicitly, and that you have some kind of writing group that is not invested in you and is a little harsher with you. You write in a vacuum, but you also need to have people around you who think like you, and don't think you are weird. You need a safe house.

"Don't forget the romance. There's romance in every single book you read."

–Marilyn Meredith

SPOTLIGHT ON SUCCESS

MARGARET M. PRICE, AUTHOR
What You Need To Know About Divorce

I have attended the Maui Writers Conference twice, and will go again this year. I travel from St. Louis, Missouri to attend the conference. Even though Maui is breathtakingly beautiful, I go there for the conference, not the setting. The first time I attended the conference, I did not leave the hotel grounds except to travel to and from the airport, because I was involved in conference activities about twelve hours a day.

My interest was writing fiction, yet at the conference bookstore the book *Is There A Book Inside You?* by Dan Poynter and Mindy Bingham caught my eye. At that time, I had not considered writing nonfiction.

I had just had a baby a few months before the conference, and I had read the book *What To Expect When You're Expecting* so many times during the pregnancy the book was about to fall apart. Since I am a divorce lawyer, I decided to write a similar book for people going through divorce. After writing the book, entitled *What You Need To Know About Divorce*, I sent it to a friend at a New York publishing house.

When I found out it would take the publisher a year and a half to two years to get the book in print and in the bookstores, I put what I learned at the Maui Writers Conference into action.

I reread the book, *Is There A Book Inside You?*, did a massive amount of research at the library, and then called Dan Poynter. He sent me his book, *The Self-Publishing Manual,* and was very helpful and encouraging. I also used the information and inspiration from Jack Canfield's talks at the Maui Writers Conference to attack the marketing of the book.

Within three months I had researched the publishing industry, started my own publishing company, completed all the necessary government and industry filings, hired a printer, and gotten my book into print. It received regional and national reviews, and can be found in libraries, bookstores, and at numerous sites on the internet.

Writing the book was only about one-tenth of the work. Self-publishing is an unbelievable amount of work. I have great respect for other self-publishers, such as Dan Poynter, Mark Twain, Richard Nixon, Ben Franklin, and many others. Although it was a great deal of work, the experience taught me much more about the publishing industry than a lifetime of simply writing could have.

Now I spend my time filling the book orders from wholesalers and the distributor, as well as from the internet sites. I also continue to promote the book. I am completing a novel this month, and will then finish writing my second non-fiction book, *What You Need To Know After Divorce.* I also teach law full-time, practice law part-time, and my son, who was a baby when I attended my first conference, is entering kindergarten this fall. So don't tell me you are too busy to write!

"Do you watch TV? How many hours a day? Cut out one. Take that one and use it to do something productive. If you were to simply write an hour a day you'd have 365 hours of writing, that's nine and a half forty-hour work weeks. Could you potentially write your book in nine and a half uninterrupted weeks? Probably."

–Jack Canfield

Kenneth C. Davis

Writing History

Halfway through college I took a job checking books for delivery to bookstores. I always laugh when I hear an editor or a publisher say he started out at the bottom rung of the book business as a junior editor somewhere. The real bottom rung of the book business is the folks who pack books in boxes. And I was one of them. But it was a great education, and a sort of introduction to the excitement of the business.

I remember my first day in this very dusty warehouse, jammed to the ceiling with books, hundreds, thousands, tens of thousands of books. But my first day, the excitement was building because Peter Benchley's novel, *Jaws*, was coming out in paperback that day. They were expecting the boxes to be delivered. And this is a huge book at the time. I don't know if you all remember how big a best seller *Jaws* was. But it was tremendous excitement at the time. And my first job, actually, in publishing, was to pack and then deliver hundreds of cartons of Peter Benchley's novel of *Jaws* to a small department store chain in New England.

As dusty and dirty as it was, it was my first taste of the thrill, the excitement of a big new book—and it does go straight to the blood. It's not something you lose. From there I went into managing a bookstore, which is another great education for a writer. First of all, again you are surrounded by books–the good, the bad, and the ugly. And you pick up an awful lot just by osmosis. You also begin to realize how tough this business is. Not only do you have the 40,000 books that keep coming out every year, the new books, but all the tens of thousands of books that have preceded you. And then if ever you do get into print, as a writer, you know there are so many other books out there to compete against.

One of the first things you learn as a bookseller is that there are those hundreds of customers who walk in every day of the week and say, "I saw a book on the *Today* show. I don't know the name and I don't know the author. Can you help me find it?" Happens all the time. That's what authors are up against in the real world. It's a very discouraging idea to an aspiring writer, I know, but it's still a thrill to be in and around the book business.

For me the other advantage of working in this small bookstore in Manhattan was that I met a young woman who was working with me and she read some of my college material. I was sort of adrift at the time–it was the '70s; nobody knew what they were really doing. And she said to me, "You're wasting your time here. You should be a writer." She later moved to *Publishers Weekly* as an editor and she got me my first writing assignment there. Figuring that this woman was smart and very useful, I decided to marry her.

So my first writing work was at *Publishers Weekly* reviewing books for the fiction and non-fiction Forecast department at the grand sum of fifteen bucks a pop. My PW work led to my first book, which is a book that preceded *Don't Know Much About History* by several years. And it's a book that unfortunately most of you haven't heard of. But it was called *Two-Bit Culture: the Paperbacking of America*. And it told the story of the rise of the paperback book in this country. The paperback book business. Many of us who have grown up in the last twenty years or so don't remember a time when there were no paperbacks, but before 1939 there were none.

So I discussed the rise and the beginnings of the paperback industry in 1939 with Pocketbook, to its domination of the industry by the mid-1980s.

But beyond that I talked about the books that changed America in that time, over the last forty years, especially as paperback books. Everything from Dr. Spock to *The Story of O*. At the time that first book appeared, "Don't Know Much About Publishing," I suppose we could call it now, but it was called *Two-Bit Culture*, my first child appeared and since my wife again had a paying job with health benefits and I'd taken three years to write a book with a $10,000 advance, less agent's commission, it seemed sensible for me to let her keep working and I would stay home and become Mr. Mom for a few years. I dabbled in book projects but I wasn't writing. And I wasn't happy. Around that time I heard of just the title of a book, a book I'd never read. The title was enough and it affected me profoundly. It was called, *Do What You Love and the Money Will Follow*. That message was enough. I knew I loved writing. I knew I needed to start writing again. But what? Again, my very smart wife had the answer. "You love history. Why don't you write a book about American history?" Which brings me to George Washington and what he said on that memorable night, Christmas night of 1776, when he was about to cross that icy Delaware River to launch an attack on the British troops in Trenton, New Jersey. He steps into the boat that's going to take him across the river. And there is General Henry Knox. He was known by the nickname Ox-Stocks because he was over six feet tall and weighed about 280 pounds. So Washington nudges Knox with the toe of his boot and said, "Shift that fat ass Harry, but slowly or you'll swamp the damn boat!"

Now I never heard that story when I was growing up in school. I certainly never read it in any of my textbooks. And it's too bad because it says more to me about Washington's earthy humanity, the fact that he was a soldier, the fact that he spoke barroom and barracks room language; it said more about Washington to me than all the hokey stories about cherry trees and prayer vigils in Valley Forge. And when I read that story, I knew that was the kind of story I wanted to tell in my history of America. That's the kind of story I wanted to write about in *Don't Know Much About History*. Because it was real. It was alive. And it was human. I must confess I'm a little bit reluctant to try and tell you how to write history or anything else for that matter. I think the best I can do is tell you what works for me and some general rules for what I think makes for good books.

The first rule of good history, I think–the first rule of good novels and any good books–is that they're about stories. Good stories. Why do we still read *The Iliad* and *The Odyssey*? They're good stories. Here's another good story. I never heard this one in grade school, either. But you all probably learned that Christopher Columbus was out to prove that the world was round. He set off sailing and–well, this is nonsense, I have to let you know this now. By the time that Columbus was around, people had known the world was round for centuries. The Greeks had proven it a thousand years before Columbus. Then, doing my research, I found this rather curious story about Christopher Columbus. He was on his third voyage. He was sailing off the coast of South America where the Oronoco River empties into the ocean and he writes in the log of his journey that he had found one of the rivers mentioned in the Book of Genesis. He said, "I have found Paradise. This is the Garden of Eden that is mentioned in the Book of Genesis." And I said, well this is rather remarkable. I never heard that Christopher Columbus discovered the Garden of Eden. So he goes on from there to write that the world is not spherical, as he believed. It's not round, but pear-shaped. And then he said, "It's like a woman's breast. And the nipple part is closest to heaven." I said, wait a minute! Columbus thought the world was shaped like a woman's breast? I don't know. Maybe he was just a sailor too long at sea. But I certainly never heard that story when I was in seventh grade. I can assure you if I had, I would have sat up and taken notes.

But a great many people will say, "That's not history. That's just a funny anecdote." But they're wrong. Joseph Pulitzer, who was a great newspaperman, a brilliant newspaperman, a yellow journalist at heart, although we honor his name with the Pulitzer Prize, was the first newspaper publisher to put funnies in the news. And people thought this was terrible and they asked him why and Pulitzer said, "First fill the pews. Then preach." And I think that's a really important idea and it's certainly one that I've tried to practice in my book.

So my first key to writing is, you have to get people's attention. Have to get them to perk up their ears, whether it's the story about George Washington crossing the Delaware or Christopher Columbus thinking the world looked like a woman's breast, people perk up their ears and they say, "Gee, I never heard of it that way before." And the way to get that attention is by telling great stories. And those stories are best when they're human stories. That simply means stories that are alive, meaningful, memorable, relevant.

I think one of the reasons that my books have become necessary—one of the reasons Americans don't know much about history and don't know much about geography and certainly don't understand the Civil War—is that schools and textbooks have sucked the life out of subjects like history. The academic writing in textbooks is a disgrace. You may have heard the stories of how political textbooks are. To get your textbook accepted in a state like Texas, one has to go through a school book board and, of course, these school book boards have come to be dominated by very conservative people who want certain things taught in the textbooks. So publishers who want their books in a state like Texas, which is a big part of the book market, tailor their books to fit these political notions.

But there's another reason. A friend of mine who writes textbooks is a very clever, witty, personable writer, who has a voice of his own. He wrote a textbook with a collaborator and it was done and it was excellent and the publisher said, "Oh, we really loved it. We're going to send it out for peer review." Peer review meant they were going to send it to thirty professors around the country. Thirty professors with really big names in this area and whose name on a consultation board would ensure sales. Well, every one of those thirty professors sent the manuscript back saying, "Gee this is really wonderful. But I've made some notes in the margin." All of those thirty professors' notes in the margins were given back to the author who was told to try and weave those things in. And he said, "Well, it wasn't my stuff, but they wanted to do it and we needed the sale so I did it." Now he had a partially watered down version of his manuscript. It was then sent out to another group of thirty professors and came back again with notes in the margin. So by the end he said, "This was just not my book. It was written by a group of academics." The professors, the academics, the professional historians, they like to speak to each other. They have their sort of own secret jargon. And it's left most of America completely out of the conversation. History for most of us was a collection and a long list of dates and battles and speeches. Most of us probably remember something like Lewis and Clark as a sort of footnote to Thomas Jefferson and the Louisiana Purchase. And it was all back there around 1803.

But then Stephen Ambrose took this story, *Undaunted Courage*, and he made it come to life. If you haven't read it, it's an extraordinary book, an extraordinary adventure story and one of the great American adventures. One of the great American tales. And it makes history come to life, the story of these two men who go out, literally where no man–certainly no white man–had gone before, and they kept with them a few people. They had a slave with them and a young Indian teenager who was pregnant and whose baby was born on the trip. It's just an extraordinary human story. That's what history is all about.

My most recent book was about the Civil War. The Civil War has been written about for 130 years. They were writing about it the minute they put down the guns. And too often that history has been about strategy and tactics and which battalion outflanked the other ones and dry words like succession and preservation of the union, and nullification. So I wanted to write about the Civil War through the eyes of the people who lived through it. So that's why when you read in one of my books about Shiloh, you're not going to read about who did the wrong thing and which general did this, but you're going to read about the sixteen-year-old drummer boy who was there and witness to terrible carnage of this war and walked out after the first day where you could barely put a foot down and touch ground because the bodies covered the earth. And he talked about seeing a young boy his own age, dressed as if his parents, his mothers and sisters had sent him out like a household pet and there he was with his hat on his breast and he weeps at the sight of this boy his own age dying. He weeps at the sight of federal and confederate soldiers, dying together, reaching out to each other as if they were trying to help each other in their last moments.

I write about Shiloh through the eyes of a housewife who followed her husband into the war. This was not typical but it was not unusual either. And she writes about being pressed into service at this terrible, terrible battle, the first really grave tremendous clash of the Civil War. She writes and talks about being pressed into service as a nurse in an amputating tent. This was, of course, at a time in American history, in medical history, when they understood anesthesia–they could put men to sleep–but they did not understand antiseptics or antibiotics. So you would get through the surgery, perhaps, and die two weeks later from gangrene. She writes about the pile of limbs that was growing. As she's standing there watching the bodies being brought in, she's wondering, am I going to see my own husband? And this is the human side of Civil War. Later on, at the end of the day she leaves the tent. She's exhausted. She's seen so much terror, so much horror. And she walks out and she feels a hand on her shoulder, turns around, and there is her husband, standing behind her. They look into each other, they embrace. There's no time for words. He sends her off. This is the kind of story I tell in my book about the Civil War. Again, it's the human side of history. Many people have heard about what Lincoln did or didn't do in the Civil War and the battles with his generals. Lincoln lost his son in the Civil War. He lost his son, Willie, who died at the age of eleven in the White House. He died from drinking the White House water which was being drawn from the Potomac River, which at that time was being used as an open sewer for the 200,000 men of the Union Army. Again, this is the human side of history that all too often, we don't hear.

So where do I find these stories? That's part of the job of the writer, the historical writer, the researcher. It takes a lot of time. It takes a lot of time going through dusty stacks in the library. One of the fears I have is this new age of on-line material, where you can instantly go and find what it is that you're looking for. But so often I find in my research when I go and look for a book on the shelf that it's the book right next to the one I'm looking for that's much more interesting. So that's my own kind of eccentric research. In the case of the Civil War we had this rich, vast treasure store of first-person accounts, letters, memoirs. Many people still have them. As I was out on tour in the past month talking to people around the country about the Civil War, people would bring up to me photocopies of their great-grandfather's letters, how they'd written home about what it was really like to be a soldier. Again, emphasize the humanity in history. It will make it alive. It will make it real. It will make it meaningful.

But beyond telling good stories, I think that good writing has to also fight closed minds. I thought it was funny a few years ago, the Catholic Church announced after 300 years that Galileo was right after all. The earth, indeed, moves around the sun. And it only took 300 years for them to realize their mistake. But this was the effect of closed minds.

Well, working on my next book, which is about the Bible, I learned about the first man to attempt to translate the Bible into English. He was working from the Latin. For that effort he was strangled and burned. I'm a little bit worried about this, actually, the occupational hazards of tampering with the Bible. But nonetheless, once again you look at history and you see the battle against closed minds. And one of the things I've tried to do as a writer, one of the things I think historians must do, what any writer must do, is force people to open their minds. We accept so many myths. The Hollywood version of history so many of us carry around with us. The myth of Washington and the cherry tree. The pictures of Jefferson as this noble man and he was. He was a genius. But let's look at the flip side sometime. How could a man who wrote "all men are created equal," a man who was dedicated to the enlightenment and these ideals of the enlightenment, the rational mind, how could such a man keep slaves? Again, human contradiction. I go back to those contradictions all the time because that's the essence of what makes history real and alive and meaningful for me.

Joseph Conrad, one of my favorite writers, once wrote in the preface to *Nigger of "The Narcissus"*: "The task which I am trying to achieve is by the power of the written word to make you see." This is the third key or the third thing I think about in my approach, to get people to look at the things they believe true. To question the easy assumption.

Another one of my favorite quotes is from William Butler Yeats, who said that, "Education is not the filling of a pail but the lighting of a fire." And I think that's what we writers have to do. We don't want to fill pails; we want to light fires. Maybe here among us is a new voice, a new talent. Apart from all the books and the movie deals that I hope you all make, the screenplays that you might sell, I hope maybe somewhere, maybe, there's a speech or a special voice here, a special voice at Maui. Someone who'll tell us to simplify and not obey unjust laws. Maybe it's the next Harriet Beecher Stowe, speaking of the Civil War, using the novel as a vehicle to express outrage at some grave social injustice. Maybe it's another Rachel Carson here among us in this beautiful place, this paradise, prepared to give us a warning against the damages we're doing to ourselves and the world. Maybe it's the next James Redfield out there, somebody with a book that will explore new insights and raise new awareness of our inner selves.

That's what writers must do. We are the visionaries. We are the dreamers. We are the people who ask not only why but why not? And that's what writing is all about, whether it's history, or fiction, or poetry, and that's what I challenge you and encourage you to do.

❦

"I believe the job for a writer is to use the marvelous ability to make people bitterly astonished at what happens to the poor as we celebrate wealth at a click."

–Jimmy Breslin

Barbara DeAngelis

Making a Difference

When I began my work of trying to transform the world about twenty years ago, I realized that most people in this country don't read. And a lot of them read things that really don't amount to much. But they do watch hours and hours of television. So I vowed that, along with becoming a writer, I would find simple words in simple ways to reach people who think that what comes out of television is the truth. And so I have.

It's been a very interesting parallel to my career as an author because when people see you on television they think they know you really well. And when they see you on television talking about love and sex and relationship they feel intimate with you. I was in an airport about two months ago. I came through security and was walking down toward the plane when this guy in a uniform came running after me and I thought, Oh gee, something beeped. And he walked up to me and said, "Excuse me." I turned around ready to explain it was my computer, it was my watch, but without missing a beat he said, "My wife can't have an orgasm." That was his opening right there. "My wife can't have an orgasm." He followed it with, "Now what I want to know is, is it something I'm doing or is it something she's doing?" I'm used to this so I didn't even bother saying, "Hello, I'm Barbara." He obviously knew who I was and he trusted me enough to share this very intimate and painful detail of his personal life with me. So without missing a beat I asked him a few questions and gave him an answer and he was thrilled. By the way, it was something he was doing. And he was just ecstatic. I mean he was ready to tear off the uniform and run home right then. It made me feel good because he felt close enough with me to do that.

I love words. My husband can tell you that. He says I wake up talking. I love words because I am a passionate person. I feel everything. I live intensely. I believe that the more passion we have the more words we need–the more our invisible world is an intense, powerful, turbulent place full of emotion, dreams, thoughts, revelation, chaos. Words are our lifesavers, are they not? They help us give some kind of order to that chaos.

My invisible world is the world I dwell in most of the time. I've lived in that inner reality, a very vibrant reality, since I can remember. And the trick has been to find a way to bridge what's inside this vastness of me, to the outside. And that's where words are brilliant. Words are bridges that bridge you– who you are, your essence–to the outside world, to your lover, to your children, to your friends, to whomever you meet. Words, for that reason, I believe are very sacred. Words are magical.

I was married to a magician once, one of my many research projects. You know, when your field is architecture, you go visit the great cathedrals of the world. My field was relationships. I got married many times. I was practicing. I didn't date much; I just would get married. I thought, why waste time? Fortunately, I've been in a wonderful relationship with my husband for seven years and I'm done practicing. But I had to get some kind of experience. And one of my husbands was a famous magician and I actually spent many years of my life being sawed in half and floated on fountains and swords. What I learned is that magic fascinates us because it seems to create something from nothing. It's that process of creation. One minute there's nothing there, then–poof!–the next minute it's a tiger! It's a rabbit! It's an elephant! It's a girl! That's what words do.

Right now you're all sitting with millions of words inside of you–thoughts, reactions, and everything. When you speak you make something out of nothing. When I sit with my lover and we look into each other's eyes and there's this flood of feeling in me, my words create a sacred bridge between us. They create something out of nothing. And the more I say them, the more juicy things get–because suddenly he can see into my invisible world. I can see into his. We are now no longer two; we are one. That is the power of words. Words make magic. Otherwise, we are living alone and separate and thinking we are the only one having the feelings we're having, which, of course, is not true.

Words are powerful and have saved my life. If you are a person who grew up with pain as I did, you know that words saved your life. Your journal, your poetry, what you wrote, who you confided to, saved your life. When you can take something that feels so big inside of you–tears, pain, grief–and with a few words paint it onto a piece of paper, it somehow makes it smaller, doesn't it? It somehow makes it more livable. It somehow makes you bigger than what it was. You become the master of the feeling instead of the feeling being the master of you. That's how words have saved me–they have made order out of the chaos of my passion.

When I was very young I lived in a very painful, challenging household, where there was a lot of infidelity and sorrow and lies and a lot of longing. And as every child, I could feel all this around me, but no one was speaking about it so I held it all inside. And that's when I first turned to words as my refuge to find my way out of this black hole of emotional turmoil. They led me out. They were my first friends, and sometimes my only friends. They were always there for me when I needed them. They took me out of what felt overwhelming and helped me make sense of it.

My very first job as a writer came when I was nine years old. I was at summer camp, lying in our little bunkhouse with eight other little nine-year-old girls. It was late at night. Our counselor was sleeping. And I heard the girl next to me snif-fling under her covers. Being codependent, I said, "What's wrong?" She said she was upset because of this boy named Bobby across the lake. She really liked him so was trying to write him a note but didn't know how to find the words. She was so frustrated she was crying because she knew that if she didn't write this note Bobby would never know she cared about him. The next day was the big dance and she wanted to give Bobby the note then. I said, "Well, I could write the note for you," and she said, "Really?" And I said, "Yeah! I love to write! What do you want to say?" So she started sort of talking and I started pulling her out—my first therapist job as well—and I wrote something like, "Dear Bobby: I think you're the cutest boy in camp and the smartest, too." I don't know what else I said, but I thought it was very clever at the time. She was overwhelmed. She couldn't believe the brilliance of my prose. She was so impressed she said, "What can I do for you? Should I pay you?" And I thought, My God, I don't have an agent. What do I do here? So I thought really hard and finally said, "How about a frozen Milky Way bar?" And so I got one. That was my first payment. A frozen Milky Way bar. I was thrilled with it. She gave the note to Bobby and it worked: They were a couple all summer. I felt wonderful. The power of my words—it was incredible.

Years later I knew it was time to write my first book, be-cause you've known since you were born that you were sup-posed to write a book. You just ignored the voice. But at some point the voice gets loud enough and it's not a whisper, "Why don't you write a book," it's "WRITE THE GOD DAMNED BOOK!" And I knew it was time.

I'd been teaching seminars for years. People were asking me for a book and I was absolutely frozen. I was petrified. And I will never forget, driving by on the way to my office, this corner in Los Angeles, where they were about to build a big skyscraper. They were digging this foundation deep into the earth, five, ten stories down, and putting in steel girders. And I watched them digging and digging slowly every day and I suddenly thought one day: "You know what? In nine months or a year, you're going to drive by this same corner that you do every single day and there's gonna be a building here because someone started it. And if you haven't written your book you're going to feel like nothing." That was it. That day I went home and I started. I did not want that building to be up before my book was finished. And I will never forget the day I finally got my first copy in the mail from my publisher of that book. I went to the corner and I stood there–people must have thought I was nuts–and the building was up and I took that book out and I just waved it. I waved it to the sky because I had built my first skyscraper.

I was turned down by dozens of agents before I found my wonderful agent, Harvey Klinger. Dozens of agents who I hope are killing themselves right now. So when you get those rejections don't be upset. Just know there will be people who one day will regret sending you that letter. I was turned down continually, until finally, finally, somebody believed in me.

My first advance was $18,000. I was so blown away I didn't know what to do first. Success is funny. Success ruins your perspective if you are not careful. As I became more successful and my advances became enormous, I found it essential to remember what I was really doing: that I was, first, a word maker. That I was trying to speak from the invisible voice inside. I couldn't let the business of being a writer become who I was, because it is very easy to get caught up in that. As I wrote, I affected people, I made a difference, and that's why I started to write–to make a difference. I didn't write to have a book, I didn't write to make money; I wrote to truly make a difference. The truth is, my books saved my life. I wrote them because I needed to read them, not just once but over and over. And I have. They have changed me and they have changed my life. And as I've changed, they have changed.

So when someone comes up to me and says, "You completely saved my life. I broke up with this terrible person, I finally attracted the right person, and I had those ten fatal flaws," I'll say, "Me, too." Me, too, because it was writing from my soul and not my head that I believe has made me successful.

But success isn't the same as happiness. It is easy when you are not published to think you will be happy when you have a book published. It's easy to think you'll be happy when you get a big advance. It's easy when you're an author and have a book out, to believe when it's on the *New York Times* best seller list that you'll feel happy then.

This is a trap we get caught up in–it's called postponing our happiness. We all do this. We're waiting for the next thing to come. Is it the weekend yet? Is it vacation yet? We race through time. We race through the moment, hoping that the next thing is going to be what we're searching for. Do I have a publisher yet? Do I have an agent yet? Do I have a best seller yet? Do I have a next best seller yet? And you know what? It will never end if you go down that road. I'll be happy when....
I'll be happy when I lose weight, when I find the right person, when my husband works on himself, whatever it is. And you're going to get that thing you thought would make you happy. You know what's going to happen? It's not going to do it. What really matters is not what you're doing, but who you are becoming. And if what you're doing is not furthering who you're becoming, you should not be doing it, including writing. Because you're not here to *do* something; you're here to *be* something–the best, most magnificent human being that you can be.

I know too many writers who hide behind writing in order to not live, who hide behind work in order to not be intimate with somebody, who use words, even in conversation, to not say anything, to avoid saying what they really want to say. Are you this person? If you are, I don't care how good your words are, if you don't match them, they mean nothing. Matching your words is called integrity. Your words reflect your being. It's who you are on the outside being who you are on the inside. If you can't live that way, it doesn't matter how great your words are. It doesn't matter how much you get paid for those words, because you're not living them. Somebody in a class yesterday said something beautiful. She said, "When you have characters in a novel and you're trying to get your characters to do something that's not in character you'll get writer's block." Elizabeth Engstrom said that. And that's the truth for us. You are the main character in your novel. And if it's not matching who you are, you just get stuck. It's as if life says, "Stop." You're stopping until you get it right.

What you write is only going to be as good, as interesting, as passionate, as moving, as who you are as a person. We can't separate the two things. In the end, what's going to matter is going to be you. No one's going to lie on their death bed and say, "Yeah, but I was on the *New York Times* best seller list." It's not gonna make one bit of difference. It's not going to matter what cars you drove, what you bought–none of that stuff's going to make a difference. What's going to matter is who you were. How did I love? How did I affect people? How did I treat my children? Did I enjoy this incredible place, this vacation place called Earth, while I was here?

This is why I say we as writers, as passionate people, as people who love and need words, must learn to live the truth, and not just write about it.

❧

"A single word, like a drop of iodine in a gallon of water, can change the color of your entire manuscript."

–Steven Goldsberry

JEFFREY R. WILBERT, PhD, AUTHOR
Fattitudes: Beat Self-Defeat and Win Your War with Weight

"I'm not the right agent for this."
"This just doesn't work for me."
"Good luck placing this elsewhere."
These are the icy hatchets that thork into the chest of a fledgling writer. I've got the scars to prove it.

Like many, I've always dreamed of becoming a best selling novelist. So, back in 1993 I sat down to write my first novel. I finished it eight months later. I was convinced I had created a masterpiece, so I set out to find an agent. Query after query brought only rejection after rejection; the few high points were the personally signed letters that made it sound like someone had actually glanced at what I'd sent. Slowly I began to realize that what I'd written wasn't a stunning debut novel–it was a stumbling first effort.

So I wrote another one. This one was much better, more polished, had a stronger plot. Completed manuscript in hand, I took a giant risk and attended the 1995 Maui Writers Conference. During my few days in paradise, I learned much about the publishing world and networked with some helpful people. I also met a couple of agents, both of whom asked to see my work. Both later rejected it, but at least I got some good feedback.

My seventy-eighth unsolicited query hit the mark. An agent was excited by my book and wanted to "take it on and sell it for a lot of money." With a good deal of enthusiasm, he went to work. Twenty editors turned him down, even one who made a paperback offer and later reneged. The agent gave up. I nearly did, too.

I wrote a third novel, but couldn't find an agent for it, so I had to soul-search. I realized that I was ignoring my personal diamond in the rough. I'm a clinical psychologist who specializes in treating emotional overeaters. I'd thought several years about writing a self-help book, but nonfiction didn't seem nearly as glamorous as fiction. I ground some gears while shifting, but forced myself to write the proposal I'd initially toyed with back on Maui. I sent out eight queries to agents specializing in health and psychology, and felt like I was fishing with juicy bait: Three agents jumped at the chance to read my stuff.

One agent snapped up the project in just a few days, and another said she was heartbroken that I'd already signed with someone else. With great excitement, my new agent shopped the proposal, but quickly got sixteen rejections. He lost interest, so I called the heartbroken agent and told her my sob story. Courageously, she took on the proposal despite its track record, helped me revise and refocus, and a few weeks later called with the words I'd ached to hear for so long: "Jeff, I sold your book."

I started out a nobody who knew nobody. Although I ran into a few anacondas in the publishing jungle, I learned that persistence pays, and that rejection endured is the sweetener of success.

"If you commit yourself to writing what your passion is, then I think your writing is going to work. Because without passion, writing is a collection of inner words on a page. It's characters without life, it's situations without vibrancy, it's places that are named but aren't real to the reader. Passion gives our writing a natural integrity, it gives it force, it displays our commitment, it evidences the risks that we're willing to take."

–Elizabeth George

Dewitt Jones

Finding Focus

I am the only photographer, I think, who gets to speak to this incredible body of people. I thought to myself, what am I going to say to these great writers? I write a little column in a magazine. Most of you in this audience could write rings around me. What can I share with you? What can I tell you? I thought maybe we'd take some of the lessons I learned in photography because they have to do with what is basic to both our tasks. And that's creativity. Creativity. That's the essence of what we do, and what is it? What is it?

When I was growing up, creativity was talked about as something magical or mystical, something very difficult to put into words and usually presented as something just out there beyond my grasp. You're born with it, or it didn't happen. And yet after spending my life in one creative endeavor I find that's not true. Creativity exists in every one of us and it's something very simple. Creativity is just the ability to look at what we see every day and see something different. In other words, the ability to look at the ordinary but to see the extraordinary.

I had a wonderful example of that this morning. I'm standing in front of the elevator on the eighth floor and as I'm waiting for it to arrive, down the hall comes a woman and her daughter, about a year-and-a-half old. The daughter has a big smile on her face and she can't wait to get to the door. She skips to the elevator door. As the door opens, she says, "Oh! ho! ho!" And I thought, God when was the last time *I* squealed when an elevator door opened?

It's that moment that we live for. That moment of seeing the extraordinary in the ordinary. When I'm being creative, I feel like I'm just about to burst, like I'm a cup that's so full it's only the surface tension holding it all inside. Sometimes it feels like an electric current. Feels kind of like falling in love. The world is extraordinary. That's what it feels like when I'm being creative–and it doesn't surprise me because I think that's what creativity is: it's falling in love with the world. And when we're in love with the world, we're in touch with a source of incredible energy. We call it passion. Passion! What most of us wouldn't give to be able to access that passion every day.

I have some techniques that I'm going to share with you tonight about how I access my passion, my creativity. Passion, the energy that drives our technique. Do you have vision? It's that vision that steers that energy into the world, that allows us to see that world with new eyes and in doing so, transforms the ordinary into the extraordinary. Passion and vision are essential to what we do as creative artists.

I began to try to focus my own personal vision so that I could stay on course in the turbulence of all that was around me in my own creative life. As I look back over my life I realize that although I probably hadn't articulated it, it had started very early–probably around the time I was a freshman in college, at Dartmouth up in New England. I changed my major from English to Drama because I really love drama and I couldn't make a living at English either, so what the hell! But there I was now, a senior, a drama major at Dartmouth, no idea how I could ever make a living at it, not really wanting to go to New York and starve, and so I listened to my intellect, figured that it was a good idea to learn how to make money, so applied and was accepted into Harvard Business School. My father said, "Yes! Yes! Yes!" And it probably would have all worked out fine except that spring term of my senior year, three of us got together one night. We just began to dream, to envision, to imagine, what we would do after graduation if we could do anything we wanted. And the visions got grander and the dreams got wilder and some time after midnight we came up with this idea of kayaking 1,100 miles up the coast of Japan. Seemed like a great idea at the time. And I said, "I'll make a movie of it!" I'd never made a movie before in my life. But I got up the next day with my first real vision–and the passion that vision brought with it.

So I withdrew my acceptance to Harvard and I applied at UCLA's film school to learn how to make movies. My father said, "We've lost him." I went out to what he lovingly referred to as "the land of nuts and flakes." I got with some of the second-year graduate students because they knew something about making movies; I sure didn't. And together we composed this great letter to the National Geographic Society about this hot young filmmaker from Hollywood–ha!–who's going to make this movie for them. Lo and behold, I get a letter back that said, "Dear Mr. Jones, we're very interested in your proposal. We'd like to have you come to Washington and when you do bring some samples of your work." So in a week and a half I made a 15-minute documentary on a little Mexican street that runs through the middle of L.A., picked it up from a lab on a Monday morning, got on a plane, flew to Washington, walked into a Tuesday meeting, said, "This is just a little something I picked off the shelf." It was still wet! And they looked at it. It was a terrible film, but it was mine! And they finally said, "Tell you what we'll do. We'll send along our Hollywood film crews to follow you guys up the coast. You take the trip. We'll make the movie." And I said, "No way. If I don't make the film, it doesn't get made." And they said, "It doesn't get made."

Lesson one. I come back to my dorm room at UCLA and I am really sick. I can *see* this film. I've got to make it! It's got to happen! And I was scared. Then I thought, what's the fear? You think they take you up behind the *Geographic* and break your thumbs if you ask twice? You've got to find a new perspective. You've got to find a new focus. You've got to find a new way to come at them. So I sat down and I wrote the president of the Society. I poured out my heart to him. Poured out my vision to him, of why I ought to make that movie. He read that letter and he caught that vision because two weeks later he called the head of the TV department and he said, "Give the kid the money and let him go." And there I was, having never made a film before in my life, about to make my first movie for *National Geographic*. Whew! So we went over, paddled up the coast. I shot the film, which was shown on TV in this country, syndicated in Europe, was on the BBC. I was a filmmaker!

And I learned something very important from that. I didn't really have the words to it until years later when I saw a movie called *Dead Poet's Society*. Robin Williams, an English teacher, stands in front of his class one day, raises his hand and he says, *"Carpe diem!"* Seize the day! Seize the day–that's what that was all about. I learned if I pushed hard enough on life it would connect and push back. I learned that I could dream the wildest dreams imaginable and at least have a chance of manifesting them into reality. And I learned it at a very deep level at a very young age. "Seize the day!" became the first cornerstone of my creative vision.

A couple of years later I'm still living out in Hollywood. I'm carpe diem-ing it up, you know. I was reading the works of John Muir, conservationist, founder of the Sierra Club, incredible writing about the meaning and value of nature. "I used to envy the father of our race, dwelling as he did among the new made plants and fields of Eden, but I do so no more. For I have discovered that I also live in creation's dawn. The morning stars still sing together, and the earth not yet half made becomes more beautiful every day." Wow! Incredible words! But it wasn't exactly what I was seeing when I went into the woods at that time in my life and I'm reading this stuff and I'm thinking, John, you are either the master of hyperbole or something's going on out there that I want to find out about. So I took off and I went into the Sierra and I lived there for 18 months and I made a movie about John Muir. The first thing I discovered was that it was *my* eyes that were clouded. That nature, and not just nature–life!–life really was that beautiful. When I was open enough to see it. And the second thing I discovered was this man Muir, I mean, what a man! Here was a man who walked into the Sierra Nevada, sought beauty, let it fill him up. He overflowed and it came out in everything he did. It came out in the way he hiked the mountains. It came out in the writings he did about the Sierra. It came out in his political activism. It came out in a huge agri-business he had in Martinez, California. It came out in his life. Muir was a man who made his life his art. And that was a staggering revelation to me. I don't know about you, but I had been raised in a community that taught me from the time I was about this high that there were two things: There was life and there was art. Art was the ultimate elective. Art was what we got to do after everything else was done. Art was creative and fun and then there was life. Life was serious. Life was hard. I was supposed to do life every day and there were a few folks over there doing art and they were a little suspect. It was a terrible definition. It defined about three-quarters of the world into never thinking they could be creative, because art was always associated with painting or sculpture and that was associated with creativity and if you weren't into that, then you weren't creative. And those of us who felt we were creative, well, we could be creative as long as we did painting and sculpture and writing but when it got to anything else in our lives, that wasn't creative. Here's Muir. He shows me it wasn't a photograph I was trying to create; it's a life! It's a life! When my cup was full, when I was in love with the world, it came out in everything I did. It came out in great photographs, came out in great business dealings, came out in the way I treated my family, service I gave in my community, came out in my life. Making your life your art. That's the ongoing project we never finish. That's the one place where we're in total control–writing it all the time, and publishing it every day.

Then the *Geographic* came to me and asked me if I'd like to do a still article for them and that began a twenty-year career shooting stills for *Geographic*. Incredible time. Wonderful time. They sent me to all these wonderful places. They sent me to Madison County, there were these bridges, I fell in love with the school marm... You wondered who it was, right? But you know the real reason I love shooting for the *Geographic*? It was because of their vision. Their vision. Every time they sent me out, what they charged me with was to celebrate what was right with the world, rather than wallowing in what was wrong. To celebrate what was right with the world. Boy, if vision gives energy to your technique, a vision like that gives you more energy than you know what to do with and it becomes a self-fulfilling prophecy. They'd send me out to places I'd never been. I'd believe that there would be beautiful landscapes to photograph. They'd appear. I'd believe that those landscapes would be peopled with wonderful folk. They'd be there. And they wanted to believe that vision, too.

I remember one time I was down on the docks in New York, taking pictures of huge men, looked as if they'd just as soon punch me out as let me photograph. I'm going, "Hi! I'm from the *National Geographic*." Guy says, "Hey! Come on home, meet the wife and kids! Stay a week!"

Why do we keep those silly yellow magazines? I'm convinced that if all the *Geographics* in the world disappeared at one time, half the houses would fall in on themselves. Cause they're supported by big yellow columns in the basement. And we say, "Well, we're keeping 'em for little Suzie's school project." I don't think so. I think when times are really tough, we sneak downstairs in our pajamas at midnight, just hold onto those yellow columns. Cause somebody is celebrating what's right with the world. So that became the third cornerstone.

I won't see it until I believe it. I won't see it until I believe it. And when I believe it I'll see it in everything. That's why that vision, that personal vision is so important. I thought my vision would be an image of what I wanted to end up. What it turned out to be was a set of principles. In my case, seize the day. Make your life your art. Celebrate what's right with the world. Principles that would allow me to live into that vision every day. Principles that would allow that vision to come out, not only in my work but in my life.

So as you spend time with the vision of your next work, spend time with your own vision. Bring it into focus. Believe it. And it's incredible how fast it will manifest for you.

"The memoir resembles a painting from the impressionist era of the late 19th century. Before that time the artists painted reproductions of life around them, using controlled lighting, always indoors. And then a small group of French artists bravely changed the way we looked at art by giving the viewer a sense of feeling–how something looked to the artist, rather than a realistic copy. The memoir does the same thing for us by focusing each stroke on the details that colored the author's memory. It's not important that you remember the details, but rather the connection that is made between those details and how they affect future choices. It's not purely history and yet, not fiction."

–Marilyn Meredith

Eric Marcus

The Story of Someone Else's Life

My talk today is about autobiographies–telling somebody else's story. If you have a considerably sized ego as I do, this can be very difficult, because it means you have to disappear into your work. Completely, utterly, absolutely. Anyone reading an autobiography that you've written about somebody else will think that personality is speaking to them directly.

I've written three autobiographies. I know I've done a good job when people come up to me and say, "How much did you help Greg Louganis do his book? Did you help him with the writing? Did you write anything?" I've grown very patient and I say, "Well, I wrote every single word but it is his story." When I haven't done my job, I recognize something in the text that doesn't sound like the subject in my book.

I want to talk about autobiographies–what they are, how you do one, and some examples from the Rudy Galindo autobiography. Rudy Galindo was an amateur figure skater. He was supposed to remain an amateur figure skater, to compete in the 1997 National Championships and the 1998 National Championships in advance of the Olympics. Of course, we assumed Rudy would go on winning, and the book was supposed to be published in conjunction with the 1997 National Championships. During the publication process, Rudy announced he was turning professional, which I thought was a good move for him because he was an inconsistent skater. Why not leave and sign up for the big money in skating tours while you're at the top of your form?

For me, it was a terrible thing because it meant the book would be published when he wasn't competing and because he'd been out of the news since Kristi Yamaguchi was his pairs partner back in the '80s. No one knew who he was. He was gone. And when the book was published people said, So? Who is he?

So first of all, what is an autobiography? It's the story about someone's life told by themselves–sometimes. Is it fiction or nonfiction or journalism? It's creative. That's the closest answer. It's selective nonfiction. It's a strange creature. It's not journalism. It's not quite nonfiction, because none of us remembers our own lives exactly as they happened. As a trained journalist, I have to remind myself that these are not works of journalism, because there are times you do things that would not pass muster with your graduate school professor in journalism.

That's because an autobiography, unlike a biography, is not objective–especially if some of the people who you write about are dead. So I had to remind myself often that it was nonfiction. You don't want to mislead anybody, but you make an autobiography what you want it to be. I have to admit having some ethical problems with some of the work I've done as an autobiographer. One of the things about autobiography that I actually like a lot is that you can bring, as the writer, your own perspective and experience to the subject's story. I don't think I'll ever write an autobiography about my own life; it would be better to have someone else write it because another person could ask me questions that I'd never ask myself. He or she would probably have more perspective on my life than I do. They would have more insight into my experiences that might take me years and years of therapy.

Ghost writing suggests no one knows who you are. My name is right there and the longer you do it the bigger your name gets. On my first autobiography my name wasn't on the cover. It should be "as told to." But even that wouldn't be adequate, because they don't just tell you their story. You have to drag every bit and piece of their story out of them. It shouldn't be called autobiography.

It sort of is biography because the process that I use in doing the book is in some ways what you would do with a biography. You have to interview the subject, and you interview people around them. You go out and get clips. The difference here is that I'm not writing objectively. I'm writing subjectively in the voice of the person who the book is about. So you're not going to read anything bad about anyone I write about unless I want to use that to show how good the person was in getting past it. Ideally, you are true to the voice of the person you're writing about.

There are different goals in autobiography, depending on what you're doing. It might be about a beloved relative whose story you feel needs to be told, or it could be about your own life. You might write an autobiography to settle scores. To make money. Unburden secrets. Educate and inspire. Rehabilitate one's image. Let's say you've done some bad things and you need to explain them. For example, Greg Louganis was HIV positive, then let his doctor sew up his head without telling him. That was sort of a hard thing to explain away. So that's one of the challenges. You have to figure out a way to present a group of facts that's interesting, protects your subject, and educates the reader.

You state your goals in the introduction. My goal in doing the Rudy Galindo book was twofold. First, I thought he had a great story to tell. I opened *Time* magazine one day and there was an article about a kid who had a terrible life. He came from nowhere and won the U.S. National Championship in his hometown in front of the adoring crowd. His sister was his coach, his brother had died of AIDS, his two coaches had died of AIDS, his mother was mentally ill, you could go on and on. And he was the first Hispanic-American to win a National

Championship. He was the first openly gay figure skater to win the National Championship. I thought this was a great story and this was a guy whose story I could tell.

It was a great story–and I was between projects. The mortgage was due and I thought: I really need this project. But I was concerned about choosing another gay man as a subject for an autobiography. I want to continue doing autobiographies and I also want to write in women's voices and straight people's voices, so I don't want to get tagged. But after some thought, I decided to write it.

I first talked to Rudy about what his goals were and what our common goal for the autobiography might be, and that's how the book begins. In the introduction, Rudy tells readers who are looking for the juicy stuff that you're not going to get it here. Now it would have been nice to have some of the juicy stuff but Rudy was still competing as an amateur at that point and it would have been impolitic for him to say anything that could hurt him professionally. It made the book less interesting. But he states that up front so anyone reading it, who might have reason to worry, knows they don't have to worry.

And then it goes on to explain what his book is for. He says, "I'm hoping that my book will be an inspiration to all people who face adversity, especially teenagers, and because of who I am, gay and lesbian people, and Mexican-Americans. I'm not, however, setting myself up as some sort of role model." He's going to tell you why he's not a perfect person so you know in advance not to expect somebody who's perfect.

He says, "The problem I have with the idea of being a role model is that I like to skate, skate, skate. And just because I won a medal doing what I love to do, why should that make me a role model? I don't belong on a pedestal, not for winning a medal. And when you're on a pedestal, people expect you to be perfect. Then you're always looking over your shoulder, trying not to make any mistakes. Everyone who knows me knows I'm not perfect. And if you don't know it now, you'll know it after reading my story in the pages that follow." So you know not to expect an angel. I think I wrote most of that.

I don't remember. The best stuff is where I can't tell the difference between Rudy and me. He probably expressed some of these sentiments but I don't think he said it in that way.

One of the interviews that I loved seeing was a gymnast interviewed on television and she was asked about her autobiography. And she said, "Well, I read some of it. I didn't have to read it all the way through because I knew what happened in the end." And I said to Rudy, "Whatever you do, read the book, so you don't say something like that." A basketball star who was asked about his autobiography said, "I was misquoted." I'm not kidding.

With Rudy, as with Greg, because they're both gay and high profile figures and I'm also gay and I've written on the subject for a long time, there are things they can say that get listened to right away. Immediately, by lots and lots of people. I can talk all I want and no one will listen to me. At least not many people. So I can, through their voices, say things about gay issues that they've experienced but are not necessarily able to articulate.

I'll give you a couple of examples of that. When Rudy says, "If the odds were against me winning the National Championships in 1996, they were against me from almost the day I was born. On September 7, 1969, Jess and Margaret Galindo, a truck driver and a part-time computer-factory assembly-line worker, welcomed me into their family. I was the last of three children. George, my handsome brother (who turned out to be gay), was ten when I was born. Laura, always my father's favorite little girl, was born five years after George.

"I wasn't handsome and I wasn't the favorite. But I guess I have a little of both George and Laura in me because it turns out I was gay and feminine. These are two characteristics that aren't much help to a Mexican-American boy growing up in a working class neighborhood. If I'd had anything to say about it, I would have been straight and masculine. But some things you don't get to choose in life."

You don't choose to be gay. You don't choose to be feminine and gay. This is who you are. And so I was able to express that point in his book in his language. Rudy also talked in a couple of places about the importance of getting a real education, using the example of his own terrible education to make a point. He also talks about the importance of AIDS education in the context of his own brother's death, and how little he knew about AIDS and how he learned nothing from the USFSA, while they have the opportunity to educate the young kids they're working with. So there are lots of different little agendas working there.

Did I ask Rudy if I could put those things in the book? I don't know if I went directly to Rudy and asked. I may have, but I said, "These are things that I'd like to do," and he also had the final pass on the book. He read the whole book and if he didn't like anything he could tell me. He only questioned two things. I had his sister read the book too, and there are things that she corrected. So try to stay as close to the facts as you can. A lot is what you leave out, not necessarily what you put in.

Some challenges you know when you go into them. Some things you don't–especially if you don't talk to the person you want to do a book on before the contract is signed. I will never, ever again do a book without talking to my subject at length. At least I know what's coming. Your subject might be inarticulate. Your subject could be dead. That's not an autobiography, it's a biography. It might be hard to explain away their crimes or bad deeds. They might not be cooperative. They might not be likeable at all. They could be immature, and you don't want your subject to sound terribly immature in a book because who's going to want to read it? So you take all that into consideration when you start talking to somebody. Who is this person? What are they like? Can I stand spending as much time as I have to with them to get this book done right? Can I smooth out the rough edges that need smoothing? Do I *want* to smooth out the rough edges that need smoothing? Because you can also hang somebody in an autobiography by letting them speak. I had that happen with a book I worked on with people who were really awful to me. They didn't want my input although they hired me to do this, so I just let them say what they liked.

Interview your subject as much as you can. If you're the subject of your book you have to get all that information on a page and you might ask someone else to interview you and come up with questions that you'd never ask yourself. Especially in areas that are too painful to talk about. So you interview your subject at great length, using a tape recorder always. You have to get to know your subject well enough to know what they would say if they could say it, because often these people can't speak well. They can't; they're not articulate. They can't say what they would like to say. So you have to know them well enough to know what they would say and how they would say it. You have to write in their voice.

I remember reading a book by Joan Rivers, an autobiography, and I started reading it and I thought, this doesn't sound like Joan. I know what she sounds like. We all know what she sounds like. And the book didn't sell. The worst is when you write a book that doesn't sound like the person. You really have to know their dialogue.

You also talk to family, friends, and colleagues. You talk to anybody who will be useful to you and anyone who will talk to you. I used newspaper clips extensively both with Rudy's book and with Greg Louganis' book, because both of them had terrible memories. When you're dealing with a celebrity, you can depend on newspaper clippings to a great extent, not just for the material but also to help stir up some memory with your subject. Photographs are great also. Go through all the family albums, anything that could possibly get them to remember something. I took Greg on a tour of his old neighborhood where he grew up. We went to each of his schools. I had a tape recorder with me and I asked him what he had thought about those things. I took a tape recorder with us everywhere. But Rudy was a little tougher, because there were fewer people to interview.

With Greg, it amounted to sixty hours on tape. That includes all the different people I interviewed. With Rudy it was about thirty-five hours on tape. And that doesn't always suggest how rich the material is—you could have forty hours of nothing. Forty hours of "I don't know." With Rudy, one of the big challenges was, "Well, I don't know." "Well, yes and no." And I would tell him I need more. He said, "Well, when the reporters ask me questions, they just take the yes or no answer." I said, "This is not a newspaper article. We're doing your book." And it took a while to explain to him what the process was and why I needed the information. Part of it was educating him about the process of writing an autobiography.

You can also get your subject to do a chronology. They know the chronology of their lives. You don't. I couldn't extract a chronology from either Greg or Rudy. Could not. I asked a hundred times. They just didn't want to deal with it. Sometimes you don't get cooperation, so I hired a researcher on both books. They put together the clip files for me and did a chronology for me as well, so I had some resources for each of the books. With Rudy's book, I used clips in a way I didn't use in other places because these are sports figures and there were specific events. The clips were very useful in recreating something. So with Rudy, to begin the book I used an extended clip about his win and why he was so incredible, because a lot of people didn't know who he was or why they should be interested in him. It set the whole stage for me. Rudy could never describe the experience the way this guy could objectively. But then the challenge was, how do you sew this clip into the book so it just doesn't stand alone? This is where your job comes in, not just in selecting the clip but also in figuring out how it might fit in.

Sometimes you take license. I tried to think how Rudy would see this clip. So I have him say: "I couldn't sleep. I kept tossing and turning, reliving the competition and the award ceremony from just the day before. The more I thought about it, the more unreal it seemed. I thought to myself, `Did it really happen? Am I really national champion? Did I just dream the whole thing?' I was so worked up that I turned on the light and looked around my room for some proof that it actually happened, that it wasn't just a figment of my imagination.

"I happened to glance at the floor and there was a copy of that day's *San Jose Mercury News* and I immediately spotted my name. The headline read, `Rudy, Rudy, Rudy! San Jose's

Galindo delivers a shocker.' I picked up the paper and started reading Mark Purdy's column."

I acquired permission to use the clip. I called the sports-writer and asked him and he said, "Oh! I can't wait to see your book!" So did Rudy wake up in the middle of the night? Certainly, he woke up and tossed and turned. Did he happen to see the paper that moment? I don't really think so. But I needed to create a device for that. Did I hurt anybody by creating that? No.

I didn't take as many licenses with Greg's book. I wasn't as frustrated. And the more frustrated I got the more liberties I took, but I never changed facts. I just massaged them a little bit.

For my research, I tried to reach Kristi Yamaguchi but she wouldn't return my phone calls. Kristi was a key part of Rudy's life. As I got to know the story I understood why Kristi and her mother would have nothing to do with me or Rudy. I needed them. And I had to live without them. No matter what I wrote or how I called, or spoke to their agent, they wanted nothing to do with this book. So I had to live without them.

Sometimes contacts you need are dead. With Rudy, that was a particular problem because his brother and two of his coaches were dead. His mother is mentally ill and not capable of being interviewed. So I was really, really limited in terms of whom I could interview.

An autobiography is a story. It has a beginning, middle and end. It has art, like a novel. And you need to think of it like that from the beginning. It's not journalism. It's not non-fiction. It's a novel. You want to grab your reader in the beginning, and you want them to turn to the next chapter. With Greg's book, every other chapter ended with a gasp! so you'd turn the page and go to the next chapter. It's real construction. It's not just someone's story spilled out onto the page.

You have to remember that you're telling a story. You want the reader to read it. It's not just for your own pleasure that you're writing this; you need to figure out who your likely readers are. With Rudy Galindo, most of his readers were going to be young, which meant there were things I couldn't say.

Especially in terms of sex. They wouldn't let me go any further than to say, "And that was my first experience with a man." No details, nothing, because they expected twelve-year-old kids and ten-year-old kids to be reading it and they didn't want them reading any of the details of his sex life.

There are other limits too. With his book I had to be careful about not including too much detail on figure skating because people are bored to death by figure skating. So if your subject is interested in bugs, and it's not central to the book, you don't want to spend three chapters writing about bugs unless it's very important to the story. With Rudy, I kept the details to a minimum. I knew there would be experts reading this but I also knew most of the readers would not really know all that much about figure skating.

There will be blank spots. There are always blank spots because people don't remember things, and that was very frustrating with Rudy. Very, very frustrating, because there were things he couldn't remember and he didn't want to remember and he was frustrated with me, and he was on a tour, and he didn't want to go into the details anyway.

I said, "Well what was it like the first time you skated?" "I don't know." I said, "Well, was it like flying? Or was it....?" "I don't know." "Did your head get light? Did you, was it fun?" "I don't know." "Well, I'm reading in a little more than that." "I don't know." And he really was pissed off at me, and I was pissed off at him. So this is what I wrote, and normally I don't do this, but he knew I was goading him a little bit when I wrote this:

"A lot of times I've been asked what it was like the first time I stepped onto the ice and I always answer by saying that it's impossible to describe. Probably the better answer is that the sensations are indescribable, because no matter what words I use, my description falls short of describing the actual experience. Taking that into account, let me say that as I skated around the rink, it felt as if gravity had dropped its hold on me. It was like flying. It was exhilarating. It made me feel alive. I felt powerful. It was fun. And I was instantly hooked." And he writes that.

Have you ever been figure skating? You know what it feels like? I've been figure skating. I know what it feels like. So I created it. He thought it was great.

There's another section where he talked about his mother's mental illness. And I said, "Do you remember what she was like when she came to visit that day when she was on leave from a mental hospital?" "Well, I don't know. I don't know." I said, "Well, was she dazed or...." "I don't know." I said, "Well, can you describe it?" And he said, "No." Well, my father was mentally ill, I know what it was like, so I could describe how she shuffled, and the look on her face and all that. So you often have to draw in your own experience to fill in the details. Often I depended upon Rudy's sister for details because she remembered so much.

Here's another example. I was with Greg Louganis at the U.S. Olympic Diving Center in Colorado Springs. The U.S. Olympic Diving Team was standing on the side of the pool watching Greg. And Greg decided he wanted me to know what it was like to look over the edge of the platform. I crawled on all fours out to the edge of the platform. I'm not crazy.

Who has the final say over what goes in? With Greg, it was easy. It was just the two of us. With Rudy, there was his sister, his manager, and her editor. The editor wanted more of Rudy's brother, so there was more of the brother. You weed out a lot of things. Inevitably you have to leave out a lot because there's so much material, but also there are pieces of stories you leave out. Rudy's mother came every day at one point in his life to bring him Taco Bell lunches at school, and he talks about how wonderful that was. The paragraph I left off was the one where he talks about the tantrums he threw every day when his mother didn't do exactly what he liked. My editor cut that out. I thought it belonged there because it was important and he acknowledged that he was a monster then, what a terrible thing it was and that he was so sorry. My editor felt it was overkill in a lot of places. But the way we dealt with it was for him to talk about it, to say he was sorry, that he has perspective on it now. He knows that was bad behavior and he's sorry for whatever harm he caused anybody or whatever hurt they felt. Was he always sorry? No. But you're not going to write in the book that he's not sorry.

You have to be very careful about the voice you create. It has to sound like your subject. If your subject speaks in two syllables, or three syllables, or always speaks in complicated words, you've got to match their language. When Greg Louganis' best friend read the book, she said it was like sitting down on his bed and having him tell the story. That's the best kind of autobiography. That's when you've done your job right. It can be frustrating to write in two-syllable words all the time, or to not have deep thoughts. But you can't write much beyond your subject.

Now, let's say you wanted to write Monica Lewinsky's autobiography. How would you get in touch with her? You start with the phone book. She's probably unlisted. Let's say you can't get the phone numbers. School friends? Her father? You know that her mother, Marsha Lewis, was at the Watergate. So you write to Monica, care of Marsha Lewis at the Watergate. That's one way of doing it. Another way is to write to her in care of her lawyers. You can't be sure that her lawyers would forward mail. You're not sure that her mother will forward mail. What would you say in your letter? That you want to represent her story. *Her side of the story.* You want to give the positive side to her story. And you tell her your credentials. That's what you would do.

What are some of the land mines that you face doing this kind of book? Lawsuits? There's a potential of lawsuits, but her resistance might be a bigger problem. Let's say she's not resistant; she's eager to do a book. The bigger issue here is, how do you take something that's been portrayed so negatively and turn it to something positive? How does she explain herself and resurrect herself? Because this would be her goal, obviously.

Your goal at this point would be to get in touch with her, to find out what kind of voice she has, whether she is a likeable person, find out if her life can be resurrected. What if she doesn't want to reveal all the details that are wanted? Well, even with the Louganis book, the editor wanted details that I didn't think would benefit Greg. People want the secrets. But there are ways of making any story an inspiration or an example. There must be.

Writing autobiographies has been very lucrative for me. I make much more money on my autobiographies than I do on my regular books. But in writing my books, I get to write my own voice.

In the end you create a book that ideally tells the story from beginning to end and makes people feel good. You've inspired them in certain ways, you've revealed things, and the book does some good. And that's my goal in doing any of these things. These books should inspire young folks. Greg's book, I know, helped a lot of people. So while I need to make a living and while I want to have fun doing it, it is also important for these books to do good things.

"Everything must serve the plot."

–Mike Sack

JANE KERN, AUTHOR
Inventing a School: Expanding the Boundaries of Learning

For me, writing my first book was a time for healing. It meant breaking away from a successful independent school I had created, initiated, and developed to do something new. It meant escaping from the stress of ongoing construction, endless meetings and fund-raising, engulfed by swarms of kids, faculty, and parents who all expected me to meet their needs on the spot with faultless solutions.

My children had grown up and moved out, and I claimed their empty space as my own, settling into my newly created home office where time had no deadlines. For three years, I lived in a near hermit state, gathering ideas that began like tiny bubbles floating to the surface to form patterns on a page.

Long periods of isolation can lead to self-knowledge, but it can also lead to self-absorption and writer's block. Without the tension between individual freedom and face-to-face communication with others, creativity can dry up just as lack of physical movement weakens muscles and depletes energy. I had to learn to break out of my self-induced cocoon to seek the company of others. I had to acknowledge that old patterns of perfectionism and a workaholic syndrome were still embedded in my psyche, censoring everything I wrote.

Breakthroughs came in several forms. A trusted friend and successful author read my manuscript and gave me encouragement and advice. When I added a short chapter on the importance of self-renewal for individuals and organizations, I recognized in a flash of insight that the chapter had literally written itself, demanding that I pay attention to my own well-being.

Another friend put a brochure in my hands and told me to sign up for the Maui Writer's Conference. Since the deadline was only days away, I filled out the forms and mailed them the next day, thinking I was going to the Maui beaches for a vacation. Instead, I spent one of the most intense weeks of my life filling up a large notebook divided into multiple topics about writing, publishing, and marketing. Best selling authors and screenwriters, editors of giant publishing houses, and top agents flooded us with a deluge of information and daily assignments, determined to transport us to victory. At the end, winning the Maui Writer's Retreat award for Best Biographical/Historical Nonfiction Manuscript gave me the incentive to begin the journey from amateur to professional.

The master of marketing, Jay Abraham, says major breakthroughs come from the correct mindset—being open and receptive to new possibilities, followed by action. If I were to state the single most important key to success, it would be to look for synchronicity—seemingly coincidental opportunities that fit right into your goals. The dedicated leaders of the Maui Writer's Conference gave me the tools to take advantage of such moments, to use my talents, and to share them with others.

PART THREE:

SCREENWRITING

What is a screenplay? Some say it's a story told with pictures. That's true, but that's only half the story. Others say it's merely a blueprint for an elaborate theatrical production. That's also true, but also incomplete, because a screenplay is an obscure and wonderful art form exclusive to the last hundred years or so. The screenplay itself–not the resulting film, but the actual hundred and twenty-odd pages of scenario–is a modern medium shrouded in the arcane protocols of technology. And compared with fiction, nonfiction, poetry, and even stage plays, screenplays are actually read by very few people–a minority of technical personnel, actors, studio executives, and obsessive fans. But at the heart of a great screenplay–such as *Chinatown*, or *The Godfather*, or *Double Indemnity*–beats the essential rhythms of great art, as well as great storytelling.

What makes screenplays different is minimalism. A great screenplay is about only two things: What you see, and what you hear. All told in the here and now. Which is precisely why screenwriting is such an immediate and powerful craft.

– Jay Bonansinga

"If you want to put someone in a place where you want to feel happy for them, feeling dignity, you've got to put them in a place, for about ninety pages, where they don't feel dignity. To do that authentically, you've got to go to where you don't feel dignity. To do that effectively, you've got to hurt. Most people don't want to hurt, so most people hold back on their main character."

–Jeff Arch

Ron Bass

Life at the Top

The common wisdom is to say that screenwriting is a lesser art, which is why while growing up I never thought of writing for screen because my heroes were Fitzgerald and Faulkner and people like that. Actually, screenwriting uses all the same tools and has all the same goals, but it's more restricted. It's got some extra rules thrown on top, which makes certain kinds of things a little harder.

The biggest difference is that fiction is essentially what happens *within* people. And screenwriting is essentially what happens *between* people. That essential difference changes everything. It's more important than the time compression, it's more important than anything else. That's the distinction. You have to re-figure out how to dramatize those things that were these lovely languid, twelve-page stream of consciousness chapters where you were inside the heroine's mind and she just told you everything in her heart. And even if you do use voice-over on screen, which I love to do, and do a lot of, and believe in, you still can't cover a fraction of that ground. So you have to reconceive it.

I can't work on novels at the moment because I work in this very strange way, different from other screenwriters. I book myself very far ahead–usually between twelve and eighteen months, but sometimes the assignments can be as much as three years ahead. I have a series of reasons why it works for me, basically because I like to write every day and write continuously and it gives me a chance to prepare things, starting six to eight months ahead, underneath the things that I'm writing. So because of that I have all these commitments and all these nice people who are anxiously saying, so, are you getting to mine in July? Or is it really going to slip to October? So I don't fit other things in the middle. I just try to do what I promised I'd do.

Sometimes it's just a promise to myself, if I'm writing on speculation. The speculative and the original are two separate things. Speculative doesn't mean it's not original. Speculative means you're not getting paid for it. It means you're writing it for yourself and you're hoping to sell it afterward. I hardly ever do that, for a bunch of reasons, only some of which are financial. If you don't know whether or not you're going to sell it at the end of the day, it's very hard not to be influenced by that fact. Very hard. I just wrote my first spec piece in a long time, *My Best Friend's Wedding,* that we're filming now in Chicago. My first spec in a real long time. And I loved it. I enjoyed writing it so I was always trying to fight against the decision: Will this make it more saleable or less saleable? When you're writing on assignment, you've got the job. You've talked to the people who you're writing it for. You know what they want, they know what you want to do, and you're freer to just let it flow.

Just because you're writing on assignment doesn't mean the project is not original. A tremendous number of things I write on assignment are ideas that I had or one of the people who works with me in development would have, and we would go to the studio and pitch that idea. They would buy it. It would go on the end of my schedule, whenever that is. And it would still be an assignment but it would be an original play.

When I was at Stanford University, I took literature my freshman year from Wallace Stegner whom you probably all know as a legendary American novelist. I said to Stegner, "I've written a novel, I really want to be a novelist. Which writing courses shall I take at the university?" And the guy looked at me and said, "Never, never, take a writing course. Never take a writing course, no matter what. No matter who's teaching it, no matter what they tell you. Even if you are smart enough to forget all the crap that they tell you, it still will have damaged you because you will have put someone in that position once in your life of being able to tell you what's right and wrong. You will have made the mistake of thinking there are rules in the back of a book somewhere." It was the voice of God. And I took it to heart. I never took a writing class. I never suffered from the lack of it. There are no rules. There is no secret that somebody knows. There is nothing you are supposed to do. It just works or it doesn't work. It's great to hear other people's opinion because they say, "I don't think this works in the third act because of this." And then you listen. And if it makes sense to you, great. You steal their idea. And if it doesn't make sense, you have to be able to put it aside with a clear conscience.

Directing is a whole different matter. I never want to direct. It is the world's worst profession. And as you get to know directors intimately in your life, many of them will tell you this. Steven Spielberg has told me on several occasions, "If I could do anything else as well as I do this, I would do it." And that's why George Lucas doesn't direct any more, because he can do merchandising and music and theme parks and other things. Directing is the least control you can have over your life, not the most. Yes, you control the script. Yes, you control what words get said, but you are stuck with the actress who won't come out of her trailer, the guy who's looking over your shoulder, the location release falls through at the last moment, it rains, the light is wrong, everyone's a prima donna, you don't see your family, it is a freaking nightmare–and I so respect and admire and am grateful for those guys and women, cause otherwise I couldn't do what I do. I would never, ever want to give up my life. I write eight or nine things a year. I travel where I want to, my kid has something at school and I get to go see it. Being a screenwriter is a neat life so long as you can live with the fact that they change your stuff and you're not the final word as to what words go on the screen. That's a tough thing to live with. And it's the big price you have to pay.

I'd love to be ten percent as good as Bill Goldman at anything. He's brilliant and does work as good as anybody has ever done in this profession. And everybody who's read *Adventures in the Screen Trade* knows that the black letter of his book is, nobody knows anything. It is really true that nobody knows anything. Unfortunately, lots of people get paid for that. There's a huge range of incredibly rich, smart, powerful, nervous people who make their living off of what writers, directors, and actors do. And their difficulty is coping with the fact that they don't know anything. That they don't really do anything but facilitate a process that doesn't really need a lot of facilitation.

The one thing that you're going to find the most difficult as a screenwriter is adjusting to the fact that you don't have control over the final words. It's a deal you make with yourself going in. If you're adult, if you're smart, you let it hurt just enough so that you keep your incentive. You keep your passion but you don't let it keep you in bed for five days in a row. You get up the next day and you write something else. But what's very hard to adjust to is that you are having to please people who you shouldn't have to please.

I was on a conference call from my home in the Napa Valley four weeks ago with six different people over a rewrite that I'm going to be doing. One of them is the executive I really do have to please. The other five are very nice young people who have very nice opinions, but you know something? You can't please six different people on something. And even though their opinions are good, they will hang in there insisting the second act should end with her shooting him because that's their contribution to the memo and that's why they've got those jobs, and boy, if Ron ridiculed that over the phone, they would be hanging their heads and maybe they wouldn't be getting a bonus. So you have to be exquisitely respectful and you have to deal with a lot of opinions that you shouldn't have to deal with.

I am incredibly insecure about every word that I write, as I write it. And so is every writer who I know and respect and have met. It's almost as good a litmus test as any when you see somebody boasting about how confident he is about his writing. I'm already kind of wondering about the guy. It's true of actors, it's true of directors. Dustin Hoffman, who I'm working with again on a project, said to me a million times, "It's a tightrope. Every time I'm afraid I'm gonna fall off and this will be the time I'll never work again." I can't tell you how many actors and directors and writers who are really legendary and rich and powerful have said the identical thing to me. I think the insecurity is necessary. It's looking for someone else's voice. It's looking for more guidance from yourself and from people around you. When you look at somebody famous who used to be a great director in the '80s, and now you look at that guy's work and you're saying, "Wow! He's just not directing stuff the way he used to. What is it?" It's almost always the same thing. He got so famous he didn't have to listen to anybody anymore and he didn't. And it makes a huge difference when you're only hearing your own voice.

I have several people who work for me in development. One of them is my sister who was the chief psychiatric social worker at UCLA. And she was my chief adviser on *Rain Man*. We also flew out a guy named Kevin Guthrie, whose brother, Peter Guthrie, was the model for Raymond Babbitt. Kevin is an actor. This script was mostly developed with Spielberg. Spielberg, Dustin, Tom Cruise, and me–sitting on Broad Beach Road for about three months. When Steven left the project then Sidney Pollack came in, fired me, brought in his usual writers, they couldn't do it, he left, Barry Levinson came in and brought me back. But where the character was really formed was that summer on Broad Beach where this guy would come in and talk like his brother and then Dustin and I would walk along the beach, sometimes with Spielberg, sometimes just alone, and we would just start talking together, just to try to catch the ear. And it's so wonderful to have the actor there with you because you know what you're putting in his mouth; you now know how he would say it.

I heard in conversations that Dustin was really unhappy with what we were doing; the character was retarded at first. Spielberg comes in, sets me down and says, "Look, Dustin and you disagree violently about this character. Dustin is right. You are wrong. Here is why. This is a love story, a love story about two brothers. How do we judge the quality of a love story? By the size and scope and interestingness of the obstacle. If this guy is retarded and sweet and loveable there is no obstacle. He's just holding this guy's hand all the time. All Cruise has to do is stop being a jerk and he'll look at him and he'll love him. If the guy is autistic, he can't love you. He doesn't want to love you. He thinks you're a tree or a book. You're an object. He can't relate to you. There is an obstacle." And I said, "Boy that is really very effective presentation but the question is, you know, can you make a guy like that loveable?" He said, "It's in the casting." He said, "Dustin Hoffman is not capable of playing this role in a way that you won't love. Write it as astringent as you can. Make him the biggest jerk, the most irritating guy. Give him every irritating thing in the world. Watch Dustin do it and you will adore this guy." So that's how lucky we got.

Luck isn't the main key, however, to getting your work noticed. Obviously the first rule is, whatever works, works. And that includes anything that can get you in the room; use it, get yourself into the room to give the pitch.

It's very hard to operate without an agent. People are very afraid of being sued. People send me stuff all the time. I send it back unopened. People stop me and say, "I've got this great story. I want to tell you." I say, "I can't listen to it." Because I may already have, or four months from now may have, an idea that you will consider similar. And it's a big, big problem. There's so much litigation these days. If you have an agent then everybody calms down, they know the CAA isn't gonna involve them in some kind of frivolous suit and it's gonna be handled in a professional way.

There are a lot of hoaxes about Hollywood. One of them is that it's difficult to get an agent to consider material. It is not. What's difficult is to have material worth being considered by an agent. They call me ten times a day except on Monday because of the tradition of reading on the weekend. On Monday I get thirty calls. They are looking for you guys. They know I have access to new writers and they call me all the time. Why do they do this if they're not looking for fresh voices, for new writers?

And what they're looking for is fresh, new stuff. Please don't rewrite your unsold thing even once. Keep writing something different. The biggest single way that people get derailed and don't become screenwriters is not that they don't write something once. They write it once, and they just keep rewriting it. It is disheartening. It is terrible to keep rewriting it. If you want to be a writer, you must do two things every day. Write every day. You have to. Write every day with part of your time, your best time, the top of your time. And with part of your time every day, plan the next thing you're writing–hopefully it's extremely different from the thing you're writing now. And figure out on a piece of paper what your writing schedule is on the thing that you're writing so that you know that three weeks before you finish you'll be able to start outlining acts one, two, and three of the next thing. And the day you finish, just reach over there where you've put the notebook for the other thing and write "Fade in." Just do that and, bingo, you are a screenwriter. You may not be good, or you may be great. You may never be sold. You may never make a living at it. But you are actually a screenwriter if you keep writing different screenplays. If you keep yourself a one trick pony, that's all you will ever be able to be.

Be persistent and be productive. Your current work may be wonderful but I swear to God, it isn't the only wonderful thing in you and the next thing you write will have all the benefit of that experience. The more things you've got, the better off you are. Really .

Hoax number two is that they commonly steal material in Hollywood. They don't. It costs $75 million to get a modest movie out. That is to say about $35 million or so to produce it and another $35 million or so just to release it. A fantastic price would be one, two, three percent of that budget for the writer. Nobody is motivated to risk all of that money on material that has not been properly acquired. Don't worry about it. Worry about writing material that's good enough that somebody might want to steal it.

Write from what you have within you. Every character and every word of dialogue you write has to come out of you. It's got nowhere else to spring from. All those characters that I've written came out of me: the psychotic murderer, the wife abuser, people of every gender, every sexual orientation, every flaw in human nature. It's all got to come out of you somewhere. So you may wind up using the same words as in the novel you're adapting, but it's only because in that sort of subliminal play-acting that goes on inside you as you're writing, those words sound right and honest and the way that character says it is coming through you. And sometimes there are tiny changes, huge changes, or it just sounds great verbatim and you're on a roll and you just do it because you sort of mind-melded with her in that character and it's coming out the same.

As for structure, you not only need to know the ending of your story, you also need to know every single thing that's going to happen before you begin. Before I write any screenplay–and I've written seventy-five, I'm finishing my seventy-fifth probably tomorrow or the next day–I always start with three sheets of paper: acts one, two, and three. Before I write my first scene, I write a complete outline, which is only scene headings. It's just numbers down a page and it's just the basic heading of what's going to happen in that scene.

Then I have a thick notebook filled with the numbers that correspond to my notes. So say, number five is, Joey comes in and catches Artie sleeping with his mother. Every time I have a thought about scene five, I'll make a note on whatever I've got handy. When it comes time to write scene five, I collect all the fives and there, over the last six months, is every damn thought I ever had of what was going to go into that scene. I read all that first and then I start to write.

And one more piece of unasked for advice: In this outline, next to the scene number, is a page budget–how many pages, to the half page, I think that scene will take. So when I get to the last scene, if it adds up to be a lot more than 139, I've got a real big problem because I don't like to turn in anything over 140. If you're a beginner, you better not turn in anything over 130.

Use that outline so that you've always got a road map in front of you for every darn thing you think is going to happen. Stop and you make yourself do that, because when I'm writing dialogue in scene one, I've got to know why. A lot of people do it other ways, but I don't recommend it.

While you want to keep focused within a single story, you might find it helpful to strike for variety within your workday. I don't write on two things at the same time on the same day but I'll be happy to have a meeting on one piece, be writing the first draft of another, be developing with my development people the fourth draft of the next, and having a phone conversation with my buyer about yet another.

Your heart gets broken so often that if you have something to go to tomorrow and it's about something totally different where the opportunity is still there, it's a lot easier than if all of your heart was in that one thing.

Lastly, you do not have to live in Hollywood to be a screenwriter. It's harder to live away from Hollywood and make money as a screenwriter, but you can be a screenwriter on the moon. If you write something great, it will get read. It will get bought. And people will come after you.

"Each scene is like a mini-story: it has a beginning, middle, and ending. The beginning introduces the conflict of the scene, the middle complicates it, and the ending resolves it. That means every scene has to have a 'hot spot,' a point in which the action and/or emotions reach an apex. Usually the scene builds towards this."

–Raymond Obstfeld

A.J. DIEHL
Best Screenplay winner for
The Currency of Souls

"It only takes one."

The four words once expressed the man's hope. Now, as he calls a crisis hotline, his words taunt him. It seems punishing that in all his years, in a world of a million possibilities, he can't catch one simple break.

The story of this man started out as a catharsis for my own doubts, my own tangle with the demon of quit-or-keep-going. It was the least conceived story I'd ever penned, and I certainly didn't think it was commercial or meaningful to anyone who hadn't smashed headlong into the cackling Oz of promise and disappointment time and again. Did it come from the most terrified, raw and fearful place inside me as a writer? Absolutely.

The Currency of Souls won Best Screenplay at the 1997 Maui Writers Conference. Some seventeen rewrites later, it went on to snare semifinal stripes in The Motion Picture Academy's Nicholl Fellowship 1999 and the Chesterfield Fellowship 2000. Those berths created interest from some wonderful companies; two have made offers and new doors have opened for my novels and screenplays. But most importantly, this story taught me that writing from the place inside that's the hardest to reach, the hardest to navigate, is the only one that really matters.

It Only Takes One Impact

Writing from this raw source led to surprises. Those who thought they knew my previous "nice" work were thrown; a tough, hardened author said my story really got to him. Witnessing that kind of gut impact with even one reader was great fuel to generate more.

It Only Takes One Coach or Mentor

The Maui Writers Retreat put mentors with boots trench-weathered in experience on the case; Don McQuinn and Jay Bonansinga taught the importance of plot motion, clarity, focus. They reminded us that aside from all business, the only way to be a better writer is to write. One tough coach who cares is priceless; Maui offered several.

It Only Takes One Insightful Critique

The most revealing analysis came from someone genuinely familiar with my genre and my intent. At that turning point, I learned how important it is for writers to find one professional sounding board they trust like no other.

It Only Takes One Yes

One of my favorite novelists, now a *New York Times* best seller, said he wrote nine full novels before he was published. I remember this every time I think of shredding my latest work.

It Only Takes One Day Left

Life throws harsh reminders of its brevity in startling ways, and so it threw me. To paraphrase Gandhi, if we only had one day left to write, what would we write? If we could only publish one story which one would it be? Sure the answer might be different in two months. We'll write that story then. But looking at the "ones" helps me put the current perspective in sharp and defining relief.

"Writer's block is the fear of sucking. It's the fear of writing crap. And that's useless because that's what writing is. Writing is writing brilliant stuff and crap side-by-side, all day long. So you don't allow yourself to have writer's block. You just keep going. Skip ahead, go to a different portion, go to something that feels fun. Skip the hard part. Leave it there. Five days later, it's not going to feel hard. Move around and go to what you want to write, but don't have writer's block."

–Steve Oedekerk

Ron Howard

A Writer's Director

I will try to share with you what I've discovered as my own personal perspective. I underline personal because this really is a process where there are so many ways to skin the cat, or destroy the studio.

I don't consider myself to be a writer. I'm a storyteller. It's a slightly different process, making a movie. The buck has to stop somewhere and somebody has to have the final word. On my movies, that's me. The reason that responsibility falls on the director is primarily because the director is the person involved with every single stage of the process. And it is extremely volatile and dynamic, and lots of strange factors come into play that impact the movie's possibilities. For that reason I feel a sense of pride of authorship on the films. But there are so many people who contribute so mightily to any movie, good or bad, and the writer contributes the most in almost every instance.

I need writers. There are writer-directors out there on their own, and in my mind, they're geniuses. I need them. I have accrued a series of early images that define my view of what screenwriters and television writers do. I'll quickly run through a couple of them.

One of the very first jobs I ever did–I was about four–was a live television show, *The Red Skelton Show*. I was a little kid in a Freddie the Freeloader sketch, and for those of you who don't know who Freddie the Freeloader was, he was a bum and he wore a hat and that classic clown look and you know, it was hilarious. It was funny. But they kept working it and rehearsing it. It kept changing. Well, about an hour before we were going to do the show and do it live–I was there with my father; we were walking around, it was at CBS in Los Angeles–I glanced into a dressing room and saw Red Skelton, pacing around in his Freddie the Freeloader outfit. But he was kinda pissed. He was going back and forth in his little dressing room. He had a reel-to-reel tape player going and there were three or four people gathered around with notebooks, kinda worried that Red was pissed, and they were playing back this radio routine from one of Red's early radio shows. They'd play it back, then he'd play it again and play it again, and say, "See how I did it in that sketch, I said the line and then there was that, and then I started to talk, and then you heard the cat yowl?" And they went, "Oh, yeah, yeah!" And that's the way he did it that night. I said to my dad, "Who are all those people?" And he said, "Those are the writers!" So I began to understand that it wasn't just about putting it down on a page. It was an ongoing process of fielding input, fielding ideas, particularly in this world of television and screenwriting.

The writers who were around *The Andy Griffith Show* were extraordinary, and our head writer was incredible. And I got to be part of the process. We would read two scripts–the one we were going to shoot that week and one for the following week. And particularly the one two weeks out, the actors were actually invited to hang around for about a half hour or forty-five minutes, and contribute, throw in their ideas, things like that. I was allowed to stay, too, even though I was a little kid. And every once in a while I would get my nerve up and throw in a suggestion. They were all rejected. One day, for the second episode of the second season, I had a specific suggestion. I said, "You know, I think a kid my age, a seven-year-old kid, probably wouldn't say that, that way." "Well, how would he say it, Ronnie?" "Well, maybe something like this...." And I did it. And they said, "OK, say it that way." This is from the head writer! I was just beaming. I remember Andy saying, "Well what's a matter, young'un?" He actually did used to call me "young'un." I said, "Well that's the first suggestion of mine that anybody's ever used." Andy said, "First one that was any damn good."

I would see the transformation in these scripts and I would see the problems being ferreted out and discussed. There were weeks when we'd come in and read the script that had been rewritten and the actors were down, and they were depressed. There were other weeks where they'd come in and read the rewrite and they'd literally stand up and applaud. I began to see that it was a very fluid, ongoing thing.

My father is primarily an actor. He's directed some theater and has done some screenwriting. My early images of him are sort of living and dying at that yellow legal pad, writing away. Typing. Sometimes triumphing and very often being very disappointed by the way people reacted to his stuff. The first credit I ever got was not an acting credit. It involved my father and an episode of *The Flintstones* that he wrote. He had been home from work one day, and he was telling me he was getting ready to pitch the *Flintstones* idea. We talked about something and I had an idea that he sort of liked and he said, "Hey! If I sell this, I'll split the story money with you." And he did. He sold it. And he gave me $200. That really was half. And he actually gave me credit, so I saw my name up there. I didn't get any residuals, but we won't go into that. That's kind of the dark side of child exploitation and I don't think that's what we're talking about. My father later wrote with a partner and as I grew up, not only was I continually around this sort of creative process as an actor but I would wile away wonderful hours watching these two guys pace around trying to sort out story problems, asking my advice, letting me read pages. It was incredible.

But I didn't really want to write. I did know I wanted to direct. At that time not very many actors managed to get the opportunity to direct. But some independent filmmakers wrote their own films and somehow found a way to get them made. So I began to believe, in my early teens, that I would have to write my way into that job. And I did. I wrote the short films that I shot on 16 mm and Super 8, and I continued to write. I wrote spec scripts for *Happy Days* that were rejected, but I kept trying. I wrote six or seven spec scripts and I tried all kinds of methods. I tried different writing partners. And one script was written entirely in the nude. I had a short break from *Happy Days*, like ten days. It was summer, I was very hot, and we were in the middle of a heat wave. I decided that my discipline was going to be waking up, before I put on any clothes or ate any breakfast or did anything, I would walk to the table, to my typewriter, and write ten pages. And in ten days I had a 100-page script. Indecipherable. Total disaster. But I learned a lot and ultimately my spec writing did pay off in an indirect way.

My father and I wrote a script that we worked very hard on and we actually came close to getting the money to make. A little comedy drama called *'Tis the Season*. I won't pitch it to you. But I'm still looking for buyers.

Roger Corman had a car crash comedy, which was a genre then, car crash movies. They're coming back as a matter of fact. He had this script, *Eat My Dust*. I read it, and I thought it was really bad. But I knew that Roger Corman was one of the few producers in Hollywood at that time looking to give young filmmakers a chance to direct. He liked to say he felt like he turned out directors for Hollywood the way USC turned out running backs for the NFL. He took a lot of pride in it. And it showed. I went to Roger and I said, "I don't care too much for *Eat My Dust*, but I'll be in it if you'll finance this script." I just wanted him to put up half the money because I thought I had half raised. I don't think that now, but I did then. And I asked him to read the script that my father and I had written. He called back in a few days and said, "This is a very good script. It's a character movie, which, you know, I don't do. But do *Eat My Dust* and if it's a success, I'll allow you and your father to write a treatment, and if I like the treatment, I'll let you write a script, and if I like the script I'll let you direct the movie, as long as you star in it." Now that wasn't a hard commitment but it was the closest thing that I'd gotten to an opportunity and we seized it, made *Eat My Dust*, and it was a successful little film, very commercial. Roger said, "Well, come in and talk to me about some ideas." So I got my yellow pad out and I cooked up eight or nine ideas and it was all kinds of things. All kinds of genres, everything you can think of, except car crash comedy. And after awhile Roger said, "You tell these stories very well, being an actor, but I'm not interested in any of them. When we were testing titles for *Eat My Dust*, there was a title that came in a very close second: *Grand Theft Auto*. If you can write a car crash comedy, which of course you can act in, with the requisite number of car crashes, that you can entitle *Grand Theft Auto*, we'll make that picture." Well that was it. That's the easiest green light I ever got. All I had to do was nod. And I went back to my father and we pounded out a draft of a movie that we could call *Grand Theft Auto* and I actually did get to shoot that movie.

I did a couple of other television movies which I co-wrote, and they weren't bad. But one day a person who I really respected said to me, "You're really coming along as a director." I said, "Oh, great. Thank you!" He said, "It would be very interesting to see what you could do with a script that someone else wrote." I said, "Oh, yeah, well that would be kind of interesting." I took about three steps and I got it. And that was an important step for me, I've come to realize. It helped define and shape my current relationship with writers, who, as I said earlier, are so important.

What I do now in relation to the screenplay is still very, very creative but it's more in keeping with sort of an editorial approach. It's really all about realizing the potential of the story, the potential of the movie, and trying to identify the shortcomings and the strengths and working with the writer and with anybody else who is a part of the creative group, to try to fully develop this script. The screenplay is a foundation.

It's a foundation for filming, which is, in fact, merely gathering the raw material for the place where the film is really made, the editing room. And that's the final rewrite. The director must, above all, remain an advocate for the movie, so it's not about protecting a vision. Not the writer's vision, not the actor's, not the studio executives', not even the director's. It's this really fascinating, sometimes wildly frustrating process of discovery.

And the question is, just how effective can this movie be? What can we do to make it great? Because someday we're all going to sit there and they're going to show it on the screen. And it won't matter what was on the page, won't matter what the weather was like the day we were shooting. Or what frame of mind the actor was in. All that will matter is what we got. What did we achieve? And so that is the daily quest.

There is no more important contributor in this whole process than the screenwriter.

A lot of people ask me, "What are you looking for in a script?" "How do you evaluate a script once you read it?" and so forth. Naturally, I respond to everything I read on a visceral level, on just a gut level. And there are so many factors that come into play to a director deciding to make a film, that you as writers can't even think about. You can't tell why somebody's going to say yes. It might be the location. It might be the type of film. It might be an actor he or she wants to work with. Once I've read the script and I've had that sort of knee-jerk reaction to it, then I'm supposed to evaluate it and give comments beyond, "Hey, pretty good!" or "I don't know." In doing that, I've devised a list of questions that I ask. It's all very imperfect and, of course, it's totally subjective. But I'll just run down the categories.

First of all, I look at the genre. I try to identify it. I ask myself, is this a popular genre, or a rather obscure one? And I don't really care, personally, because I'm happy to make a genre movie, happy to make a movie that's difficult to define. That doesn't worry me as a director. But I like to know. And if it is a genre that you can identify, and that an audience is going to be able to identify, then I think it's kind of important that you fulfill the promise of the genre at the very minimum. And if it's not fulfilling that promise, the sort of understanding that an audience has—an expectation—that may be a problem.

Then, of course, I want to know about characters. I love actors. When I go to a movie, I love characters. All my favorite movies are the ones that are really character driven. Are they memorable? How are the conflicts? Is there a sort of a heavy-weight match here? Do they really stand out? What's extraordinary about them? Are great actors going to want to play these parts or is it an ensemble piece? These are all questions that I'm interested in and I'm very excited when the rating in that category is high.

Then there's structure, which is very hard, particularly in a one-read, to really analyze. I have come to believe that it really is about suspense. Whatever the genre, whatever the tone, if it's pulling you along, if there's a question that's asked at the beginning of the movie and you're not quite sure what the answer is going to be, then that's great. That's really what gives it tempo and drive.

Then I look at an area that I call fanatic resonance or popular relevance. What is the movie about? What does it have to say? What's the point of view? Is it deep? Or is it something that we all really relate to?

Freshness is very important. Very hard to come by but invaluable.

And then the toughest of all is the resolution, because endings are brutal. If you don't care for the way the movie resolves itself, it may plague the movie. And that's a real problem.

And the last thing I look for are memorable moments. Great movies are made up of four or five memorable scenes. Many scripts can be very undisciplined, all over the place, but if they actually have great moments that you can't get out of your mind, well that's something extraordinary and that's something to begin building on. If the movie's good and it reads along fairly well and you can't find any of those, you can't identify any of those highlights, then that's a problem.

As I said, this is all very personal, but it's about beginning a process of asking the tough questions, because you can't be afraid of the answers. You've got to have the courage to step out there, to ask people you care about—and most importantly, ask yourself—to define those questions and bring them out, work hard on behalf of the movie and the audience. If there's anything that I try to do every day, it's just simply keep that in mind.

And of course, that's what working with the writer is all about, because that really is where it begins.

"I've been doing something that I thought I'd invented myself and then I discovered in a conversation with Jim Cameron and then I read an interview with George Lucas where he talked about the trick that Francis Coppola taught him and it turns out everybody's doing the same thing. We never read what we write. I know that sounds preposterous but the point is you don't edit while you're writing. We don't even dare look at what we're writing until it looks like there's around a hundred pages. It sounds nuts but when you have a hundred pages and then you finally look at them, you have the aesthetic distance to edit yourself."

–Steven deSouza

Barry Kemp

Just For Laughs

Everything you will hear me say today is mostly true, and that only means that to everything there are exceptions so don't take this as the gospel, but as near to the gospel.

How many of you would like to write for television? I'm going to guess about half. How many here want to sell an idea and have somebody else write it? Most of you, probably. I ask you that because there is an old saying, "Ideas are cheap and execution is everything." That is especially true in television. People tend to think that writers and producers and studios and networks are looking for ideas–and they're not. They are looking for writers to have ideas, because somebody who is producing has more ideas than they have time to produce them.

They are looking for writers. The reason concepts are easy to sell is because there are so many of them. It's only the uniqueness of the writer and the point of view of the writer that makes any concept special. I would say that most, not all, but most breakout, trend-setting hits have a very specific and unique voice either coming from the author or possibly from the stars, especially if they're a stand-up comic. And if you think back to the shows that we tend to think of as trend-setting–*All In The Family, Roseanne, Seinfeld, Home Improvement, Ally McBeal, Cheers, Everybody Loves Raymond*–those shows are so specific simply because of the personality involved.

The catch-22 in television is that networks get nervous the more specific a show is. It's a little bit easier with a stand-up comic because they can see it. They have seen his act, or her act, and they think they know what they are buying. But if you come in as a writer and you're presenting an idea, the more specific that idea is, the narrower it will make that band in their minds, and that will make them a little nervous. So they tend to go for the slightly more generic idea, then ask you to write it in a very specific manner.

If you think about it from a network standpoint, television has undergone a change based almost exclusively on the number of channels that now exist. When there were only three networks, this really was not so much the case, but now that you've got so many networks, the demographics of television have become so much more important than they used to be. So while they want your idea to be broad, and they want your writing to be specific, they also want it to appeal only to people between the ages of eighteen and thirty-four exclusively. And that's all they care about right now, because where the major networks used to control ninety percent of the audience, they now control less than forty-five percent of the audience. So they want a hundred percent, or as close as they can get to a hundred percent, of the forty-five percent of the audience that they have left, because they want to keep their advertising rates up. So that's the business behind the business.

Second thing I want to cover is that it doesn't matter where you live if you're trying to get started. You commonly hear that you have to live in L.A. if you want to write for television. That is not true. You'll probably have to move to L.A. if you want to work a lot, but you do not have to live there to get started.

I was living in Phoenix, Arizona, when I got started. I've hired people from Washington, D.C., Virginia, Iowa–it doesn't matter where you are when you're trying to get launched. The key to getting started is not to have an idea but to write. Simply know the way to do it. Almost everybody gets started as a result of spec scripts, and I would encourage you to write a lot. When somebody became interested in my first script, I had written twenty-three spec scripts, and fourteen of them were for television. It was the fourteenth one that I had written, an *All In The Family* spec script that I showed to Jim Brooks, who immediately thought I was better than I was simply because he didn't know I had written twenty-three scripts. He thought, like most people, "Well, he has probably submitted his first or second script so he's probably got potential." And I didn't want to tell him any differently.

Whatever you're sending, send your best. Don't send everything, just send what you truly think is your best work. Last week I received a submission from a writer in Florida who sent a three-page list of different screenplays he'd written. That means nothing, so you don't want to take any of those. But here's a trick that came to me by accident, and I've shared it with others and it has been successful for them. What I submitted to Jim Brooks, who was working on the *Mary Tyler Moore* show twenty-some years ago when I got started, was an *All In The Family* script. I didn't do it consciously; I did it because that was the best script I had. I had just written it and thought it was the best work I had done, and he read it. But an amazing thing happened. If I had submitted a *Mary Tyler Moore* show episode, there is a very good chance that Jim would have read that and said, "It's not really our show." Because there's no way anybody is going to know that show as well as Jim does. But Jim didn't know *All In The Family* any better than you or I do. He watched *All In The Family* like everybody else. And he thought, "Boy, he really nailed *All In The Family*." So he hired me. I cannot remember an instance where I have *ever* hired a writer who had submitted specs for one of my shows. I almost always hire them based on reading spec scripts that they've written to other shows that I admire.

If you're attracted to a show—for the style of the show, the uniqueness of the storytelling, the writing behind it, whatever it might be–there's a good possibility that similar shows have similar sensibilities, and chances are the writers and producers of those shows tend to admire the same shows you do. So you're going to be on pretty solid ground if you submit specs with that in mind.

Not everything is a series. For the most part, series are created around characters, and movies are created around stories. Now that's a very broad generalization and we can spend some time shooting it down, but if you think about it, when you're creating a series you're trying to find a hundred stories to tell with a handful of characters. So it's really important to consider, "Can I write fifty hours of these people?" If you're fortunate enough to have a show run for two hundred half-hour episodes, that's one hundred hours of stories you have to tell.

So those people have to be pretty compelling. And the depth of those characters, the history behind them, has to be pretty well thought out before you start wading into those waters. It doesn't do a whole lot of good to think of a great premise for a series and find out five or six weeks into it that it doesn't hold water, that there's nothing there to sustain it.

I generally spend six months or more with an idea before I actually decide to pitch it to a network, because I really have to be certain in my own mind that, first, I can write a hundred episodes if need be, and, secondly, that I can stay interested in it that long. Sometimes you will think of a great idea, and two weeks later you've cooled on it. Five to six months later if I'm still excited about the idea then I'll go ahead and pitch it, and I'll pitch it with confidence.

One thing to bear in mind is how long a series needs to be in production before you can start doing episodes about the supporting characters. Research has told us that everybody who is ever going to watch a show is going to watch it in the first eight weeks it's on. Almost never do people catch up with a series in the second, third, or fourth year. So if you take that principle, your first eight episodes should be some version of the pilot eight different ways. Imagine that a friend sees a new show and loves it. They tell you, "There's a show about a coach and his daughter. She has come to live with him. It's got some good family stuff in it and you really ought to check it out." And the next week when you see it it's about some tall blond assistant coach who is going with a woman's basketball coach, and you think, "That wasn't the show you told me about." It's very important in the first eight episodes that you find eight different ways of doing the pilot and not having anybody realize you're doing the show eight different ways. From that point on, you can do whatever you want.

Now we come to some technical matters. Would it be better, you may wonder, to get a script to a series you like and try to duplicate that format, versus simply watching the show? There is a generally accepted format for film shows, and there is a generally accepted format for taped shows, and they are slightly different. There are software systems that will give you the basic tape format. And the basic multi-camera film format and single-camera film format for a television show looks just as it does for a feature script. For half-hour scripts done on tape for three-camera film, there is a slightly different form and, as I said, there is software that you can buy so you don't have to worry about it. But you could probably write to any show and I imagine they would be happy to send you a sample script. We've done it hundreds of times.

There is huge value in it. If you're going to write to a show and ask for a script, ask for a copy of the table draft, the first draft, and ask for a copy of the script that they shot because they will be dramatically different. Not only will they differ simply because they have had a chance to rewrite the show and throw out the stuff that didn't work and incorporate stuff that does. But also one of the things you'll really notice is the way transitions disappear. When you take a script to the table on a Monday morning, if you're doing a show on a Monday-Friday schedule, you're writing that script to be read; you're not writing that script to be shot. And you put in all the transitions so that everybody–from the networks to the cast–can understand what the moments are in the show. And over the course of the week you begin to eliminate those transitions because actors can make them in a move, with a look, and it doesn't need to be as talky. So the script gets shorter, and you'll almost invariably say, "Gee, this reads better than the rewrite." But when you see the rewrite it will play better.

There's also the question of star appeal. In a situation like *Newhart*, where you had an established star, did I go to Bob and say, "Let's do a show together?" Or did I just get an idea for a show and think that Bob would be good in it? Again, there is no hard and fast rule here. I can tell you that in the case of *Newhart*, I had just come off three years of *Taxi* and Bob wanted to do another series. MTM made a deal with CBS for Bob to do a new show for thirteen episodes. They came to me and asked if I would be interested in creating a series for Bob Newhart and Suzanne Pleshette called *Mr. and Mrs. Hartley*; it was going to be a sequel to *The Bob Newhart Show*. I could do anything I wanted except I had to keep those two characters. I told them I wasn't interested because I thought that series had really already been done. They came back a few weeks later and said, "OK, it doesn't have to be *Mr. and Mrs. Hartley*. Could it be Bob Newhart and Suzanne Pleshette in anything you want to do?" So I thought about that, and I said, "You know, if you got Bob and Suzanne together, and I really like Suzanne a lot, but that is still going to be *Mr. and Mrs. Hartley*." So I passed again. But you know, I was twenty-nine, and what did I have to lose? So I kept saying no and they finally came back and I think they were confused that I was saying no, but at any rate, they came back and they said, "What if it's Bob Newhart and anything you want to do?" I said, "That sounds good."

I really don't know what makes a series, but I'm pretty sure I would know what isn't a series. So as I'm thinking about ideas for this particular project I'm saying, "That's not it," "That's not it." Then when I'm out of "That's not its," whatever I've got left hopefully is it. So I started with Bob; I just had an image. I had never met him. I had an image of Bob in sweaters. And for some reason–hey, you start someplace–I started with a sweater. And I saw him in a den with a fireplace, and I saw him in New England. So he and I had our first meeting together and I said, "I don't have a lot–I've got it set in

New England." And he said, "I was thinking of the Pacific Northwest." I was trying to think of something positive so I said, "So we're both talking America!"

Fortunately they'd decided early on that they were going to let it be a writers' company and not an actors' company, so they said, "It's going to be in New England. Just go do it." From there I began thinking of New England, and I started thinking of, I don't know, I thought of Holiday Inn. I was just trying to think of images of New England. I had never been to New England, by the way. I created a whole image of what I thought New England should be like. I had this idea of Holiday Inn, and I had an idea of the play, *George Washington Slept Here*, and sort of put all of those elements together and began to see him as a writer because that seemed to fit with the image of him working in the study, and that is how it all came together. Then I went to New England after I had written it, to verify that I was accurate.

I don't know if I was inspired to be a writer. I just loved it. I wrote all the time when I was a kid without ever thinking about it as a career, and then I went to the University of Iowa. I was majoring in speech and the performing arts, and acting in plays and things like that. And at some point I had an idea for a play, and so began to write it. And I found as I was writing that when I was in rehearsal for a play I was acting in, I couldn't wait for the rehearsal to get over so I could get home and write *my* play. I thought you should spend most of your time doing what you love doing the most. I love writing a lot more than I like rehearsing.

And while I love writing and working with other writers, I've changed over the years in how many writers I hire to help me with a series. I used to work with a room of seven or eight, counting me. There are some shows that hire as many as twenty. You can teach basic structure things but you can't teach talent, and if somebody has the talent, you don't need to teach them much of anything, and if they don't have the talent, all the time in the world and all the teaching isn't going to help, so the staff has become smaller and smaller over the years. Now we usually use three or four.

I think people who write funny see the world as a funny place. I know you've probably heard that before, but I think it's true. For example, a couple of years ago I was pitching an idea to Fox with another writer. I was going to supervise the idea and the pitch was going really well, and people were laughing and falling all over themselves, and we thought, "We've nailed this!" They said, "That is really funny! Is there any talent involved?" I said, "Yeah, I thought it was me but I think I know what you're asking." Because in television, the word "talent" generally refers to actors. It doesn't refer to writers, directors, or producers. So that is what they were asking. I've heard the term for years and suddenly at that moment I was sort of offended. I thought it was kind of funny.

I also remember when I was twenty-one or so, my grandmother was living with us and she had Alzheimer's, and it was very sad. One day I was home taking care of her while my family was out of town and a note came for her. Now her sister had recently passed away and my family had elected not to tell her because they said there is really no good that could come of it, and she won't remember it, and she'll just be upset. But we went ahead and sent flowers from her but didn't tell her. So the note was to thank her for the flowers she had sent for her sister's funeral, and she completely fell apart, and wailed, "My God, my baby sister is dead and nobody told me." She was inconsolable. I had no idea what to do. She went back to her room and within five minutes, I heard her whistling and she was coming down the hall singing, "There is nothing quite as good when you're tired of chopping wood as a nice piece of gooseberry pie." And I said, this is good, this is good. What I didn't anticipate was that when she would sit down she would reach into her housecoat and pull out the note again. "Oh, my God," and she went through it again: "My baby sister's died and they didn't tell me." So I thought, gee, I've got a find a way to get that letter away from her because I don't know how many times I'm going to go through this. So I followed her back to her room and got rid of the letter. My point is, I think humor comes from just looking at life and thinking, "this could be a tragedy, but instead I think I can make something out of this," and make a dollar.

There is, absolutely, a relationship between humor and pain. I think that people who see the world as a dark place write tragedy, and people who see the world as a funny place write comedy. And they talk about the exact same thing.

Different people bring different qualities to their work. When I'm looking for a staff writer, the qualities I look for begin with, first and foremost, whether they can execute the same idea we're trying to execute. You like everybody to be on the same page. If a person is really a good writer, you'd like them to work for you for a year or two, to lessen your load of writing the show, and then ideally you would try to launch them into doing what you do. I mean, it's the theory of multiplication, and it works, and that is really gratifying. So what you look for, after the ability to write and the ability to be a team player, is the ability to be a leader. Leading a writing room is like throwing a party every day. You are the person who has to keep everybody up–the cast, the crew, the staff– and if you go too much into yourself and withdraw, and don't keep throwing that party, you're not going to get an awful lot back. It's not going to be a lot of fun, and eventually people will just separate and say, "You do it."

The other thing I look for when I'm casting a room, and I cast a room the same way I cast a show, is different talents. I don't want six people who all write great jokes, and I don't need six people all to write stories, so if someone is particularly strong in the story side and somebody else is strong with one-liners, I will try to make them part of the staff. I generally look for strong writing and story sense far before I look for comedy because if you write it real, and you write it great, you can always find a joke. But if you're writing the joke first, and you have to build it back, sometimes it's a lot harder.

Either way, it has to be a team approach. I start off every season of a show by doing what I call a writer's camp, usually in May. Sometimes we will meet in a hotel, sometimes we'll meet at the beach. We go someplace away from the studio and spend anywhere from three to five days talking about all the possible things we could do that year. One year it was for *Coach*, which was about a man whose life was out of balance. Over the course of however many episodes it was going to run, the writers were going to have to create a baby-step attempt to bring his life into balance. We were very calculated about the fact that when one part of his life would come into balance, another part of it would go out. So if his relationship with Christine was working, his team was not. If his team was working, the relationship with his daughter was not. So there was always one edge of the flap that was always up. And eventually, over the course of 200 episodes, we got all the flaps down.

So in the case of that show, I would generally come in at the start of the year saying, "I'd like us to begin this season here, and I'd like us to end twenty-two episodes here, and now let us talk about what we can do within the confines of that arc, that piece of the puzzle." It all begins with the pilot. If you think about a series, you think about a pilot. A pilot episode is the foundation for the series, but you have to remember that if you fear the series is going to be a hundred episodes, that pilot episode is 1/100th of the puzzle. It is not a microcosm of the entire hundred episodes.

That's generally the problem you run into when you're trying to explain that to a network, because you have explained the series to them, all 100 pieces of the puzzle, and then they wonder why they're not seeing all 100 pieces in the twenty-two minutes they've given you. You'll touch on it. I mean, you can go back and look at a pilot and say, yeah, for the most part, at the end of a hundred shows I could see where all those seeds were planted. But it's very important when you are starting each season to understand that each particular episode is a piece of that total puzzle. That's what you are trying to create; that's the body of work.

So that's what we do to start off a season, and we generally try not to get too far ahead of ourselves. I used to try to write nine or ten episodes at the start of the season, thinking we would get ahead. But that doesn't allow for any potential cast changes, any discoveries in new cast, any discoveries of things in relationships, and suddenly some things start working that you didn't expect, and you want to expand on that. So if you get too far ahead of yourself, you really cut yourself off from what other possibilities there are. So, now we generally go into a season not much more than four to six episodes written, even though we may have twenty-two episodes blocked out.

When I pitched *Coach*, the network was very interested in me doing a series for them and very interested in me doing *Coach*. They thought it was a great idea. The only things that they objected to were: (a) that he was a football coach; they would prefer that he coach basketball, and (b) under no circumstances should it be Craig T. Nelson, and (c) that they didn't like the title. Other than that, they were fine. They were on board and ready to commit. And every single step along the way I had to quit. Well, if you wanted it to be a basketball coach, get somebody else to write the show. I'm not going to do it. "OK, it can be a football coach, but it can't be Craig T. Nelson." No? Then I quit. "Well, it can be Craig T. Nelson, but it can't be *Coach*." Well, then I quit. "All right. It can be *Coach*." And so they fired the president of the network–true– for not being able to get me to change it, even though the show made about half a billion dollars for ABC during its run.

But, before you can quit, you need to break in. If you don't want to break in by writing a spec script, and if you have what you think is a really great idea, how would you go about trying to sell it? It's going to be very difficult because the first thing networks are going to ask is, who is going to execute the series? Who's going to be there day in and day out, running it, casting it, writing it, having the vision? You have basically two or three roads you can follow. You can take it to a writer-producer and pitch it to them and hope they will take it to the network and make it their own–and you must know that in doing that, they are going to take it over. You will get some credit and you'll get some money for it, but the bulk of it is going to go to that entity. Or you could try pitching it to a studio and letting the studio champion it and go find the writer-producer. The result would be the same. The studio might be a little bit more willing to undertake an idea because they are not going to write it or produce it themselves. Your third avenue would be to go directly to a network, and the network will then go out and find a writer-producer to run it. So you're going to end up at the same place, regardless.

It's probably not any better to pitch to agents if you don't have any experience. There are a couple of agents who specialize in taking on either new writers or people who don't have a lot of experience, but for the most part, agents are for something that they know they can sell. I'm not saying it is impossible, but it's probably not the best way to go. Agents in television don't read as much. Studios read a lot.

In television, the producer has almost total creative control. That's why so many writers become producers–it is the way you control your work. And yes, we have complete control to change the casting or do whatever we want to do.

"What about those cases like *Thelma and Louise*, where we go through the whole journey but the heroes end up dead? Another example is *Butch Cassidy* where obviously they're going to be shot to pieces. And yet they lived on somehow. The freeze frame immortalizes people. And so they live in our memories. Just like when someone you love dies, yeah the physical body is dead, but they live in your memory. *Thelma and Louise*, classically, technically, is tragedy. A happy ending is a comedy; an unhappy ending where the heroes end up dead or they fail, is a tragedy. And in the tragedy, you're always asking yourself the question: Who learns something? And that usually is the hero. But when the hero doesn't learn because they die, or because they never got it, somebody still learns. The audience learns."

– Christopher Vogler

SPOTLIGHT ON SUCCESS

JANA WOLFF, AUTHOR
Secret Thoughts of an Adoptive Mother

Under Mrs. Bricker's right elbow was a sack of skin that would dance when she wrote on the blackboard. There's more, though, that I remember about the teacher we called The Flapper: she was my first publisher. Released in 1961 as a first-edition paperback with a very small print run, *The Ant That Drove* garnered positive reviews from discerning third-grade readers.

Neither an advance nor a publicist was assigned to my first book; and no one told me that I couldn't be both author and illustrator. With its very own Dewey decimal, my book could be checked out from the library nook at the back of the class-room—giving me reason to believe that Radburn School was far more influential than Random House.

Thirty-six years after third grade, I was published again. With nary an illustration, and a plot much less bold than the one about an ant who could drive, my second book sold sur-prisingly well and actually was, for a time, the number one best selling nonfiction book in the State of Hawaii.

I was moved to write my second book by the same forces that prompted the first–a good story. But this time I was lacking in two things I had when I was eight: time and confidence. I made the time, between five and six a.m. Monday through Friday, and made up for the lack of confidence by telling myself that, no matter what else happened that day, at least I had written for an hour. It was like the credit you give yourself for twenty minutes on the treadmill.

I knew I would not be so lucky to get published a second time without really trying. So I signed up with the symphony of sycophants and pitched my good story at the Maui Writers Conference. Most of the important people I spoke to said: "Good story; it's been done." But two of them–one an editor, the other an agent–said "Good story." Period. Sixteen months later, I was published.

The leap from manuscript hawker to title-page signer is quantum. More than the difference between first and second place, it's the difference between wanna and be. No one can take this achievement away from you; no matter how miniscule the advance, how pathetic the publicity budget, or how bad the cover art.

The problem–for which many aspiring writers would give not only their eye teeth but also their incisors–is that you feel the pressure to write and publish another book well before your jet lag's worn off. The risk in being a single-book author is that you can quickly become your own remainder. Once published, you may not be able to rest on your laurels; but I've learned that you can loiter there for a year or so, forestalling the terror about your next book with the glory from your last.

"The movie can be violent, the book can be very violent, and at the same time, enlighten you about the human spirit. I think Mailer's *An American Dream* captures something in the American psyche. It was a very, very violent novel. Did its violence say something about the human spirit? Absolutely it did. And when I finished reading it, did I feel debased, demeaned, corrupted in any way? No, I didn't. I felt that through showing me the motivations for the violence, I learned something about the human spirit. I could be better as a result of learning it. Shakespeare is probably the bloodiest playwright in history. If we applied the same yardstick to Shakespeare that some people are trying to apply today, where do we stop? I think it's very dangerous to even begin."

—Joe Eszterhas

James Orr

A Day in the Life of a Screenwriter

If I were to show you a day in the life of a screenwriter, this would be it. Maybe I'd light a cigar. It'd be very boring. There's lots of talk about theory and I like to talk theory, too. But at the stage of entry-level writers, there are so many mysteries about the process–how things are done, why things are done, where you should put your energies–that if you're not reasonably informed you can waste a lot of time and a lot of energy doing the wrong thing. So I'm going to try to tell you some things based on experience and hindsight that, frankly, I wish somebody had told me when I was starting out.

My favorite way of looking at Hollywood, even now as an established writer, is what I call the Vegas casino metaphor, because Hollywood's sort of like a casino. You come up to it for the first time and you look inside and you see very glamorous activity going on. Very colorful, looks like a lot of fun. More money than you've ever dreamed of would be flying around a room. And needless to say, you want to get into this casino. So you walk in the casino and you look around, wide-eyed. Glamorous, attractive people seem to be living a very high life, and enjoying it. And you're a novice player. Maybe you've played a little bit at home on your computer or black jack, poker, video stuff like that. But you've never really been in serious action. So you're looking around and you're trying to figure out how to get into this phenomenal action, how to get a piece of it. The first thing you notice is that there are a lot of games to play. And there are a lot of games to play in Hollywood. And like the casino, all the games in Hollywood are stacked against you. All the odds are not in your favor but, like a casino, some games are less stacked against you than others. And the smart player who's coming into the casino for the first time finds the game he's most likely to succeed at, even though, like Las Vegas, you can still lose even with the best odds.

I'm going to tell you the only four ways screenplays get written in Hollywood. There are no other ways. And once I tell you about each one of them, who does them, what's involved in it, and how it works, then you'll see not only where you are and where you should be addressing yourself, but also where you one day might get to.

We all know what the "spec" script is. It's a script that you write; it's your idea, it's your passion, it's something you spend time on. You put it together and once it's together no one owns it except you. You've done it for free, and now you go out and try and sell it.

A "pitch" is an idea but instead of writing it as a spec script and taking six, eight, ten weeks to write it, you come up with the essential parts of the story. And you go to a buyer–a producer or a studio person–and you pitch them your idea. And you hope they like it enough to say, "OK, here's X amount of dollars. Now write the script." So the difference between that and a spec script is obvious. The spec script you write for free; with a pitch you get someone to pay you to write that script. But essentially it's the same process. It's your idea. And you try and sell it.

The next level is "the assignment." An assignment is not your idea. It's someone else's idea, usually the studio's or an executive at the studio. Or something they bought, or a book, or a sequel they want to make, or something they have. So they go out into the pool–a community of writers–and they find writers who they believe will best write the material they have. The assignment pool tends to be, for obvious reasons, experienced writers–people who are known in the community, people who have certain talents, who have been slotted in a way. This guy's a comedy guy, so if we've got a comedy we go to him. Or we go to these guys who are comedy guys. This guy's an action guy. This guy's drama. This guy's great with women's stories. So depending on what it is that the studio has and wants to see made, they will go to that group of veterans and try to assign the material. The process is actually very simple. You get a call from your agent. The studio says they want to talk to you about an idea of theirs. You go. You have a meeting. You listen to the studio's idea. You decide whether you like it or whether you can do it well, or whether it's something you want to spend time with. You go back home, you call your agent, you say, "What's in it for me? How much money?" He says X amount of dollars. That has a big impact on how much you like the idea, obviously. And you decide whether or not you're going to try it. This level of activity in Hollywood can be very lucrative but it is reserved for that pool of writers who are known and who have written and have proven themselves and either had movies made or have had movies bought. There are a lot of writers who make a fortune and have never had a movie made. They just sell their material, constantly, and it never gets made. So if you're perceived as a good writer, a good craftsman, a good journeyman writer, then you'll fit into this assignment level and you can make a fabulous living. I know one guy who does just three assignments a year and the rest of the year he grows grapes in Sonoma Valley. He makes a lot of money.

The last area that is significant in writing in Hollywood is one of the most interesting ones, and that's the "rewrite." As small as is the pool of talent that gets to do assignments, it's an even smaller pool that gets to do rewrites. And it's probably the most rarified part of Hollywood screenwriting. It's also, for time spent, the most lucrative. People who do rewrites on a regular basis can make up to $100,000 a week.

And that's a lot of money. You spend three weeks on a re-write for Sylvester Stallone, and you walk away with 300 Gs, I mean, you know, what do you do for the rest of the year? So that's a very rare and a very small pool. And that pool is defined by people who have had some kind of glamorous, sexy success. You win an Academy Award, you write a hit movie–$100 million plus–you're going to get rewrites galore. You are perceived as the hot new flavor of the day. You are going to get rewrites forever. I remember the guy who wrote *Ghost* years ago. Big movie; made a lot of money. Everybody loved the movie. He got an Academy Award nomination. After that movie he did two years of rewrites at $100,000 a week. And then he made another movie and we haven't heard from him since. Maybe he left with all that cash, I don't know. Even veteran writers who've been in the business for twenty, twenty-five, thirty years, sometimes don't get to that level. As I say, it's a very, very serious piece of Hollywood business.

Now those are really the only four ways that writers work. The first two are your ideas in some form or another. The second two are others' ideas where you're hired to execute something specific.

In the beginning there is only one game in the casino that you should play, and that's the spec script. That's the only game you can win. Not that there's any guarantee you will win, but it's the only one you have a chance at winning. The others are completely off limits; don't even think about them. I know some people think they can pitch ideas, but if you've never written anything or never sold anything, chances are no one will hear your pitch. And if they do hear your pitch and they like it, and that happens from time to time, they may buy the pitch and then tell you to go away and hire a writer to write it. And the guy at the assignment level will come in and write your idea–because they don't know you can write. They'll pay you for the pitch but it's a small amount of money.

There are exceptions to every rule including the rules I'm telling you. Going back to the casino metaphor, you don't play the exceptions. You play down the middle. You play the pass line; you don't play the numbers. Play what you can win.

There are exceptions, but I wouldn't play them if I were you. I would focus on the spec script.

With the spec script there are some rules you should all pay attention to. Simple things. These are nuts and bolts things that I'm going to throw out because some of you may know them, some of you may not.

I did a kind of an armchair study of spec scripts that were sold over a two-year period awhile back. I wanted to see what dominant type of spec scripts sold. Spec scripts are bought every week. Every Monday morning you read in the trades about this script and that script, et cetera. And by far the most dominant genre for spec script sales is the comedy. There are a lot of reasons for that. One is that there's always a need for comedy. It's a genre that never goes out of style. Horror comes in, goes out; action comes in, goes out. Romance comes in and goes out. But comedy of some sort is always there. The other thing about comedy is that they're not expensive films. They're not *Waterworld*. It's much easier for an executive to buy your comedy spec script knowing it's going to cost $15 million instead of buying your *Star Wars Revisited* spec script that's going to cost $50 million because he's now going to take your spec script and sell it to his boss. Sell it to actors. Sell it to the audience. It's much easier to sell something that's not expensive. So comedy tends to be the dominant market for spec scripts.

The second most-sold spec script is the action genre. *Speed* is an example. *Speed* made a lot of money, and it's a very simple notion—kind of a rip-off of *Die Hard* but on a bus. And it launched this guy's career in a very major way. Now he's writing everything there is to write, all in that genre. But essentially it was a very simple notion; it was easy for a reader or an executive to grasp and sell to the next level up. To some extent, you're always deputizing the person you are talking to, to sell to somebody else. You have to give them the tools to sell and usually that's three or four lines of your script, something to grab somebody and make it clear what it is. So *Speed* is a classic example of that because you say, "*Die Hard* on a bus, blah, blah, blah. Goes below fifty, it blows up." An executive will hear that and he writes the script himself in his head. He doesn't even need to read anything. So action tends to be the second most-sold spec script.

Now some of you may be saying, "Well I don't write comedy or action." You're in trouble. The personal dramas. The artistic dramas. The melodramas, romances. Those things don't sell at the spec level so well. They often come from the other levels. Those simple, accessible lean ideas that are clearly commercial are what sell the most. And until you get to the other levels–which I'm sure you will at one point in your career–when you can start to write those other movies, you have to focus on what is real. So it's some version of action or some version of comedy at the spec level.

Now some more nuts and bolts: This is what an executive does with a script that needs reading for the first time. Most scripts get read on the weekend. It's called the weekend read. It's a very big tradition in Hollywood. Most executives who are reading scripts go home with upward of fifteen or more scripts to read, which is daunting because most scripts take ninety minutes to two hours to read. A lot of big investment time, especially weekend time. Most scripts are read as people are eating bagels and cream cheese or sitting around the pool. And the first thing that happens, the script is picked up, the person goes to the last page to see what page number it is. If it's more than 120, chances are it goes into the pool. So lesson number one, make sure scripts are 120 pages or less.

Then they'll flip through it and look for white space. White space is all that space around the dialogue and the action. They like white space. That means less reading. So that means no novelistic descriptions. That means no long speeches that take a full page. Plenty of white space. These people are better at reading menus than they are at reading scripts. And you need to help them–and menus are very concise, you know? Salmon, grilled. Start writing like menus, and people will read your script. It doesn't mean they're not going to read it if it's over 120 pages. It means they're gonna be reading it now begrudgingly, which means your script has to work harder.

I'm talking spec scripts now. Keep your speeches short, keep your descriptions lean, hard, drop pronouns if you have to.

Now that you've gotten over that hurdle, your reader is now going to read your script. Truth is, he's *not* going to read your script yet. The truth is, he's going to read the first fifteen to twenty pages. If in the first fifteen to twenty pages you haven't grabbed him, you haven't dazzled him, you haven't stood out from the other fifteen scripts he's got, it goes into the pool. People think pools are for swimming; they're where you throw the scripts. One of the secrets of southern California. So your first fifteen pages are the most critical pages of your script. Not that the other hundred pages don't also have to deliver. They do. Usually the first fifteen minutes tells you, the audience, what you're going to think about the movie.

So now you have a great fifteen pages and a decent hundred pages following that. You're under 120 pages and you've got a lot of white space. Now, your script gets read. And probably read in the best possible way that it could be at the time. And hopefully, it's being read by an executive, although it's very possible that it's being read by this unique breed of subterranean pod people called "readers." I've been in the business fifteen years and I'm still amazed by readers. First of all, you never see them. Never. I've never met a reader in my entire life. You read their reports and you see their names on scripts they've read for you, in which they synopsize the script so you can read two pages instead of the whole script. And then they give comments at the end about what they think of the script, and then at the very end they recommend or not recommend. They say, "Pass" or "Consider" or "Fabulous."

And I swear, the thousands of reader reports I've read, I've never met a reader. I don't know where they come from. I don't know where they live. I don't know if they're of this planet. I'm totally confused by readers. But the interesting thing about them is they're very underpaid. They're all frustrated screenwriters themselves. And they have enormous influence. I can't tell you how many times I've been in a situation where a piece of material's going around and a studio is considering buying it or not buying it and the executive will say, "Well, how was the reader's report?" And if you say the reader's report was phenomenal, then the executive may look at the script. But if the reader's report was bad and you say it wasn't very good, chances are the executive's not going to look at it. So that's a major influence. Doesn't mean the script's bad. Just means the reader's report was bad. These are things that are out of your control but you have to know about them.

Rejection is more common for veterans than acceptance and when you get your first thousand rejections you can't help but ask, "Why did they not like this?" Ultimately you stop asking that question. Ultimately you get into a Zen place, frankly, where it either works or it doesn't. And you don't take it personally. You should try your best not to take it personally. Because it'll really scar you and lead to many things like divorce and alcoholism.

So now you've got a guy, he's read your script. You've done all these things that I'm talking about. You find the best game in the casino. You still may end up in the pool. And that's the chance you take. You play a game of chance. You have to accept the fact that you may lose. Otherwise, don't play the game. Don't come into this casino if you're not prepared to lose. Don't go into any casino, real or figurative, if you're not prepared to lose. Because that's part of the process.

The other thing that comes up a lot when I talk to new writers is how to get people to read your script. You get whoever will read your script to read your script. And that means, *whoever*. From your brother, to your best friends, to the secretary you know who is the assistant to the junior vice-president of the valet company that does all the bar mitzvahs for all the movie executives in Hollywood, and, hopefully, if this assistant likes it, you'll get all the way through the network and it'll end up on the passenger seat of somebody's Mercedes. I've heard some very inventive ways to get people to read scripts. The secretary who reads your material today may be a junior executive tomorrow—and I can't tell you how many times that's happened.

It isn't so much that people are looking for a specific kind of script. They're just looking for good material. A good story. Something that's commercial. Something that's marketable. Hollywood is always looking for new blood, new material, new ideas. Always. There are people whose sole task at agencies is to find the new talented writers.

Very, very few writers sell the first script they wrote. Usually the spec script they sell, which sounds like it's their first script because you never heard of them before, is the third, fourth, fifth, tenth. I say, "Write three and throw the first two away." And then show the third around. Because you have to work things out. Ten years from now when you're an established writer you're going to look at that first script and you're going to be embarrassed. The more you do it, the better you get. So get to that level of a spec script. Make sure you are putting your best foot forward.

My company gets scripts all the time that don't have agents attached to them. An agent will be an asset because he'll get your script to more people than you could possibly get it to. Often a spec script does nothing except get you an agent– which, by the way, is a major accomplishment. So let's say you have a spec script, you write it and it doesn't sell anywhere. It's just floating in every pool in town. But you get an agent out of it. You move on to the next script. Get to script number three and get it out there.

Television is a tougher industry to crack than movies. Television is a kind of closed club of people who have done it year after year after year. They have been around forever and they know the process, they know the players, and breaking into television is harder than breaking into movies. So again, with the casino metaphor, you've gone into the casino and you picked a tough game. You haven't picked the easiest game. You haven't picked the hardest game, either, but you haven't picked the easiest game. So you need to make a decision, step back and see the big picture and say, "OK, I've got this idea. I really like this idea but is this really the game I want to play?" Because the odds are going up. I would urge you to consider the casino metaphor in finding the easier game because you don't want to waste your time.

A new writer has zero control. Here's what's going to happen: You sell a script. God bless you, you sell a script. You make some money. First sale. Celebration, champagne gets opened. The script will be rewritten by someone other than you. Your spec script will go down to that level. The spec script you wrote I'm going to rewrite. For more money than they paid you for the script. And that's the law of the jungle.

❧

"Good dialogue hides as much as it reveals."

–Linda Seger

Mike Scully

'Toon Master

When you're writing, I think you really have to be hard on yourself. The greatest feeling in the world is to have a finished script in your hand. The hard part is to open it back up and be honest with yourself. "Is this good? Is this the best that I can do?" We do it on *The Simpsons* constantly.

We write and rewrite and rewrite those shows up to the very last minute. Up to a few days before they air, we are still changing jokes to match the animation of the character's mouths. We could easily let it go as is, but if we've got something that could be better, funnier, anything we can do to make it better, we do it.

Everybody has his or her own method for handling when they get stuck writing, whether it's a joke or a story point. I will sit at the computer and stare at the screen until I have it, and I have sat hours and hours and refuse to break away from the computer because I know me. I know once I walk away, I'll go in and click on *The Nanny* and I'm done for the night. It's too easy to get it out of my mind. Just get something down on paper. You can always go back and fix it later.

The only thing I never write in any of my scripts is "jokes to come." That's a bad habit to get into. It allows you to move on but then you get to the end of your script, and you go back over it and you find, "Whew, I've got a lot of jokes to come!" And you're back in the same position again and now you hate it because you remember what it was like when you were on that page before.

I've been writing for thirteen, fourteen years professionally. I came out to Hollywood in 1982 with a dream in my pocket and a song in my heart. I didn't know anybody in Hollywood, I didn't have an uncle who ran a studio, I didn't have a friend who was working on a show, and I didn't go to Harvard, which is a big way in for a lot of people now. If I can inspire you in any way, I will confess to you that I went to college for one day. And that's all. I say that not out of pride but just to show you that anybody can do this if you work hard enough.

I walked into college after high school; that whole summer after high school, I just didn't know what I wanted out of life. Finally, on August 30th, I realized I had better do something. I signed up for school and went in the first day and the teacher had her name written on the board and suddenly it was high school all over again, except this time I was paying for it. That's when I drew the line, and I went out and decided to get some life experience instead.

And I got a lot of it. I worked a lot of really crappy jobs. I flipped burgers, I sold shoes, pumped gas–I did a billion things. Live as much life as you can because as you get older, those are the things you are going to draw from to write stories. They make some of the best stories you'll ever write because they really happened to you. So I recommend getting married, having kids. Do whatever you can. A lot of people ask me where *Simpsons* stories come from, and I answer that they come from all sorts of places but the number one place is the writers' own lives.

For example, there is a show I wrote where Bart wants a video game. When I was his age, they did not exist. But anyway, it was a video game he wanted really, really badly, and it was Christmas time and he was hoping he would get it for a present, and then he found out his parents couldn't afford it. So he went to a store and he's just staring at this game. I used to go into a bakery across the street from our school and I would just sit there and stare at the sugar cookies, hoping the lady would give me one because I had no money. So I had Bart go into the store and he is just staring at this game, and he wants it so badly, and he sees a bunch of his friends in the store and they're shoplifting some very obvious things, like footballs under their shirts. And they tell him, "This is the only way to get stuff!" And the character from the video game starts to come alive to Bart–it was the Mario Brothers–and it said, "Go ahead."

It's a real moment of truth for Bart, and it's also one of the moments where we break the preconceived notion that Bart is a bad kid. He's not. He's a smartass. But he's not in his heart a bad kid. He finally decides to go ahead and take the game. He puts it under his jacket and he gets out of the store, and he's like, "Yeah, I did it, I made it," and boom, this big hand comes on his shoulder and it's the store detective. I remember that moment. I'm almost forty-three now; I was twelve at the time. I remember that moment, that hand, I knew it wasn't a pal of mine who wanted to say, "Hey, Mike, how are you doing!" I just knew I was busted. I was taken up to the store detectives; it was the most terrifying day of my life. They were going to call my parents, and it was just awful. And what happens to Bart in that show is what happened to me. His parents were not home when they called. He is riding his bike home when the store detectives leave that message on his family's answering machine, and he races. He sees his parents' car coming from one direction, and he races there. He gets home in time to switch the tape, and they never find out what he did.

Now he's living with it but he feels like it is easy street, until Marge wants to take the family in for their Christmas picture. And she takes them to that store, and this also happened to me–my mother wanted to take me shopping for back-to-school clothing. I said OK. "We're going to Bradley's," she says. "Bradley's?" I had been forbidden from going into the store again. I walked in, you know, twelve years old, and I felt like everybody was looking at me. Anyway, it's in that scene–and this was where my own experience and Bart's differs–that Marge finds out. The store detectives spot Bart and they put in the videotape of him stealing and it comes up on all the monitors in the TV department. It's a great emotional moment because you see Marge is just crushed, *just crushed*. When the third act starts, Bart is expecting to really get his butt kicked and screamed at, and it doesn't happen. Instead, Marge just kind of dismisses him and says, "I don't know what to do with you." It's like she has given up. And that hurts much, much more than being yelled at or being grounded. It's a feeling that he is now questioning: Does his mother still love him; did he blow his mother's love? And for emotions, that's a good one.

He even goes to his friend's house and starts hanging out with Milhouse's mom, trying to help her around the house, and finally he just says, "Tell me I'm good!" And I think everybody can identify with that.

That's just an example of pulling a story out of your real life. You don't have to follow it beat for beat what happened to you. You're allowed to take liberties and embellish, but that script was so easy for me to write because I was reliving the terror all over again. I was getting paid for it this time, but it felt very real and honest to me.

Not every story is going to come like that. Sometimes you just come up with an idea. *The Simpsons* is also known for commenting on things going on in the country, and we try to hit those quite a few times a year. Sometimes we get to them; sometimes the trend goes before we get to do the show. We had planned a great show two years ago where Homer joined the Promise Keepers, and we had it all worked out. I made the mistake of putting it real late in the season. And it all kind of fell apart and now the card just sits there, and I get sad every time I look at it because I know it could have been a great episode.

We like to talk about things on the show that other shows don't talk about. We do a lot about religion. Sometimes people think it's done in a blasphemous and mean-spirited way, and it's not at all. First of all, nobody on TV does religion unless the show has an angel in it, in which case they are kind of forced to do religion. I don't know every single show on television, but I think *The Simpsons* is the only family on television that goes to church every Sunday. It doesn't mean they jump out of bed and say, "Is it time for church yet?" They deal with it more realistically. Homer's kicking and screaming, he doesn't want to go, it's his day off, he doesn't want to get out of bed, it's 7 a.m., but he goes. He goes with his family and he sits through it, and whether or not he gets something out of it remains to be seen.

But he persists, which is what you as writers need to do. When I got out to California, I wanted to write for *Taxi*. Jim Brooks, to me, is the Woody Allen of television. I thought he wrote the smartest things, and I just wanted to work for him. So I bought old copies of scripts from TV shows to learn the format, then sat down and wrote my first spec script. I went out and mailed it directly to the show and, to this day, I'm amazed how the script was back in my mailbox, rejected, before I got back to the house. It literally seemed that fast. I felt like I had poured my heart and soul into this thing for months and it was back so quickly. It just said, "Thank you, but this doesn't suit our needs." Boom, and it was over.

So I went for a month or two then sat back down and did another one for *Taxi*, a whole new story. And this time it actually took a couple of weeks before it was back in the mailbox. You have to look at things with a positive attitude as much as possible because you're going to get a lot of rejection. A lot. And it came back, and this time it had an extra paragraph. It said, "You might want to try Gary Marshall's show. You write very joke-oriented comedy, and his shows do that." I felt that it was nice of him to give me that advice. I loved Gary Marshall stuff, but I didn't take his advice and I wrote another *Taxi* script. And this time around, the script didn't come back. It finally came back after five months, saying, "We're developing a similar story line." And then I saw the episode a couple of months later. I could say, oh, they ripped me off, but nothing will come from that. There's always the legitimate possibility that they had the story line in development. Yes, there is the possibility that somebody is going to rip you off. You've got to take that chance. You've got to trust people. And coming from Hollywood I know that sounds crazy, but you do have to throw your stuff out there and let people see it.

I went through trying to get agents. If you're looking to get an agent, ask The Writer's Guild of America for a list of agents. They will have little marks on it as to which agents will read new material. If you have a friend or a connection with a more established agency, maybe you can get it through the friend, a personal recommendation. My first agent experience was the Tina Marie Talent Agency. I had sent scripts all over town and she called me up saying, "I love your script. I want to represent you." The address was in Hollywood, which you know, I said, "Wow, she's in Hollywood!" I went to the address on Western Avenue in Hollywood and I got there and there was a sign outside that said, "Nicky's Hairstyling." And there were no other buildings around. So I went in and said, "I'm looking for a place called Tina Marie Talent Agency, but this is the address." He said, "Oh, yeah, it's my sister. She's in the back." So I walked to the back and she's behind this curtain with head shots of the most famous stars in Hollywood on the wall as though she was representing them all. In any case, she was very nice. She represented my scripts. At that time, the loopholes were closing up as far as people reading scripts without agents. It's virtually impossible now to get it done. So I thanked her for that, but it didn't work out with her.

I went through a lot of agents. These are people you trust your career to and, by doing that, you're really trusting your life, so you want to make sure you feel comfortable with the person, which is hard in the beginning if you don't have a lot of choices.

One agent took me to breakfast and said, "All right, I want to sit down with you and do some strategy on your career issues." So we're doing that over breakfast and he said, "All right, what's the name of that show with Roseanne Barr?" I said, "*Roseanne.*" He said, "Right, right." I realized this man knew nothing at all about television. Now, if you land with a big name agency, you don't know if you're going to get the attention you need. They frequently will go with their bigger name clients because those bring better commissions. So you want to find somebody who seems really excited about you and your material, but it helps if they know the names of a few of these shows.

Once you have an agent, don't count on the agent to do it all for you. You've got to hustle yourself. If you just sit at home and wait for the agent to call with a great job, chances are it won't happen. You've got to go out and make your own contacts, too. That's one reason I did audience warm-up for shows, so I could meet the writer-producers of the shows. Eventually I had to step out of it because they were just looking at me as a warm-up guy, but I did make some connections.

I also worked in a mug store in Glendale, California, doing personalized coffee mugs all day long, sticking names on mugs, people coming in, saying, "Do you have 'Lupe'?" "No, I don't." They always expected their name to be in the stock shelf for some reason. But one day, someone called from the show *Alice.* They were doing the final show and they needed 500 coffee mugs that said "Mel's Diner" on them. I thought they were going to send over a couple of runners to pick up the mugs, but two writers came over so I started talking to them. I always had my scripts under the counter, ready to go. They couldn't understand why I was so helpful to them because there were cartons of mugs and I'm saying, "No, no, let me do this." It was pouring rain. I got all the mugs in the car for them and then said, "Oh," and I pulled out the script–and I could see it in their eyes. You know, they were so mad like they'd been had, but they agreed to take the script and read it. And they called me a couple of weeks later and said, "I've got to be honest with you, I was really pissed off when you handed me that script, but I like it." They had me come in and pitch stories to them and they have remained friends.

You've got to work it a little yourself, and you've got to know where to draw the line between persistence and pushiness. You don't want to frighten people. You know, don't follow people really closely. They don't like getting in the car and having you pop up in the back seat. They don't like that. I remember Gary Marshall telling a story of a gas station attendant. Gary used to get gas there every morning and every morning the attendant would wash the window with pages of his spec script. And then Gary took it and read it. If you can find that line, you kind of make somebody laugh.

In L.A. on television there are maybe 2,000 jobs. You've got 7,000 people who are trying to get them, and they all want to be on the best shows. But even on a bad show you can learn a tremendous amount. I've been on many, many, many bad shows. You learn a lot about how *not* to do things, and you take note of that. That has allowed me to gain trust in my own instincts. There were times when something felt wrong but they'd been doing this a long time and I was the new guy, so I kept quiet. Then later on I realized, gee, I was right. That makes you begin to trust your instincts.

As far as spec scripts go, find a show that you like and write it. Then find another one. Don't count on one script because the first thing they are going to ask you, if they like your first script, is, "What else have you got?" They always want to see your second sample. It's one of the things that makes no sense, because many times you send the second script over and they say, "Well, we really liked your first one a lot. We don't like this one as much." "Yeah, that's why I sent the other one first!"

No matter what, you've got to have a good story to hang everything else on. The jokes are a lot of fun, but the jokes have to come second. You might think of a few while you're coming up with the story, but you should really have your story nailed first. Then once you know what everybody's attitude is going into any situation–where the conflict stems from– all your jokes will come off of that. Some of my favorite *Simpsons* episodes are the Homer-Lisa conflict shows because they're such opposite extremes but they have to deal with each other because they're father and daughter. There is a big emotional connection between them. There's an episode where

Lisa becomes a vegetarian and it really sets them at odds. What was so great about that particular episode was that they were both wrong. They were both being intolerant. Eventually they reached an understanding.

Write as honestly as you can write. I'm a big stickler for honest jokes. I remember seeing a *Murphy Brown* episode years ago where she wasn't invited to the White House because the last time she was there, she had President Bush in a headlock and gave him nosebleeds. And they hung the whole show on this incident, which I could not believe could ever happen. And when you hang your whole show on something unbelievable, you're going to find it a lot harder to write and you're not going to be satisfied at the end.

There are about 700 people who work on *The Simpsons*, between the studio and Hollywood and then our child labor sweatshop in Korea. It takes nine months to produce one episode. The script writing takes about two months, then we record the voices and then the animation starts; the actual animation takes six to seven months. We're always working at the same time on five or six shows that are in various stages of production.

We don't actually have discussions about whether people will get a particular joke. We figure if it makes us laugh and we can find ten other people who think it is funny, we put it in. When you begin to water your show down to make sure everybody will get every joke, you've got *Three's Company*.

You've got to do what you think is funny. We're aware of the audience, we're aware that kids are watching. We try and make sure there is stuff in there for kids and have adults be entertained also. We try not to be too reckless in certain things. We've actually pulled back on the language on the show because I thought it was getting a little out of control with no point to it.

When I was a kid, I thought *Rocky and Bullwinkle* was a show about a talking moose and a flying squirrel, and that was funny enough for me. I didn't need anything else. But as I got older, I started listening to the jokes. They're very, very smart jokes. It's really the best of both worlds.

If you want to work on series television, you've got to move to Los Angeles. I'm sorry to be the one to have to tell you that. It's just a fact of life. You can write your spec scripts from home, but if somebody likes it and wants to do business with you, you're going to have to be in L.A. It's a hard decision for a lot of people to make. I'm from Massachusetts and it was difficult to leave my friends and drive across country, not knowing what I was doing, but you just have to do it, and that's that.

"One of my least favorite things is writing a treatment. People come to these sessions and say, 'I have ten treatments.' And I say, 'Well, instead of ten treatments, you could have one screenplay.' A treatment is not a sales tool for a beginning writer. It's neither fiction nor fowl. It's not prose. It's not poetry. It's not a screenplay. You cannot tell someone to write a screenplay from a treatment. I write treatments after I have the movie deal."

–Steven deSouza

MARK BAKER, AUTHOR
The Psychology of Jesus

I've been trying to write this book for over twenty years, I just didn't know it. I went to graduate school, published professional articles, and started submitting proposals to publishers for years until I realized that I wasn't going to get anywhere without an agent. I even had my wife personally call over thirty publishers to find that almost all of them did not even accept unagented manuscripts. So, I bought *The Writer's Handbook* and began the agonizing process of introducing my book ideas to agents who universally began to reject me. It was depressing having several graduate degrees and years of experience as a psychologist, yet having to endure rejection after rejection because I was a novice in the book publishing industry.

Convinced that I needed a personal encounter to land an agent, I signed up for the Maui Writers Conference with the specific goal of forming a relationship with just the person to help me transform my ideas into books. Although I did create several relationships with potential agents, the fate of my writing career finally took a turn for the better when I found out that Julie Castiglia, a well known literary agent, was going to be vacationing on Maui the same time I was there for the conference. Talk about serendipity. I offered to buy her lunch and give her a ride to the airport if she would let me pitch her an idea I was working on, and she agreed. Painfully, she didn't like my proposal but she loved another idea I had had for years, which wasn't in proposal form yet. It took several months to get this idea into shape, but within a month of signing a contract with Julie I had a deal with Harper, and a nice advance.

One of the things I learned from this process is that I was trying too hard to write a great book. I had studied at a psychoanalytic institute and a seminary and I was trying to write the next *The Road Less Traveled*. Once I stopped trying to write someone else's book, my book became obvious to me: a contemporary psychoanalytic perspective on the teachings of Jesus. This is the thing I know the best, which makes it the most natural book for me to write. I think I was afraid not enough people would be interested in my book, so I found myself trying to write one for everybody else. That didn't work. Fortunately, Julie could see the book I really wanted to write before I was even clear about it. I have just finished writing the first draft, and I loved doing it. I've spent the past two decades becoming an expert in this one area, and I'm grateful for the opportunity to share my ideas with others. I know this is exactly the book I was supposed to write all along. It just took me a few years to realize it myself.

"We spend a lot of time on character names. Our editor told us if the names are wrong she puts the manuscript down. If she can not immediately get an image from the character's name she is no longer interested. She doesn't even look at the premise of the book. If those names do not evoke images, she won't bother to read the first half of the manuscript because she doesn't have any images of the people."

–John Saul

Christopher
Vogler

The Writer's Journey

This all started with my appreciation for myths and fairy tales. Luckily I had a mother and a grandmother who read to me, and I loved listening to those classic fairy tales and doing thought experiments while I was listening to the stories. I loved to create a bubble in my mind in which I'm that little girl going through the woods or I'm the little boy who separated from his parents or I'm the young prince on the road. And I just loved imagining those roles and thinking about them as movies.

It was all preparation for a phase of my career when I spent about ten years working with Disney trying to figure out what new animated stories to tackle, what appropriate things should follow the great tradition that Walt Disney had started. So I began to see, even as a kid, that there were certain patterns and similarities.

If you start looking at myths as I did, first with the Greek and then the Roman, you'll see these are related. There's a kind of family tree to this thing. They're all connected. Other scholars have done a lot of study on the differences from one culture to another, but I was interested in the similarities. And

I followed that trail through the Scandinavian folklore and the Celtic myths and then the myths of Asia and Africa.

And along the way I was always fascinated by the culture of the movies and seeing again the same kind of patterns, especially in characters. There were certain character types who were doing certain jobs in the script and those showed up repeatedly across all genres and in movies from all over the world. I was fascinated by this. And all this was to blossom when I got to film school and somebody pointed me in the direction of a book called *The Hero with a Thousand Faces* by a man named Joseph Campbell.

It's pretty well known that Campbell was a big influence on George Lucas and the *Star Wars* series. When the first *Star Wars* movie came out, I had just read Campbell and I was blown away that Lucas had also read Campbell and had taken that as a kind of outline. It gave it an extra edge over all the other movies that were out. There was something extra in this material.

So I began working with the ideas. I wrote a term paper for a film class that tried to explain the almost religious experience people were having going to see this film and others like it, like *Close Encounters* and *E.T.* I had figured out a couple of the parts, and then Campbell came along and just gave me the whole toolbox. He had done all the work. He had read all the myths and had arrived at some kind of a basic pattern that seems to underwrite all stories. In fact, it's how we define a story unconsciously. This is how we comprehend something, how we experience a narrative and recognize it as a story—because it has this shape to it, this pattern to it.

This was a tremendously helpful tool for analyzing scripts, and I became a professional script analyst. That is a job in Hollywood—somebody who reads scripts, breaks them down, reacts to them, and analyzes them for their story content and their commerciality. I found this tool a lifesaver for that job, and also a great template for designing stories. Not just structurally, in terms of what happens next, but in terms of what's going on psychologically at the deeper levels.

Obviously this works for adventure stories, where people are going on some kind of journey physically. That's the basic metaphor that underlies this whole concept: The story is a journey of some kind. You could say that life is a journey or a series of journeys, and stories are about the journey from one phase of life to the next phase. Maybe it's going from childhood to the teens. Maybe it's going from being single to being married or alone in life, and then developing your relationship. Or joining some kind of a group like an army squad or a team of spies or something, and traveling from place to place.

It works equally well even if there's no physical journey. When it's a stationary piece about emotions, about somebody going through some transformation or transition in life, there's still a metaphorical journey. Metaphors are very important in getting some use out of these ideas. I think that's really what's going on when people read a story or see a movie: They are looking at a metaphor. The writer is trying to understand some human quality and so they create the story and the story automatically becomes a metaphor for that particular human quality or that aspect of life or that transition in life, and people like to compare.

That's what metaphors are about, the comparison between one thing and another. We learn how something works, or what the relationships are among things, by comparisons. People like to compare their behavior with the behavior of the characters in stories, and they're always doing some kind of self-measurement. How am I doing in relationship to the protagonist or the hero of that story? Sometimes the watcher feels that they are doing better than the character in the story and they get some comfort from that. Then there are times when we watch movies or hear stories or read stories and think, gee I wish I could be as elegant or clever or sexy or dashing as those characters. We compare ourselves, and it becomes a metaphor in our own lives.

I think everyone has one or two of those movies that sort of sum up their life at a certain moment and that actually gave them ammunition or a model. I had friends in Vietnam who said the only way they got through that experience was thinking in terms of Jimmy Cagney movies. Or John Wayne movies. And they would get into a kind of John Wayne swagger when they had to go out on point and that helped carry them through a difficult experience, by having some kind of a metaphor to hang on to.

I want to give you a couple of quick run-throughs at two different levels of magnification. The first one is the long shot, where you see the whole story as four major movements. Now most people talk about movie structure as three-act structure. But I see it really as breaking down into four major movements. And this, by the way, applies very well to the structure of novels, or short stories, or thirty-second commercials. It really doesn't matter. This idea of the hero's journey has validity, no matter how long the story is.

The four movements are, let's say, a circle or the face of a clock that's divided into four quarters. I think that in the ancient world people looked at the cycle of the year as a drama, a life and death drama, beginning at the winter solstice when things were darkest, then the light slowly starts to creep back again, the days get longer and longer–gradually through the spring and summer. That was the growth of the hero. The sun was the hero of the tale that was repeated every year. And then the sun reached its zenith and began its decline in its old age and went through death and then rebirth.

Death and rebirth is critical to this whole concept. It's really the mainspring of the whole idea. The first quarter, the beginning of the story, has to do with a certain action that the hero must perform that is usually an act of separation. The hero has to go away from the ordinary world, the known world, the world that's comfortable, and begin the journey by an act of separation. And then there is a line that runs across this circle that separates the two different worlds: an ordinary world and a special world, because most stories seem to take place in at least these two different worlds.

Often the heroes are uncomfortable or uneasy in their normal world but that is what they know. And then often they are moved to leave that world and go to some kind of special, scary unknown, just like going to the Maui Writers Conference. You know, you leave your ordinary world, you separate from that and you enter this special world where things can happen to you and you can experience some change.

The job of the first act is to tell us who the hero is, what his background is, and get him out of that and into the special world. But always there are exceptions. This is very flexible. And there will be stories where maybe you want to begin, for some narrative reason, at the ending. Show somebody who's up against the wall and now we try to figure out how they got there. It may take you unt.... of Act Two to trace back to the roots of the thi.... gin the story again. That depends entirely on .... e and the needs of the story.

So the hero breaks aw.... on some new journey. The next good mover.... ross that threshold into the special world, is g.... at special world in an act that's called descent. There is always a feeling, even if you're not literally descending but are climbing a mountain or something, that still you are surrendering and taking the plunge into that new world. You're diving off the edge into the unknown. So we use that term, "descent," to describe that process of letting go and taking the plunge into that new world. And at the bottom of that circle there is a moment of punctuation, almost, in which the hero usually encounters Mr. Death.

Death is a character, in a way, in most stories and it's a missing piece in a lot of stories where writers are just beginning to learn the ropes. I don't necessarily mean physical, literal death. It could be death of the enterprise. Death of the game. The death of hope. If it's a love story and nobody actually dies, still, it's not a great story unless there's that moment when it looks like the two lovers are never going to get together. If you're just going down the garden path and falling deeper and deeper in love, that might be nice but it isn't a very interesting story unless there's tension and doubt and you actually create the condition in which the audience believes there's no way they'll get together.

When you're watching sports it's not a terrifically good game when our team is ahead at halftime by sixty-five points, and at the end of the thing we're ahead by 125 points. The really good games are the ones where our team is down by sixty-five points and the quarterback has broken his leg, and clearly the referees have all been bribed and there's no way we can possibly win this game. And yet we win anyway.

So the idea is to create that situation where it looks like there's no way we can win or that there is a death. And then that third movement is a movement that Campbell calls initiation. This means beginning again, often with the beginning halfway through or three-quarters through the story, but what is meant here is that the hero is beginning a new life because he or she has died. The old life has passed away and new life has to begin. There is always this sense of death and rebirth.

This is a very ancient pattern. In the old days, in Babylon and Egypt at the very birth of religion, religion and drama were very closely related and they would create this effect of death and rebirth at the solstices and the equinoxes—at those turning points of the seasons, which are like dramatic turning points in a story. They would bring about this feeling of death and rebirth by covering up all the statues in the church. In the Catholic Church, they still do this around Easter. They cover all the statues, they put out all the candles, there's no celebration for a period of time, and everything is allowed to take a little rest. And Christ is in the tomb and then he's reborn and there is that period of renewal.

That initiation is that period of time when you're sort of getting your legs back and figuring out, "Well, what am I going to be now? I've gone through the experience of most of the Maui Writers Conference and I die. My idea of myself has died." This Conference is like that scene in Don Quixote, when he confronts the knight of the mirrors and all he sees is himself, but it's the most horrifying thing he can see. So you're all confronted by hundreds and hundreds of versions of yourself—variations of yourself. And you see all of your flaws and all the annoying things about you reflected back. And that has a transformative effect on us.

The final phase is the phase of return, that last quarter. And in the return, the hero of the story tries to figure out how to go back and bring something with him or her from the special world, a little souvenir or some lasting change that has a radiating effect. It comes out from the hero, maybe by talking about it, preaching it, or acting on what has been learned, so that it begins to affect in a rippling kind of way the people in the immediate family and down the block. And eventually the whole world can be changed by the inner change of the hero. It's very important in this mythological or heroic system that the hero do that and not be selfish. Not keep what has been learned inside, but get it out there and let other people know or act on it somehow so that it is shared. The hero is supposed to be–in the mythological way of looking at things– the one who sacrifices and looks out for the welfare of others. The word "hero" means, in Greek, to protect and to serve. That's the long shot.

And now I want to zoom in, get into a close-up and just take you real quick to those twelve stages. Again, this is very flexible. This is a form just like the sonata is a form or the symphony is a form. Or a pop song is a form. That doesn't constrict great composers. They can create infinite variations on these things and pull interesting strings from time to time.

This is a form, not *the formula.* And this is the mistake that people make; in fact, a lot of studio executives make this mistake. They say, "Oh, goodie! Somebody has written down all the rules. Now we don't have to think anymore!" So they use this thing, unfortunately, like a club to hit the writers in the head and say, "Uh, you know, he says in the pamphlet that this is supposed to happen by roughly page forty. Well, it didn't happen in your script till forty-one. So take a page out of there so it will fit in the cookbook."

It's not a recipe. It's a map. And if you're driving from one place to the other, you don't drive with the map pasted to the windshield. The map is just a guideline. It's something that you consult before you set out so you generally know where you're going. It can help you plan to hit the high spots–that'd be a nice place to get to the extreme of where we're going, and then we'll turn around and head back from there. Maybe we'll go off on a tangent over here and see that site or that site. And then when you get on the road the fun part is getting lost, when maybe you get the thing out of the glove compartment and see where you got off track and can get back on. Or the hell with it–throw the thing out the window. I want to emphasize the freedom about this. It's a guideline. Suggestions. But they are backed up by thousands and thousands of examples and there's something deeply right about them that everybody understands. The audience knows this stuff better than the writers do. They know it intuitively. It's programmed, first of all, by the many stories they've heard and seen. But it's also hard-wired into the human nervous system. It's part of the definition of being a human being. So it's hard to get away from it.

The first part, again, is that of the ordinary world. And here you introduce the hero. That's the function of this part, to make an introduction between the hero and the audience. And this is pretty heavy magic because you are trying to establish a bond. I feel very strongly that there is a connection that comes out of the solar plexus of every person in the audience when actors are up on stage or a Greek orator is speaking. They can pull those threads out of the guts of every member of the audience and pull them together into a bundle and steal that audience like a bunch of horses in a chariot race. Very exhilarating feeling when you're on a good night, and you got 'em, and they're all awake and they're cable-ready. You don't have to coax them. They're ready to plug into that hero.

But you have to make the hero attractive in a certain way. I don't mean beautiful or handsome necessarily, but like us in some fundamental way. There are many techniques I describe in the book for creating a hero who is sympathetic, which may mean very badly flawed. Because sometimes the more neurotic the character is, the more we recognize they're like us. And so you're sympathetic. Another little tip here: Take something away from the hero at the beginning of the story. Subtract something. Steal something from the hero, or show the hero's missing something. If something is missing, that sets off a certain urge or energy in the story. The story wants to complete that energy.

The next is the call to adventure. This is usually paired with the third movement, the refusal of the call. Heroes typically early in the story get a call–sometimes it's a little phone call–to adventure. Either it comes from inside and he's fed up and can't stand the problems of his life anymore, or it comes from outside and there is some impulse that says, hey let's undertake the adventure. Typically the hero's response is to refuse. Now this is a rule that's broken sometimes because you have a class of heroes who are gung-ho. They are committed. They gotta go. They don't care about anybody's blockages or fears. They want that adventure. But the more common case is that the hero says, not for me. You're not conning me into that one again.

If the hero is gung-ho, something still has to be communicated to the audience, which is that this is dangerous. This could kill you. This has an element of fear. So, often that job is given to another character in the story, who says, "Wait! Stop, hero! You can't go there! Don't you know the way is littered with the bones of all the guys who tried to do this before? Nobody's ever been able to do this." Those are called threshold guardians. That's one of the archetypes, shapes, or patterns that show up again and again. And I'm sure everybody in the room knows the threshold guardian archetype very well. That's the voice inside you that says, "I want to go to Maui but I can't afford that! I can't take the time away from work! I want to write scripts, but it's hopeless." You hear it inside, you hear it outside. Other people say, "Isn't that an awfully competitive field? And don't you have to know a lot? And you could spend years writing the stupid script and then you still have no guarantee you're going to make any money." You hear these voices and that's that threshold guardian energy.

The hero goes through that stage, where they're stopped temporarily by it, so that has to be overcome. And that's where you get to the next stage.

Often writers will bring in a character or an energy that is that of the mentor. The mentor is a hero who's been around the block before. They've already done this circle a few times and they know this is survivable. It's dangerous, it's scary, but you can do it. They become guides. They draw the maps, they give the heroes guidance, and one of their big functions is to give something to the hero: advice, training, practice, magical weapons or equipment, or just the benefit of their experience.

Let's go to that threshold that cuts the story roughly in half. And here the hero commits; he or she takes on the adventure and takes the plunge. Sometimes they have to be pushed by the mentor, sometimes they pull up their socks and dive in on their own. Sometimes they're driven out of the ordinary world because it's not comfortable any more. Often there will be some condition that develops in the ordinary world that makes it impossible for the hero to stay there any more. They're on the run. They're suspected of murder. Something's been pinned on them so they have to hit the road. So that gets the story really rolling. Make that happen as fast as you can. If you can do it in the first ten pages, that would be great.

That lets you into the second act, and now you've begun to encounter some of these things that are new and special. And that leads you to that stage I called tests, allies, and enemies, where the hero is tested in certain locations–often a bar or a saloon or a cantina, because that's a good place to find out what's new about a new place. If you want to find out what's going on in the town, go hang out in the bar–the Western heroes know that. They head right for the saloon and find the road is polarized between two major camps or forces. There are the cattle ranchers and the Indians. Or the railroad men and the religious reformers. And the hero has to choose sides and figure out who's a friend and who's an enemy. The hero has to figure out the rules and the new currency, what's valuable in this new world, what's the leeway, what is the special language of this world, all these new things. And the hero will be tested.

The next phase I call approach. It's almost as if the hero has just finished all the business of the ordinary world and this person has set foot across the threshold into the new world and now they have to pull themselves together and face the big thing, the big event, the greatest fear. Often there will be love scenes here, because it's an opportunity to bring people

together and build a team and find out more about the characters. In the Disney animated features, they're very basic. The
classic ones–Peter Pan, Pinocchio, and so on–are extremely
frantic and frenetic and they just churn up a lot of nervous
energy, but then every once in awhile they slow down and
they go into big close-ups with huge eyes in the hero's face.
It's a getting-to-know-you scene. These are opportunities to
build and deepen characters a little bit before we go into the
big battle, the main event that's coming up.

And that is stage eight. The ordeal. It's an extreme point
of tension. It's a big breakthrough. It's a big battle that seems
to kill the hero or the hero's hopes but you still are going to
have to top this one later on. So, the nature of this is death
and rebirth. Those two things very closely link together.

A super way to understand this is to think about the game
of peek-a-boo with babies. Kids love to look deeply into the
eyes of adults. And in peek-a-boo, you make that bond and
you get the kid looking at you goo-goo-eyed and then you
break the bond. You sadists! You put something between you
and the baby: a pillow or blanket or something. And the baby
reacts characteristically and physiologically. Babies will first
react by kind of giggling and teasing and trying to look around
and trying to resume that contact, which is very important to
them. It's a way of reassuring them that they are alive, that
they have something adults want to be in contact with. But
you frustrate that and the baby reacts–first the little chin starts
to wrinkle up and the breathing starts to get a little faster. You
can traumatize a child doing this. And then, if you have any
mercy, you resume the contact–and watch what happens when
you do this with a kid. Do they just go back to, "Oh, mommy's
back." No, no, they go to a higher level. They start giggling.
They have a nervous laugh and reaction. Like, "Oh, I thought
you were gone. In fact, I was beginning to think you were
dead–which means I'm dead."

So the audience is like a baby. And you are playing peek-
a-boo with the audience. You are making a bond in the opening act. You are causing the audience to project part of themselves. This is the eye contact. It projects something out of the

solar plexus into the character and then you cut that cable. You cut that umbilical cord and there are the pangs of separation. Let 'em dangle for a while. Not too long. Could be just two or three frames of film, where the hero is clinging by the side of the train and they go through the tunnel and the train comes out of the darkness and the hero's not there. And you think, Where'd he go? You start freaking on some subterranean, psychological, physiological level. That cable has been snapped and suddenly you're thinking, Well, I can't be nobody in this movie. I have to be somebody. Who am I gonna be? And this is what Hitchcock was playing with in *Psycho*. He hooked you up to very neurotic Janet Leigh who has stolen some money, and she's in love and they've got a hot relationship. So all of these chambered reasons to connect with her have gone when he cuts the cable. And this is a one-time thing that a creator can do. But it leaves you wondering, when she's knifed, who am I in the movie? I've got to hook up with somebody, but there's nobody to hook up to except the psycho, OK? There's nobody there! There's nothing good at the Bates Motel. So Hitchcock moves you into the mind of the psycho. I mean that's really getting dirty with the audience.

You can't do that every time. Usually, you bring the hero back on screen. You find as you pan down from the side of the train that there's a convenient little railing there that he's caught onto and he's hanging underneath the train or he's landed on the siding somehow, or they caught him and they're dragging him in. And that's the pay-off of the cliff-hanger.

If you get that one, you've got a real good start on this. The next movement is reward and that, in a way, is the rebirth. It's the moment when you come out and you're relieved and you've gotten through it and often the heroes are patting themselves on the back or celebrating or there's a love scene here because you've survived death. You've faced the greatest fear and now you deserve to be loved.

The next movement is the road back. This is that moment when you look back on the whole thing and say, "Now there was some reason I was on this journey. Oh, yeah. People were starving at home. And we had to go in and kill the dragon and now we've got to drag home some of that dragon meat and have a barbecue." So the hero is recommitted to finishing the adventure.

In the life of the writer, all these stages are duplicated. It's why I call the book *The Writer's Journey*, because writers go through these things, too. The writer has to get through the special world, go through those opening stages of figuring out what you're going to write and who your mentors will be. Then you take the plunge into the special world of the story and you go through your death–your concept of what you thought it was going to be, which is always different from what it really is.

And then there's that moment when you commit to finish. Choose a particular form and drive it home. Sometimes the hero has to be pushed. Sometimes they have it within.

Whatever, the time will come when it's time to leave this special world, which can be very attractive. It can be a lot of fun there. It's different, it's exotic and you may be tempted to stay on Maui; many people do. Many people come to the conference and just never go home.

But most of us have to go back–so that is the idea of that turnabout. Like with the first threshold crossing, you're crossing that threshold again and there's a certain action that you see very often here, which is the chase scene. The chase scene has a function of waking the audience up. People tend to fall asleep during the three-quarter movement and in that last quarter you have to wake 'em up, you have to speed toward the curtain. "Racing for the curtain" is what they say in the theater.

So the hero enters into the last phase: The return. And here are two major movements–resurrection, and return with the elixir. The resurrection is almost a replay of the ordeal, but this time everything is at stake. You know, you could really blow it here if you don't get everything in its proper place. People can regress, they can go back to their old behavior, they can mess up and blow the whole thing in the last moments. It's a dangerous moment, that moment of return. You can do everything right and if you trip on the doorstep on the way back into your house and break your leg, it can turn from a victory into a defeat. Or if you chicken out on your resolve that you made here at the Maui Writers Conference, it can be for nothing. So it's a dangerous moment but it is a moment, if it's done properly, in which we see the hero's complete transformation on all levels.

It should be a final test. It's like a final exam in which everything the hero has done so far is put to a final test. Did you really mean it, or were you just on vacation? Is this a real change? Or was it just something you flirted with? Did it go down through all the levels of your being or was it just a superficial thing? So the heroes are put through a final test. And that might be going home and having people say, "Well, that was a total waste of time, wasn't it?" And, "I bet nothing happened to you there," and try to invalidate your experience—that's one form of the test.

The final movement is return with the elixir. Elixir is a word from Arabic that means a powder. It's like a magical potion, a powder that heals all wounds and cures all ills. It's the universal panacea and it's like the Holy Grail. It's something that proves that you went, like a souvenir, but also has some kind of transformative power. It might be knowledge, it might be experience, it might be some metaphor that you carried back with you. It might be even seeing a person who has a certain energy field around them that has an affect on you.

That's the idea in a nutshell.

THE CONTRIBUTORS

Mitch Albom is a best selling author, nationally-syndicated columnist, host for ABC radio, and television commentator. He is the author of seven books. *Tuesdays with Morrie*, his most recent, was a *New York Times* number one best seller, the largest nonfiction book in America for 1998. Two of his other books, *Bo* and *Fab Five* were also *New York Times* best sellers. Mitch has been named number one sports columnist in the nation twelve times by the Sports Editors of America (APSE) and has also received five first place APSE honors for feature writing.

Jeff Arch's spec screenplay *Sleepless in Seattle*, was nominated for Best Original Screenplay by the Academy, the Writers Guild, and the British Academy. Since then, he has been working non-stop for virtually every studio in town, on original stories, book adaptations, and rewrite assignments. His production rewrite of Disney's *Iron Will* starred Mackenzie Astin and Kevin Spacey. His romantic comedy *Sealed With A Kiss* aired on CBS. Jeff is currently developing *Cross Country*, a road drama; *The Same River Twice*, a romantic comedy; and *The White Guy*, a comedy for television.

David Baldacci has written four novels, including *The Simple Truth, Total Control, The Winner,* and *Saving Faith,* all of which have been national and international best sellers. His fiction has also appeared in *USA Today* magazine, Italy's *Panorama* magazine, Great Britain's *Tattler* magazine and the *New Statesman.* Mr. Baldacci's first novel, *Absolute Power,* was made into a major motion picture.

Dave Barry became so famous for his humorous columns in *The Miami Herald* that he won the Pulitzer in 1988. He has written what he calls "a number of short but harmful books," including *Babies and Other Hazards of Sex, Dave Barry Slept Here: A Sort of History of the United States, Dave Barry's Book of Bad Songs, Dave Barry in Cyberspace, Dave Barry's Complete Guide to Guys, Dave Barry Turns 50,* and *Dave Barry Is from Mars AND Venus*, and his first novel, *Big Trouble.*

Tad Bartimus: While pursuing her journalism career, Tad co-authored *Trinity's Children*, contributed to *Mid-Life Confidential: The Rock Bottom Remainders Tour America with Three Chords and an Attitude,* served as Atwood Professor of Journalism at the University of Alaska, and is a volunteer writing coach at Hana Hawaii High. Her critically acclaimed book, *Requiem*, chronicles the work of Vietnam war photographers who died in the conflict.

Ron Bass: Ron is one of the film industry's preeminent screenwriter-producers. He won an Academy Award for the screenplay for *Rain Man* and most recently acted as co-writer and co-executive producer with Terry McMillan on *Waiting to Exhale*. He also wrote or co-wrote *The Joy Luck Club, Sleeping With the Enemy, When a Man Loves a Woman, Black Widow, Gardens of Stone, Dangerous Minds, My Best Friend's Wedding, Entrapment,* and *Stepmom.*

Jay Bonansinga: Screenwriter, novelist, and filmmaker, Jay recently adapted his own supernatural thriller novel, *Oblivion*, for Universal Pictures. Jay's latest suspense novel, *Bloodhound*, is currently on the stands in paperback from Signet Books, and his 1997 hit man opus, *The Killer's Game*, is in pre-production at New Line Cinema under the title *Godforsaken*. Jay has been a Bram Stoker award finalist, as well as the recipient of the Silver Plaque from the Chicago International Film Festival.

Jimmy Breslin: Pulitzer Prize-winning columnist for *New York Newsday*, Jimmy has been covering New York for more than thirty years. He is the author of many best selling novels and nonfiction books, including *The Gang That Couldn't Shoot Straight, World Without End, Amen, Table Money,* and *Damon Runyon: A Life.* Jimmy has also made a name for himself as a playwright, TV commentator, talk show host and NYC political figure.

Terry Brooks: With over fifteen million books in print and sixteen consecutive *New York Times* best sellers, Terry has been called "the Master of Fantasy." A practicing lawyer when his first book *Sword of Shannara* was picked out of the slush pile by revered science fiction/fantasy editor Lester del Rey, Terry retired from law in 1986, nine years after "Sword" became an instant best seller. Last year, Terry published *Star Wars: The Phantom Menace*, an adaptation of the George Lucas movie. His latest book, *The Voyage of the Jerle Shannara: Ilse Witch*, was published in September.

Jack Canfield made his mark in publishing with the phenomenal success of *Chicken Soup for the Soul* and the twenty-six *Chicken Soup* sequels (including the recent *Chicken Soup for the Golfer's Soul*) which have crowded the *New York Times* best seller lists for over three years and have sold over forty-five million copies in twenty-nine languages.

Jackie Collins: With 200 million copies of her books sold in more than forty countries, Jackie is one of the world's top-selling authors. Her first book, *The World is Full of Married Men* became an instant best seller. After that spectacular debut came a long list of hits including *The New York Times* number one best sellers *Hollywood Wives, Lucky,* and *Chances.* Over the last three years she has *published Thrill!, Dangerous Kiss, L.A. Connections,* and *Lethal Seduction.* Author of twenty-four international best sellers, Jackie is currently writing *Hollywood Wives–The New Generation.*

Bryce Courtenay exploded on the literary scene with his first book, the international best seller *The Power of One*. It was translated into eleven languages, and became a successful movie. His subsequent novels, *Tandia, April Fool's Day, The Potato Factory*–now a mini series–*Tommo & Hawk, Jessica* and *Solomon's Song*, the last of *The Potato Factory* Trilogy, also landed on the best seller lists. Other works *include A Recipe for Dreaming, The Family Frying Pan,* and *The Night Country. The Power of One–Young Readers' Edition* was published in 1999.

Kenneth C. Davis is the best selling author of the Don't Know Much About© series, including *Don't Know Much about History, Don't Know Much about Geography, Don't Know Much about the Civil War*, and most recently, *Don't Know Much about the Bible*.

Barbara DeAngelis: One of America's leading experts on relationships and personal growth, Barbara is a popular television personality and author of numerous *New York Times* best sellers. Her books include *How to Make Love All the Time, Secrets About Men Every Woman Should Know, Are You the One For Me?, Real Moments,* and *Chicken Soup for the Couple's Soul*.

Steven E. deSouza: One of Hollywood's busiest writers, Mr. DeSouza's action-packed screenplays include *48 HRS., Die Hard, Die Hard 2, Commando, Richochet, The Flintstones, Beverly Hills Cop III, Possessed,* and *Tomb Raider*.

Michael Eberhardt: The author of *Body of a Crime* and *Against the Law*, Michael is a criminal lawyer with an international reputation for winning the longest murder trial acquittal in US history.

Elizabeth Engstrom has written six books, including *Lizzie Borden, Lizard Wine, When Darkness Loves Us, Black Ambrosia, The Alchemy of Love* and *Nightmare Flower,* which received a Bram Stoker nomination for fiction. She has edited three anthologies, and has written over a hundred short stories, articles, and essays. She is director of the Maui Writers Retreat and its Department of Continuing Education.

Joe Eszterhas is one of Hollywood's highest paid screenwriters. In 1993, Columbia signed him to adapt *Gangland* for $3.4 million. His movies include such blockbusters as *Jagged Edge, Flashdance, Basic Instinct, Sliver, F.I.S.T., The Music Box,* and *Betrayed.*

Richard Paul Evans currently lives in Salt Lake City with his wife, Keri and their five children. His self-published book, *The Christmas Box*, was bought by Simon & Schuster for an eye-popping $4.2 million. Richard has written five novels and two children's books, all of which have been national best sellers.

Ernest J. Gaines' books include *A Gathering of Old Men, In My Father's House, A Long Day in November, The Autobiography of Miss Jane Pittman, Bloodline, Of Love and Dust, Catherine Carmier,* and the 1997 best seller *A Lesson Before Dying.* He was elected to the American Academy of Arts and Letters, received *the Chevalier in the Ordre des Arts et des Lettres* in France, was awarded an NEA grant, a Rockefeller, a Guggenheim, and the prestigious MacArthur Foundation Fellowship for a lifetime of literary achievement.

Bud Gardner is a Jack London Award-winning writer, professional speaker, business writing consultant, and former TV writing instructor. He wrote and sold sixty articles before taking over the Writing-for-Publication program at American River College in Sacramento, California. Since then, his students and seminar participants have sold more than 3,000 articles and 112 books, earning more then $3 million from their writing, reaching an estimated 500 million readers worldwide. In June 2000, Bud, Jack Canfield and Mark Victor Hansen co-authored and published a new book, *Chicken Soup for the*

Writer's Soul, a volume dedicated to the Maui Writers Foundation.

Julie Garwood: With more than twenty million books in print and fifteen *New York Times* best sellers, Julie Garwood is firmly established as one of America's favorite fiction writers. Her first novel, *Gentle Warrior*, was published in 1985. Since then, her books have appeared regularly on the top lists of every major publication in the country. One of her more recent novels, *For the Roses*, was adapted for the Hallmark Hall of Fame presentation, *Rosehill.*

Elizabeth George has written ten novels of psychological suspense, all of them set in Great Britain (*A Great Deliverance, Payment in Blood, Well-Schooled in Murder, A Suitable Vengeance, For the Sake of Elena, Missing Joseph, Playing for the Ashes, In the Presence of the Enemy, Deception on His Mind,* and *In Pursuit of the Proper Sinner*). Elizabeth is the recipient of the Anthony Award and the Agatha Award for best first novel, as well as France's *Grand Prix de Litterature Policiere* and Germany's MIMI, an international award for mystery fiction.

Steven Goldsberry: Associate Professor of English at the University of Hawai'i, Steven is a recipient of the Cades Award for Literature and a Michener Fellowship. He is the author of the novels *Maui the Demigod* and *Luzon*, and the books *Over Hawai'i* and (with his wife U'i) *Sunday In Hawai'i.* His work has appeared in *The New Yorker, The American Poetry Review, The Iowa Review, McCall's, Windsurf, ALOHA, Manoa, Honolulu,* and the German *GEO.*

David Guterson's first novel, *Snow Falling on Cedars*, ran a consecutive seventy-six weeks on the New York Times best seller list and won the PEN/Faulkner Award among others. His new novel is called *East of the Mountains.* He is also the author of a collection of short stories, *The Country Ahead of*

Us, the Country Behind, and of *Family Matters: Why Homeschooling Makes Sense.*

Tony Hillerman, former President of Mystery Writers of America, is a former farmer, infantryman, truck driver, police reporter, newspaper editor, college professor, and author of 20 books, including five which made the *New York Times* Notable Books list and a half dozen national best sellers. Honors include Ambassador Award of the Center for the American Indian, Special Friend of the Dineh Award of the Navajo Nation, Grand Master and Edgar Allan Poe Awards of the MWA, Golden Spur of the Western Writers of America, Media Service Award of the U.S. Department of Interior, and the French *Gran Prix de Litterature Policiere.*

Ron Howard: Named Director of the Year by the Directors Guild of America, Ron gained fame as a young actor on the big screen in *The Music Man* and *American Graffiti,* and on TV's *The Andy Griffith Show* and *Happy Days.* He directed his first feature film at age twenty-three, and has gone on to such works as *Night Shift, Splash, Cocoon, Parenthood, Backdraft, Far and Away, The Paper, Apollo 13, Ransom, EDtv,* and *How the Grinch Stole Christmas.*

Susan Isaacs is the author of eight best selling novels including *Compromising Positions, After All These Years, Lily White,* and *Red, White and Blue.* Her screenplays are *Compromising Positions* and *Hello Again.* Susan's first foray into nonfiction was *Brave Dames and Wimpettes: What Women Are Really Doing On Page And Screen.*

Dewitt Jones is recognized as one of America's top professional photographers. He was a freelance photographer for *National Geographic* for twenty years, has published eight books, writes a column for *Outdoor Photographer Magazine,* and has directed two Academy Award-nominated films.

Barry Kemp began his career as a writer for the TV series *Taxi*. He created *Newhart, Coach, Fresno* and co-created or produced ten other series, including *The Popcorn Kid, Princesses* and *Delta*. Barry produced the feature film blockbusters *Romy and Michelle's High School Reunion* and *Patch Adams*. Barry is the recipient of multiple WGA, Emmy, Golden Globe and People's Choice nominations and in 1999 was the recipient of the Valentine Davies Award from the WGA.

Elmore Leonard: A writer of legendary status, he has published thirty novels. His titles include *Hombre, The Big Bounce, Fifty-Two Pickup, Stick, LaBrava,* and *Glitz*. The recent smash movies *Get Shorty* and *Jackie Brown* were based on his books.

Craig Lesley: Winner of three Pacific Northwest Booksellers Association Awards, The Western Writers of America Best Novel of the Year, and the Medicine Pipe Bearer's Award, Craig has authored *The Sky Fisherman, Winterkill, River Song,* and *Storm Riders*; and edited *Talking Leaves: Contemporary Native American Short Stories,* and *Dreamers and Desperados: Contemporary Short Fiction of the American West*. He received an NEA Fellowship, a Bread Loaf Fellowship, and two National Endowment for the Humanities Fellowships to study Native American literature.

Eric Marcus is a former associate producer for both CBS and ABC's morning news programs. He is the author of *Breaking the Surface*, the number one *New York Times* best selling autobiography of Olympic diving champion Greg Louganis. He is also the author of eight other books, including *Making History, Is It A Choice?, The Male Couple's Guide, Together Forever, Why Suicide?,* and *What If Someone I Know Is Gay?*, a question and answer book for young readers.

Bob Mayer has written nineteen novels under four pen names including Robert Doherty and Greg Donegan. His *Area 51* series has been on *USA Today's* best seller list and his *Atlantis* series is wildly successful. A new series, *Psychic Warrior* has just been launched.

Don McQuinn: Don is a well-known Pacific Northwest writer and teacher, and the author of nine novels, including *Targets* (a Book-of-the-Month Club selection) and the best sellers *Warrior* and *Witch*. He is currently at work on his next novel.

Marilyn Meredith is an instructor for the Writer's Digest School, the author of two historical family sagas based on family genealogy, *The Astral Gift*, a mystery with a supernatural twist, *Deadly Omen* and *Unequally Yoked*, the first two books in the Deputy Tempe Crabtree mystery series. She is also the author of several electronic books.

Dan Millman is a former world trampoline champion, gymnastics coach, and college professor. His books, including *Way of the Peaceful Warrior, Everyday Enlightenment, The Laws of Spirit,* and *The Life You Were Born to Live* have inspired millions in twenty languages and have influenced leaders in the fields of health, psychology, education, business, politics, entertainment, sports, and the arts.

Raymond Obstfeld teaches English literature, film, and creative writing at Orange Coast College and is the author of more than thirty novels in many genres, including espionage, western, futuristic adventure, occult thriller, mystery, young adult, and mainstream.

Steve Oedekerk has written and directed films, including *Patch Adams*, starring Robin Williams. His writing credits include: *Act Ventura: Pet Detective, Ace Ventura 2: When Nature Calls* (which he also directed), *The Nutty Professor, Nothing To Lose* (which he also directed), and *The Dubbed Action Movie,* a wild comedy feature for Fox which he is also directing and starring in.

James Orr: One of Hollywood's most successful and respected writer-director-producers, James Orr, along with his partner Jim Cruickshank, is responsible for a cumulative box office of over a half billion dollars worldwide. Their writing and producing credits include such famed movies as *Three Men and a Baby*, *Mr. Destiny*, *Tough Guys,* and *Man of the House.*

Joe Ortiz: Joe was nominated for the Julia Child Cookbook Award in 1993 for his book *The Village Baker.* He followed the volume with *The Village Baker's Wife,* which he wrote with his wife Gayle, and which was inspired by their renowned and award-winning California eatery Gayle's Bakery. Joe's newest books include *Shakespeare on Golf* with John Tullius, and *The Gardener's Table* with Richard Merrill.

Ridley Pearson: Following his debut with *Never Look Back*, he published *Blood of the Albatross, The Seizing of Yankee Green Mall, Undercurrents, Probable Cause, Hard Fall*, and *Chain of Evidence.* In 1991 he became the first American awarded the Raymond Chandler Fulbright at Oxford University, where he researched and outlined *The Angel Maker* and *No Witnesses.* His latest novels are *Beyond Recognition, The Pied Piper*, and *The First Victim.*

Katherine Ramsland has published fourteen nonfiction books, among them biographies of Dean Koontz and Anne Rice, and an undercover expose of the vampire subculture, *Piercing the Darkness.* Her forthcoming books are *Writing for Bliss* and *Ghost Hunt.* Recently, she worked as a research assistant for FBI profiler John Douglas, exploring unsolved murders, and is working on a book for writers on forensic psychology.

Michael Sack collaborates with authors, developing concepts and story lines. He has worked with John Saul over the past twenty-one years. He has also published numerous magazine articles in the field of psychology, maintained a newspaper advice column, and authored *The Single Parent Survival Guide.*

John Saul: John's first book, *Suffer the Children*, appeared on the best seller lists throughout the country. Subsequently all of his books, including such psychological thrillers as *Guardian*, *The Homing,* and *Black Lightning*, have made the *New York Times* best seller list and have been published worldwide. His six-part serial, *The Blackstone Chronicles*, also appeared on the *New York Times* best seller list and its CD-ROM computer game was nominated for Adventure Game of the Year in both 1998 and 1999. An earlier novel, *Cry for the Strangers*, was produced by Gerber Productions and MGM as a CBS movie. His newest book *Nightshade* is a current hardback best seller. He is also engaged in a multi-media development deal with Middle Fork Productions and The Shooting Gallery.

Mike Scully: Emmy Award-winning writer Mike Scully joined *The Simpsons* as a producer in April 1993. Since then, he has written several episodes, including *Lisa's Rival, Two Dozen and One Greyhounds, Lisa On Ice, Team Homer, Marge Be Not Proud, Lisa's Date With Destiny,* and the "Homega Man" segment from *Treehouse of Horror VIII.* In 1997 he became executive producer and show runner for seasons nine, ten and eleven.

Linda Seger is an internationally known script consultant, seminar leader, and author. Her clients have included TriStar Pictures, MGM/UA, Guber-Peters Entertainment, Ray Bradbury, etc. She has lectured around the world, and is the author of six books on screenwriting and filmmaking.

Nicholas Sparks is the best selling author of *The Notebook, Message in a Bottle, A Walk to Remember,* and *The Rescue.* He lives in North Carolina with his wife and three sons.

John Tullius is the director of the Maui Writers Conference, the author of thirteen books, including co-author of the national best sellers *Body of a Crime* and *Against the Law.* He has written scores of articles for dozens of magazines including *Cosmopolitan, Playboy,* and *Town and Country,* and was a contributing editor for *Tennis Magazine.*

Christopher Vogler is a story consultant for major Hollywood studios and is the author of *The Writer's Journey: Mythic Structure for Writers.* Most recently he was a development executive at Fox 2000, where he worked on the feature films *Courage Under Fire, Volcano, Anna and the King,* and *The Thin Red Line,* which was nominated for seven Academy Awards. Vogler is now a producer for Fox 2000.

Susan Wiggs has won many awards for her work, including the RITA Award from Romance Writers of America for Favorite Book of the Year. This author of twenty novels is a popular speaker and teacher at many writing conferences, and was featured luncheon speaker at the Romance Writers of America National Conference in Washington, DC in July of 2000. Her recent book, *The Horsemaster's Daughter,* spent two weeks on *The New York Times* extended best seller list and two weeks on the *USA Today* list.

The Maui Writers Conference takes place during Labor Day weekend every year. For more information about the Conference, the Manuscript Marketplace, the Retreat, its Department of Continuing Education, or to order tapes of these or other presentations, contact:

The Maui Writers Conference
PO Box 1118
Kihei, Maui, Hawaii 96753
808-879-0061
www.mauiwriters.com